To the UTTERMOST ENDS of the EARTH

To Lolly, the "Muse," who has always believed; so, therefore, I write.
And to Pierce, for whom I write, for his legacy and mine.

P.K.

To Vivienne Vun Kannon, whose adventures have just begun.

T.C.

To the UTTERMOST ENDS of the EARTH

The EPIC HUNT for the SOUTH'S MOST FEARED SHIP— and the GREATEST SEA BATTLE of the CIVIL WAR

PHIL KEITH *with* TOM CLAVIN

HANOVER
SQUARE
PRESS

HANOVER
SQUARE
PRESS™

Recycling programs
for this product may
not exist in your area.

ISBN-13: 978-1-335-47141-3

To the Uttermost Ends of the Earth

Hanover Square Press
22 Adelaide St. West, 41st Floor
Toronto, Ontario M5H 4E3, Canada
HanoverSqPress.com
BookClubbish.com

Printed in U.S.A.

THE COASTAL BLOCKADE

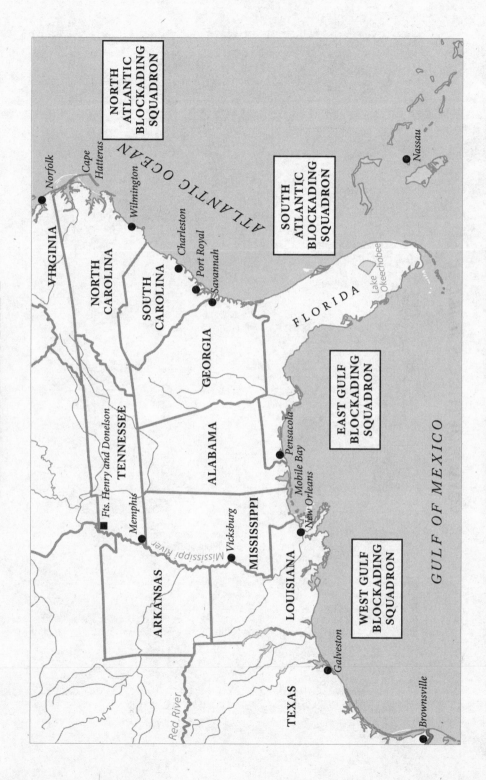

NORTH ATLANTIC BLOCKADING SQUADRON

SOUTH ATLANTIC BLOCKADING SQUADRON

EAST GULF BLOCKADING SQUADRON

WEST GULF BLOCKADING SQUADRON

ATLANTIC OCEAN

GULF OF MEXICO

VIRGINIA

NORTH CAROLINA

SOUTH CAROLINA

GEORGIA

FLORIDA

TENNESSEE

ALABAMA

MISSISSIPPI

ARKANSAS

LOUISIANA

TEXAS

Norfolk

Cape Hatteras

Wilmington

Charleston

Port Royal

Savannah

Lake Okeechobee

Pensacola

Mobile Bay

New Orleans

Fts. Henry and Donelson

Memphis

Vicksburg

Mississippi River

Red River

Galveston

Brownsville

Nassau

VOYAGE OF THE CSS *ALABAMA*

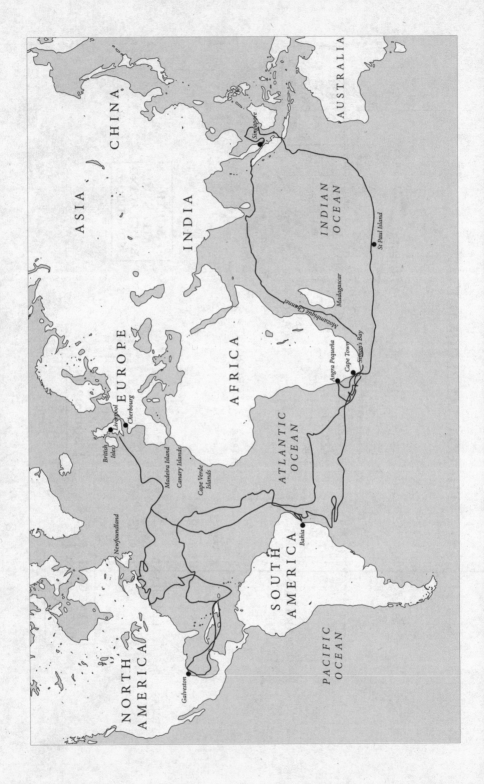

CONTENTS

PROLOGUE

*What did I get my Medal of Honor for? Oh, I suppose they had
one left over so they had me take care of it.*

John Bickford, June 1922

I was definitely not meant for a life at sea, Sherwin Cook told himself as he bobbed across Gloucester Harbor. The dinghy he was
clinging to swayed perilously, or so he felt, and the little put-
put outboard that pushed them forward spewed fumes that assaulted his nostrils and choked his lungs without letup. Much
more of this and he was going to be puking his guts out over
the starboard gunwale.

It was hot for June and the noonday sun was beating down.
His sweat output increased, which only exacerbated the nausea
rising in his gut. Cook dreaded being on the water—he even
avoided swimming pools. There was no choice, though, if he
wanted this interview because there was no way out to Rocky
Neck except by boat. He had hired a local fisherman to ferry
him across and as he unsteadily settled himself in the old salt's
puny craft, he instantly regretted his choice. The small boat

reeked of fish guts and the gnarled, sunbaked old codger didn't seem to smell much better himself. But the price was right, two dollars and fifty cents round trip. Since he had to pay his own expenses, the cheap ride would leave more commission in his pocket. As Cook tried desperately to keep his breakfast down, the pier at Rocky Neck finally came into view. If he could last another five minutes, he might make it.

Cook's quarry that day was an aging Civil War veteran by the name of John Bickford. It was early June 1922, and the old veterans of the Civil War were rapidly slipping away to be with their mates in the great hereafter. Bickford was nearly eighty, Cook had been told, and he was reportedly in decent shape and had not yet lost his marbles. Cook wanted to interview Bickford about two story lines: First, his participation in the most famous sea battle of the Civil War, the duel between the famous Rebel raider CSS *Alabama* and the Yankee sloop of war USS *Kearsarge*, in 1864. Second, Bickford was rumored to be the last survivor of the seventeen Medal of Honor awardees from that battle. As a freelancer for the *Boston Evening Transcript* Cook had been commissioned to get Bickford's narrative, but also as an amateur historian, he was keenly interested in capturing the old man's tales.

As the dinghy mercifully touched the Rocky Neck pier, Cook noticed a tall, older, and beefy gentleman sauntering down the dock toward him. He wore a jaunty sailor's cap, cocked to one side of his head, and sported a broad smile under a bushy white mustache. He walked with a slight limp, but briskly and otherwise unaided.

As Cook struggled to ascend the rickety pier-side ladder, a hand reached down to help. The young reporter grasped it and noted how strong the grip was. Once standing on the pier, and grateful to be on a solid surface, Cook retrieved his leather portfolio from the boatman.

"I'll be back at 1600," the craggy fisherman announced. "Don't be late or you'll be spending the night. And I'll be collecting double if I have to fetch you back tomorrow," he cackled with some glee.

"Don't worry. I'll be here at…4:00," Cook calculated from the nautical time reference. He was already dreading the return trip.

"Name's Bickford." The older gentleman on the pier smiled. "John Bickford."

The two shook hands. "I'm Sherwin Cook. From the *Boston Evening Transcript*. Pleasure to meet you, sir."

"Well, Mr. Cook, let's get you out of the sun and have something cool to drink. Please follow me."

Setting a brisk pace, Bickford escorted his guest down the pier and up a short rise to a tidy and pleasant-looking cottage overlooking the harbor. Neatly trimmed rose bushes framed the front porch which accommodated a settee, a rocking chair, and two wicker chairs with cushions.

"Please sit where you'd like, except the rocker. That's the chair I need for my bad back. Made some lemonade this morning. Care for a glass?"

"Yes, please, that would be splendid."

Bickford ducked through the screen door, which closed with a slam. Cook settled into one of the cushioned chairs and took out his handkerchief to wipe his brow. He was beginning to feel normal again and his stomach was settling.

The view from the porch was magnificent. It faced west, which ought to provide gorgeous sunsets on clear days. Several sailboats dotted the harbor, cruising along hither and yon, capturing the gentle airs. A dozen fishing boats sat at anchor, a couple of which had seagulls swirling near their sterns as crews cleaned the detritus from the morning's catch from their decks. Below the cottage, to the left, was another short quay, and tied up all along it, on both sides, were a dozen small boats that looked to be the type that could be rented for the day.

The screen door swung open again and Bickford emerged with a large tray upon which were two tall glasses of iced lemonade, some crackers, a large hunk of cheese, and an uncut salami. He set the tray on a small table between them.

"Here you go. Something to wet your whistle. And a small lunch if your stomach will allow."

Was that a sly smile of recognition on Bickford's face?

"Thank you very much. Quite nice. Perhaps I'll have a cracker or two."

Bickford grasped one of the tall glasses and set it in front of him. He pulled a silver flask from his shirt pocket, unscrewed the top, and poured two fingers' worth of a golden liquid into his lemonade. He then offered the flask to Cook.

"Sun's over the yardarm somewhere," Bickford chuckled, using the sailor's universal excuse for being able to imbibe at any time of day.

"No, thank you," Cook replied, his stomach flipping over. "I think I'll pass...for now."

Bickford downed a generous swallow and began to rock. "So, I understand you want to hear an old sailor's tales about the 'War of Northern Aggression' as our friends down South called it."

"Yes, please, in particular about the Battle of Cherbourg. My editor wants a good story about that fight, your participation in it, and how you got your Medal of Honor."

Bickford took another long sip, and almost as if on cue, began his recitation. Cook had taken out his writing pad and pencils and was already furiously scribbling away. For the next three hours, between more sips of lemonade, bites of cheese and crackers, hunks of salami, and more "lemonade," John Bickford's remarkable story unfolded. It began with him answering his country's call to arms in 1861, his enlistment in the navy, and assignment to the USS *Kearsarge*. It continued with his young man's unauthorized and dangerous spying on one of the enemy's ships and with the remarkable story of the famous battle between the *Kearsarge* and the *Alabama*. Cook learned, too, about Bickford's rapid rise through the ranks, his assignment to a blockade ship on the Cape Fear River after his *Kearsarge* tour, his debilitating malaria that forced him from the navy, and his later life, including his work, marriage, rowdy *Kearsarge* reunions, and—sadly—his becoming a widower.

As the sun sank a little lower, and the clock moved toward 4:00 p.m., Bickford finally ran out of steam—or maybe it was the "lemonade."

The old man pointed toward the harbor. "You see that string of boats tied up down there, over yonder? That's my 'fleet.' I'm the admiral of my own fleet!" he guffawed, slapping his knee. "I rent the boats out. Sometimes I go, too, if they need a hand. Tell my sea stories for extra tips. Sometimes they know who I am, sometimes not."

He paused for a moment, silently contemplating.

"I'm almost the last one, you know. Only three of us from the *Kearsarge* left now."

The two-cylinder "pock-etta, pock-etta" of the old fisherman's outboard broke the silence. It was time to get back to the mainland. Bickford walked Cook down to the pier, a bit more unsteadily this time. With a glint in his eyes, and rosy cheeked, Bickford bid his guest adieu. Cook promised to send, by post, any article that might be published.

Lastly, Cook pointed toward Bickford's shirt. "Say, Captain Bickford, would you mind? For the ride back?"

Bickford laughed heartily and handed over the silver flask. Cook drained the last two fingers, returned the container, then climbed down into the dinghy.

On June 21, 1922, the *Boston Evening Transcript* published a long article with Sherwin Cook's byline titled, "A Survivor Recalls the *Kearsarge* Fight." The piece featured a large photograph of former Acting Master John Bickford, U.S. Navy, wearing his Medal of Honor.

Almost five years later John Bickford, proud old sailor, heroic warrior, and "admiral" of his own fleet, sailed off into the sunset one last time, on April 28, 1927, age eighty-four. He was not just one of the seventeen men who were awarded Medals of Honor for their actions in the duel between the USS *Kearsarge* and the CSS *Alabama*—Bickford was the last living crewman to earn America's highest military honor in the greatest sea battle of the Civil War.

ACT I:
THE RAIDER

I don't care if you have to chase that pirate to the uttermost ends of the earth!

Gideon Welles, Secretary of the Union Navy

1

When the Civil War began in the spring of 1861, Raphael Semmes hoped to become captain of a ship. And not just any ship, but a fighting ship—a powerful vessel that could bring the contest to the enemy and prevail. The odds, however, were not favorable. And no one, not even Semmes, could have believed that he would become a noted hero of the Confederacy, a maritime version of Robert E. Lee.

One big hurdle for Semmes to overcome was that the administration of President Jefferson Davis might consider him too old to be a seafaring captain. It was not unheard of in the early days of the Civil War for a land-based commanding officer to be over fifty, and even have great responsibilities. A very public yet extreme example was the Union's commanding general at the start of the war, Winfield Scott, who had become a general during the War of 1812; his next birthday would be his seventy-fifth. On the Confederate side, Lee had turned fifty-four that January. Commanding a ship at sea, however, was a particularly strenuous job, and a captain could go for weeks without a respite. Semmes would turn fifty-two in 1861, and with few captaincies available, one could assume the nascent nation would rely on its young firebrands to further the South's military cause at sea. But unlike the eager Rebel naval officers in their thirties and even twenties, Raphael Semmes had wartime experience to back his claims.

He was not a native-born Southerner, though Maryland, where his family had lived as slave-owning tobacco farmers for generations, had strong Southern leanings. Catherine Middleton Semmes[1] had given birth to her first son, Raphael, on September 27, 1809, on the family farm twenty-five miles south of Washington, D.C. Another son, Samuel, was born two years later. Then the stability of the family shattered. The boys' mother died soon after Samuel was born and their father, Richard Thompson Semmes, remarried and uprooted the family, moving his new bride and sons to the Georgetown section of Washington. Several years later, when Raphael was fourteen, there was a new tragedy when his father, just thirty-nine, died.

Apparently, the Widow Semmes's plans for her future did not include continuing to be a stepmother because she sent the two boys back to Maryland to live with their uncles in Prince Georges County, east of Washington, D.C. Uncles Raphael and Alexander Semmes were both merchant ship captains and business owners. Uncle Benedict Semmes was a physician and a rising politician in the county.[2]

Uncles Alexander and Raphael—the latter having the nephews living with him—were the primary influences on the younger Raphael (Uncle Alexander was lost at sea in 1826). They encouraged his interests in a career on the water, beginning by teaching him how to swim in the Potomac River. But the influence of Benedict Semmes, a member of the Maryland

1   Catherine Semmes was a descendant of Arthur Middleton, a signer of the Declaration of Independence.

2   This particular uncle was named after the Benedict Semmes who had accompanied Lord Baltimore on his voyage to America in 1634.

House of Delegates, was of great value too. He passed on to Raphael a passion for reading and writing. While the young-ster's main enthusiasm would be for sailing the sea, a love of books made those long days and nights not only tolerable but enjoyable. Also, because of his passion and industriousness, with his uncle as guide, Raphael received a better education than a local school in Prince Georges County might have given him.

As sporadic as his formal schooling was, Raphael did have the opportunity to study Latin, science, and history. Politics was a frequent subject of conversation at the Semmes residence, especially when prominent lawmakers like Henry Clay of Kentucky visited. Already there was support for states' rights in the family.

The clan's religious beliefs were also very important to the teenager. The Semmes family had been Roman Catholic at least since the first Benedict Semmes had set foot in the New World. With his aunts and uncles and cousins, Raphael attended Holy Trinity Church in Georgetown. According to the biographer John M. Taylor, Semmes "came to view Catholicism as an im-portant part of his cultural heritage and to regard his Catholic forbears as a driving force behind the growth of political liberty in both Britain and America."

Benedict Semmes was also instrumental in getting his nephew's naval career off to a good start. Raphael was just sixteen when his uncle, by then Speaker of the Maryland House of Delegates, secured for him an appointment from President John Quincy Adams as a U.S. Navy midshipman.[3] Finally, he could be off on the sort of adventures Uncles Raphael and Alexander had told him about. No doubt another reason for the teenager setting off to sea was that even the living conditions aboard a wooden ship would be more congenial than his own household, given

---

3 Semmes would express his gratitude publicly twenty-five years later when he dedicated his first book to Benedict Semmes.

that his Uncle Raphael and his wife, Mary, would eventually raise thirteen children of their own.[4]

Once at sea, however, young Raphael realized he should have counted his blessings. Life aboard a ship, especially for prolonged periods, meant enduring confined and foul-smelling quarters, food on the verge of being rancid, "fresh" water in barrels that gave off a sickening odor and tasted worse, encounters with rats and a range of maddening insects, salt beef and pork that could make one gag, jaw-breaking biscuits, and never knowing if the next storm to strike was the one that would spell doom.

Midshipmen had one boot in each shipboard world: they were the lowest ranking of the officers yet were senior to all the enlisted men. They dined and lived with the officers but spent most of their time getting the crew to attend to orders and their assigned tasks. Despite all the challenges, for a man foreseeing a career in the navy, living on a ship at sea was also an academy.[5] A midshipman learned everything about how a ship operated and was taught navigation, seamanship, signals, rules of the road, naval regulations, and other essential skills. His teachers were both his superiors and the senior petty officers with years of experience. Midshipmen visited places that heretofore had existed only in travel journals and their imaginations. Acquiring and practicing discipline was very important too, not only for the midshipmen themselves but also making sure it was applied to the crew. They learned how to cope with fear and crises, such as when the ship was battered and tossed about by storms and it seemed that only Providence could save it from catastrophe.

For the next six years, Semmes was a junior officer in good standing, adapting easily to the rigors of life aboard U.S. Navy ships, which at that time, in the 1820s into the '30s, was still a

---

4   His brother, Samuel (1811–1867), would grow up to attend Georgetown University and become a lawyer and a Maryland state senator (1855–1866).

5   There was no national service academy for the navy until the U.S. Naval Academy at Annapolis was established in 1845.

navy based on sail. Below-deck living conditions continued to be claustrophobic, uncomfortable, and fetid. On deck, when midshipmen like Raphael Semmes were on watch, the weather ranged from blistering heat to bone-chilling cold depending on the latitudes. Semmes, the son of a farmer, took it all in and thrived.

In addition to his embrace of a wide and watery world, voyages allowed Semmes to broaden his intellect. He was required to learn the sciences of the sea, but at ports of call he searched for books, some to enhance his necessary studies but also novels to be read for pleasure. He found he enjoyed writing as well. Visiting islands and cities—some exotic, others exciting for their beauty and legendary attractions—was pleasurable enough, but for Semmes, writing about his experiences in journals compounded the joy of being a seafaring lad.

He was land bound for a time while attending a required navy school for junior officers at the Norfolk Navy Yard in Virginia, a forerunner of the U.S. Naval Academy. After this, he passed a series of tests—with the second-highest score in his class—that left him ready for promotion to lieutenant. But this was 1832 and the United States had not been at war since the conclusion of the War of 1812 eighteen years earlier. The good news was not losing soldiers and sailors in combat; the bad news was a lack of opportunity for ambitious officers. Semmes, nearing his twenty-third birthday and not having political connections higher than Uncle Benedict, was confronted with the likelihood of fewer voyages, less adventure, and surviving on half pay.[6] By this time his brother, Samuel, had become an attorney, and Raphael decided to become one too.

He "read for the law"[7] and after passing the bar in Florida in

---

6 A bright spot was an assignment in Norfolk to maintain the chronometers of navy ships in port, which led to a lifelong fascination with the instrument.

7 In the nineteenth century "reading for the law" or studying law books and being tutored by practicing attorneys was still a common and accepted way to become a lawyer. Law school was not a requirement: Abraham Lincoln became a lawyer in the same way.

April 1834, the twenty-four-year-old Semmes settled in Cincinnati to practice. He had friends in the Queen City who were also newly minted attorneys. His legal career was still in its infancy when he became involved in a significant case. Several young Ohio men opposed the view of an abolitionist publication so vehemently that they destroyed the presses. They hired Semmes to represent them. The prosecutor he opposed in court was Salmon P. Chase. To the latter's chagrin, Semmes's defense was successful. Less than thirty years later the two would square off again—in a way—with Semmes being a Confederate Navy raider captain and Chase being the secretary of the treasury in Abraham Lincoln's cabinet.

Also, while in Cincinnati, Semmes fell in love. He was residing at the home of Electra and Oliver Spencer, and they had a daughter named Anne Elizabeth.[8] The attraction was mutual, and before long it became clear that they would marry. The future was also clear: In Ohio, Semmes would grow his practice and, with Elizabeth, a family. His father-in-law was a Methodist preacher, which at the least would be useful in making connections. But the U.S. Navy intervened to alter the immediate future.

Semmes had not quit the service but had been placed on indefinite leave to pursue the law, so when he was summoned back to active duty in March 1835, he had to leave Anne and Cincinnati. Still a passed midshipman, he was sent to join the crew of the USS *Constellation*. This was quite a comeback for his naval career. The thirty-eight-gun, three-masted frigate had been built and launched out of Baltimore in 1797, and its name had been chosen by President George Washington. Its most famous engagement came two years later when, although the two countries were not officially at war, the *Constellation*

---

8   Oliver Spencer's childhood included being kidnapped by Indians when he was ten and adopted by the tribe. He was adapting quite well but seven months later a British agent encountered the boy and bought him from the Indians. For years afterward, Oliver was paid visits by his adopted Native American father.

defeated the thirty-six-gun frigate *L'Insurgente* of France in the Caribbean. The ship later participated in the First and Second Barbary Wars and distinguished itself against the British in the War of 1812.

Constellation's mission in 1835 was to sail to the West Indies and protect American shipping from pirates. The following year *Constellation* transported supplies and soldiers to Florida during the Second Seminole War. As part of this endeavor, Semmes was given command of a small cargo ship, the *Lieutenant Izard*, used to get supplies ashore. This opportunity came to an unfortunate end in October 1836 when, while towing a barge of goods, the *Lieutenant Izard* ran aground. It would soon be deemed a total loss.

Nonetheless, the following year, Semmes completed his posting on the *Constellation* and was promoted to lieutenant. This allowed him to return to Cincinnati with some measure of achievement. He was welcomed well enough by the Spencers that they gave permission for their daughter, only seventeen years of age, to marry a man a decade older. That the ceremony took place in May 1837 at the Episcopal Christ Church was probably a concession to the Spencer family but Anne herself converted to Catholicism soon thereafter, to please her husband.

Though there were strong and genuine feelings between Raphael and Anne Semmes, the marriage would often be a troubled one. The difference in religion was but one factor. Another was Semmes being a navy lieutenant. He could have left the service for good to focus on his law practice but apparently he could not bring himself to do so. This meant that from time to time he was drawn back to active duty, with most of his postings being at bases along the Gulf of Mexico. For Anne, this meant either her husband being absent or accompanying him in a climate much less comfortable to her than Ohio. It also would mean and become increasingly significant that she and her family were living in the South. This was solidified in 1841 when Semmes bought property for what became the family estate known as Prospect Hill in southeast Alabama. From that point on Semmes would consider Alabama his home state.

The lieutenant was home often enough—mostly working as a land-bound navy surveyor—that he and Anne started a brood of young Semmeses. First came two sons named Samuel (1838) and Oliver (1839), then daughters Electra (1843) and Katherine (1844). Eventually there would be a Raphael Jr., too, in 1849. But in the fall of 1843, it was back to sea when he was assigned to a new class of ship, a steamer. The USS *Poinsett* was instructed to deliver an emissary of the U.S. State Department to Veracruz, allowing Semmes to visit Mexico and record his impressions about the country.

Upon his return, he resumed the sedate and not nearly as stimulating life of a landlubber. In 1845, soon after the birth of Katherine, Semmes was off to sea again, this time as first officer of the USS *Porpoise*. The ten-gun brig was tasked with patrolling the Caribbean. During its travels, the crew learned that war had broken out between the United States and Mexico. In July 1846, the *Porpoise* was ordered to Veracruz where it was to become part of the navy squadron stationed there. Finally, in his late thirties, Semmes would experience combat.

At first, however, there was very little action to write home to Anne about. The squadron, commanded by the War of 1812 veteran Commodore David Connor, was assigned to blockade Mexican ports and guard against attacks on American shipping. While tactically sound, this chore was routinely boring. Making the experience more frustrating was receiving reports about victories by U.S. forces on the mainland. If only war had been declared against a country with a navy worth fighting.

Semmes's mood certainly improved in October when he received his own command. He would captain a brig named the *Somers*, and its 32-pounders, ten of them, packed a wallop. Unfortunately, the ship had the reputation of being haunted. In

November 1842, only seven months after it was launched at the New York Navy Yard, while en route to the West Indies, several members of the crew were accused of mutiny and three were hanged.[9] Longtime crew members subsequently claimed that on some nights the ghosts of the executed men visited their former below-deck berths.

Semmes soon distinguished himself as captain of the infamous vessel. The *Creole*, a Mexican ship, had managed to run the blockade and sail into the port of Veracruz. Under the cover of darkness on November 26, Semmes sent his first officer and seven others in a rowboat into the harbor where they set fire to the *Creole*. Most of the ship and its cargo were destroyed.

The captain had very little time to bask in congratulations. Only two weeks later, the *Somers* was sunk. On the morning of December 8, the sighting of an unfamiliar sail prompted Semmes to give chase. The *Somers* did not get far when it was struck by a sudden and vicious squall. The ship was blown so much over to starboard that its yards were in the sea. Water began to flood the ship and with the storm continuing to batter the *Somers*, there was nothing to prevent it from sinking. In the brutal chaos two of the lifeboats were broken up, leaving just one to accommodate the survivors. Semmes, making good use of the strength and skills he had acquired years earlier swimming in the Potomac, dived into the roiling water and swam to a floating plank of wood, joining his first officer in clinging to it. The squall began to sweep them away.

---

9   One of the alleged mutineers was a midshipman, Philip Spencer. He was no relation to Semmes's in-laws, but he was the son of John Spencer, Secretary of War in President John Tyler's cabinet. The "Somers Affair," as it was known, remains the only mutiny aboard a U.S. Navy ship. A lieutenant aboard the ship was Guert Gansevoort, who it is believed informed his cousin Herman Melville of events on the *Somers*, which later informed the short novel *Billy Budd*. Additionally, the U.S. Naval Academy was founded as a direct result of the Somers Affair. Appalled that a midshipman would consider mutiny, senior naval officials ordered the creation of the academy so that midshipmen could receive a formal and supervised education in seamanship, discipline, maritime law, and related matters.

The career as well as the life of Raphael Semmes might have ended right there but for the intervention of Midshipman Francis Clarke. He had steered the one remaining lifeboat to nearby Green Island, unloaded crew members, and set out again into the turbulence. Clarke caught up to his captain and first officer, James Parker, finding them close to drowning. He hauled them in and made for the nearest ship, the *Endymion*, a British warship. As Semmes and Parker recovered, they learned of the magnitude of the disaster.

The *Somers* was gone, and with her went thirty-nine of seventy-six crew members. Though a natural disaster, the captain would still be held responsible. Ironically, the abrupt appearance of the squall and its mercilessness worked in Semmes's favor. During a court of inquiry, the surviving officers supported their captain's argument that he was not at fault, that nothing could have been done to save the ship in such a maelstrom. The court agreed and Semmes was found blameless.

With his command having been lost, Semmes was given a posting as a lieutenant on the USS *Raritan*. A few days later, he welcomed into his cabin another lieutenant, a fellow by the name of John Winslow. He, too, was a Southerner, at least by birth, having been born in North Carolina, though raised in New England. Winslow had also just lost a ship, the *Morris*, which had hit a reef while on blockade duty. As Semmes and Winslow bucked each other up, a friendship bloomed.

General Winfield Scott arrived in Mexico in late winter 1847. Semmes noted in his journal that the embarkation of troops had gone smoothly, then added, perhaps to feel less left out of the anticipated action: "The officers of the navy, although cut off by the nature of the war, from any participation in its glories, none the less willingly discharged their duties to the government, and aided their more fortunate brethren of the army, to gather fresh laurels for their common country."

With his army outside Veracruz that March, General Scott made plans to seize the city. Because he had outdistanced his artillery, Scott needed to borrow guns from the navy squadron, which was then co-commanded by Matthew Perry.[10] The commodore required that navy guns be operated by navy men, so officers of the fleet were deployed along with six 32-pounders, which were transferred to land and hauled to within firing distance of Veracruz. One of those officers with a chance for "fresh laurels" was Raphael Semmes, who had been chosen to assist the army with the loaned ordnance. Semmes, in turn, was introduced to an army officer coordinating the guns' placement, Captain Robert E. Lee.

The bombardment commenced on the 24th and ended the following day when the Mexican garrison in Veracruz surrendered. If Semmes was disappointed that the battle had been so brief, he was cheered by another exciting assignment—to journey deep into Mexico as an emissary to its president, Antonio López de Santa Anna. This was the same Santa Anna who eleven years earlier had massacred Davy Crockett, Jim Bowie, William Travis, and the other defenders of the Alamo.

The purpose of the mission was to protest the treatment of Clay Rogers. He had been a midshipman serving under Semmes on the ill-fated *Somers* who had been captured during a middle-of-the-night attempt to destroy a Mexican powder magazine. Word had reached the James Polk administration that instead of being incarcerated as a prisoner of war, Rogers was to be tried as a spy.

This was a different kind of adventure indeed, and a rescue mission of a former loyal officer as well. Semmes set off in early April 1847 accompanied by another navy officer, Francis Seymour, and escorted by army cavalry. The first leg of the journey

---

10 The fifty-one-year-old Perry helped establish the curriculum at the U.S. Naval Academy and came to be considered the "Father of the Steam Navy," but is mostly known for opening up Japan to the Western world with his first visit there in 1853.

would be to catch up with the American army which was making good progress into Mexico from Veracruz and would soon score a victory at Cerro Gordo. Along the way, Semmes noted in his journal the intriguing plants and flowers he observed as well as his experiences, such as writing about spending one night in a small village they encountered along the way:

He and Seymour "put together very comfortable beds, on which we soon fell asleep, lulled by the pattering of the rain on the palm leaves of the roof, the occasional chattering of the guinea fowl, and now and then a little of the national music of the country—the braying of a donkey."

The mission did not proceed smoothly. When Semmes and his entourage caught up with the army, General Scott brushed them off at first. Then Scott reconsidered—no sense irritating the navy when there was still a chance their services could be of use. Then it had to be ascertained if Rogers really was going to be put on trial. It turned out he was finally counted a prisoner of war and in no imminent danger. Still, holding a flag of truce, Semmes met with a Mexican general to negotiate a prisoner exchange. No one knew that back in Mexico City, Rogers had simply walked away from the prison and was already on his way to Scott's position, eighty miles to the southeast. When Rogers arrived safe and sound, Semmes's mission was quietly abandoned.

Semmes was not keen on going back to the boredom of blockade duty. Instead of returning to Veracruz he dawdled at General Scott's headquarters and was rewarded with an invitation to join the staff, no doubt aided by being able to speak Spanish fluently. He thus was able to accompany the American army when it began its march toward Mexico City to deliver a knockout blow.

Nearing the country's capital, Semmes was a member of a scouting party who found a passage that would allow Scott to forego a head-on attack into the city's defenses in favor of a flanking assault. At the same time and from another direction, an American army commanded by General Zachary Taylor also threatened Mexico City. In August, Mexican forces were defeated in several actions, and on the 20th a Mexican emissary arrived at Scott's headquarters to request a truce. Negotiations ensued, with Semmes as a translator. However, when Scott suspected that Santa Anna was simply trying to buy time, the war resumed.

Semmes and Lieutenant Ulysses S. Grant worked together to position artillery for what was expected to be the climactic assault on Mexico City. But it turned out that the attack on Chapultepec fortress on September 13, 1847, broke the defenders' back. Santa Anna surrendered, and with that the war with Mexico entered its final stages.

Semmes received several commendations for his services in the campaign, which helped to put the ignominious end of the *Somers* well behind him. The bad news was that with the war over and no other similar conflict on the horizon, there was suddenly an overabundance of idle navy lieutenants. Semmes went home to Alabama where he slipped back into the roles of husband and father and lawyer.

And there was some rather awkward news awaiting him: When Semmes returned home to Prospect Hill, the twenty-seven-year-old Anne was eight months' pregnant. During the time of conception her husband had been at Veracruz. The baby delivered the following month, her fifth, was named Anna Elizabeth Semmes. Though the marriage remained intact, as a young child Anna Elizabeth was exiled to the Academy of the Sacred Heart, a Roman Catholic boarding school near Philadelphia. Other than scheduled visits, Anna Elizabeth would not return to live with her mother until Semmes shipped out during the Civil War.

Though immersed in his law practice, Semmes could not resist taking on another occupation, that of a writer. Relying on his memories of recent events and his journals, Semmes wrote a book that would be published in 1851.

Service Afloat and Ashore During the Mexican War was not simply a memoir. The author's ambitions were grander than that. He first offered a history of Mexico, then details about the country's people, sympathetically portraying the poor. He detoured to his thoughts about American expansionism and politics. And he finally got around to providing details of his observations and exploits during the war. Upon publication, *Service Afloat* would receive glowing reviews, more satisfying to Semmes than mundane law matters.

The navy was not completely done with Raphael Semmes, though. He was given command of the *Electra*—a storeship that coincidentally shared the name of his mother-in-law and daughter—and this job was as boring as blockade duty. He soon requested another assignment and was made an inspector of clothing and supplies at the Pensacola Navy Yard. There was a brief escape from this drudgery in February 1849 when he commanded the USS *Flirt*, a schooner, which was dispatched to patrol waters off Mexico, but that made him homesick. He was back in Pensacola when he became involved in a legal action that would prove significant for him.

Four midshipmen on the USS *Albany* were to be tried for refusing to obey orders. One of them was Francis Clarke, the same junior officer who had saved Semmes's life when the *Somers* had sunk. Obviously, Semmes could not ignore Clarke's plea for help, and he signed on as their defense attorney. One of the other accused midshipmen was John McIntosh Kell.

While it is likely Semmes would have represented Clarke and his *Albany* comrades anyway, it helped that he believed in the defense. The midshipmen had refused to carry out orders they considered demeaning and insulting. They had been treated by the captain as nothing more than cabin boys. Semmes argued eloquently during the trial, but the naval court was not swayed. The four young men were convicted and dismissed from the navy.[11] Twelve years later, Kell would serve aboard a military

---

11   Clarke was reappointed a passed midshipman in 1851, promoted to master in 1855, but died at sea of disease the same year.

ship again—this time a Confederate one, and under the command of Raphael Semmes.

Disappointed in the verdict and the autocratic nature of the U.S. Navy, Semmes returned to Alabama. But the family was together in Mobile only a short time.[12] In November, Semmes and his wife and by now a gaggle of six children relocated to Mobile so he could focus on his law practice. As Semmes settled in as patriarch of the large family, his view was that unless a foreign power displayed enough belligerence, his career as a military man on the water was likely over.

---

12 Semmes had moved his family to the city from the somewhat isolated Prospect Hill, which perhaps, like Anna, prompted memories of his wife's infidelity.

2

Raphael Semmes thought he was through with the navy, but the navy was not through with him. He just was not needed on the water. While the conflict over slavery roiled the nation during the administrations of Franklin Pierce and James Buchanan, the decade of the 1850s was a mostly peaceful period internationally for the United States and many of the navy's ships of war were left sitting at their docks or semiretired in a reserve fleet.

As he tried to grow his practice in Mobile, Semmes kept a hand in naval affairs by serving on court-martial panels. He occasionally requested sea duty—perhaps a reflection on the shifting levels of domestic bliss—but he was rejected. Still, despite relative inactivity, in September 1855 he received a promotion, to commander.[13] One result was the navy, the following year, finally granted his request and he was made captain of the U.S. Mail steamer *Illinois*. There was not much adventure to be had on it, though, as the ship's purpose was only to transport mail. In

---

13 Promotion in the nineteenth-century navy, much like the army, was seldom based solely on merit, but rather how long one served and vacancies above an individual created by death, disability, or retirement.

November, Semmes was assigned to a position even less scintillating, as an inspector of lighthouses along the Gulf of Mexico.

An unanticipated consequence of his diligent if not flashy service was further promotion to secretary of the Lighthouse Board. As this was a subdivision of the Treasury Department and under its direct supervision, the job could not be telegraphed in from Pensacola or Mobile. Semmes relocated to a basement office in the Treasury Department in Washington, D.C. One might think the land-bound commander, just turned forty-seven and separated by nearly a thousand miles from his family, would have been living a nightmare scenario. However, in a letter to his eldest son, Samuel Spencer, he claimed to be satisfied with the work and the social and cultural advantages of a city that straddled the North and South and that dwarfed Mobile. He would be secretary of the board for the next two and a half years.

During this time, Semmes's views on slavery and the suppression of the South were evolving. His family had owned slaves and he had now spent over fifteen years as a landowner in the Deep South and was himself a slave owner. However, his wife and her family were from a Northern state and leaned toward abolition—yet at Prospect Hill in Alabama, Anne had gone along with slave ownership. Semmes looked at the North as haughty and often bullying the South. He was not a supporter of those advocating Southern secession, but he did believe in states' rights and self-determination, probably recalling some of the political discussions at Uncle Benedict's home.

Semmes did his job as he continued to wither on the vine as a seagoing officer. Little about him foretold his spectacular future. As the biographer John M. Taylor notes, the land-bound captain "gave few indications at this time of the dynamism that he would bring to the Confederate Navy. He projected no charisma or martial presence."

Everything changed on January 11, 1861, when Alabama seceded from the Union. The state had not been the first to do so. That distinction was held by South Carolina, which in short order was followed by Mississippi and Florida. Two days after Alabama joined them, Semmes visited the Washington, D.C., home of one of the state's two senators, Clement Clay.[14] There, he informed Clay of his intention to resign from the U.S. Navy and put himself at the disposal of the emerging Confederate States of America.

However, Semmes had hesitated before doing so. One reason had to be the personal cost to himself—and his family—of leaving a secure position and the advancement possibilities with the Union in a war that appeared inevitable. While Semmes sympathized with the plight of the put-upon South, its cause could crash and burn swiftly, and he would have ruined his naval career. Another impact on his family was being a native Marylander whose children's grandparents were Northerners. Such an act as resignation could affect his children and of course his marriage to a native Ohioan.

There may well have been a third reason—the dim prospect of there being a Confederate Navy to serve in. After over a decade of relative peace the navy of the United States was not formidable, but at least it was a navy.

Early in 1861, the entire U.S. Navy consisted of eighty-nine ships, forty-six of which were laid up in reserve and crewless. Half of the mothball fleet were so decrepit and obsolete that they were, in reality, unusable and fragile hulks. One active ship, the USS *Michigan*, was on permanent Great Lakes duty. In truth, she was too big to get out of the Great Lakes and go to sea. That left forty-two hulls on active duty that were manned and equipped sufficiently to take to sea and perform their assigned missions. Half of the serviceable ships were wooden sailing vessels in an age that was turning to steam and iron. The largest and most powerful Union warship at the beginning of the Civil War was the USS *Powhatan*, a two-hundred-foot-long side-wheel steam

---

14   A third cousin of the famous Henry Clay.

frigate that could chug along at eleven knots, top speed. She was armed with eleven Dahlgren smoothbore cannons, which made her a formidable foe—but she was still wooden hulled and sported masts and sails for backup.

The navy had begun the year with approximately 7,000 sailors of all ranks and nearly 1,200 commissioned officers, from midshipmen to captains. That number was about to change drastically. In the aftermath of states seceding, 350 officers resigned, defected, or were dismissed as they literally jumped ship to join the nascent Confederate States Navy. Nearly 2,000 enlisted sailors did the same. When the new U.S. secretary of the navy, Gideon Welles, first toured the Navy Department he found dozens of empty desks and piles of papers, some skittering across the floor, left behind by the officers who had quickly traded sides and vacated their posts. The entire Navy Department was in complete disarray.

A handful of the U.S. Navy's active-duty ships were in the Pacific. At least one frigate was stationed at all times at the Isthmus of Panama to protect the gold trade trekking back and forth over the pre-canal land routes from the Pacific to the Atlantic. Two frigates were assigned to San Francisco, and one or two additional warships were constantly busy scouting and maintaining an American presence in the Far East. The remaining vessels were transferred to the East Coast to take a more active part in the expected war effort.

Despite the inadequate status of the U.S. Navy, the Confederate Navy that Semmes contemplated joining was almost laughable in comparison. Still, on February 14, his period of indecision ended. At the time, Montgomery in his home state of Alabama was the capital of the Confederacy, and from it Charles Conrad, the chairman of the Committee on Naval Affairs, sent Semmes a telegram requesting his presence. With this invitation in one hand, he signed his U.S. Navy resignation letter with the other.

He bade goodbye to Anne and the children still living at their rented home in Washington, D.C., and took a train south.[15]

Semmes stepped off the train in Montgomery on February 18. There he called upon Conrad to pledge his loyalty to the Southern cause. Next came a meeting with the new president of the Confederate States of America, Jefferson Davis. Up north, Raphael Semmes may have been only a member of the Lighthouse Board, but in Alabama he was an experienced naval commander who had cast his lot with a rebellion that was, in his mind, true and just.

Davis explained the obvious: He could not put Semmes out to sea to fight for the South because there were practically no decks to set under his feet. What the Confederacy needed most urgently was…well, everything. President Davis told Semmes his stay in Montgomery was to be short-lived because his mission was to return to the North as a secret purchasing agent. Of highest priority were weapons and other items that would help fight a war. The surrender of Fort Sumter to Rebel forces was still almost two months away, but few Southerners doubted that once the defeated James Buchanan was out of office and was replaced by Abraham Lincoln, there would be retribution for secession.

So, Semmes reversed course—physically, not philosophically. Though he had resigned from the U.S. Navy, not all his contacts were aware of that fact; so, he was still received at the facilities he wanted to visit. First was the Tredegar Iron Works and state arsenal in Virginia, then he was back in Washington to tour the government arsenal. Semmes was both a spy and purchasing agent. What was about to drop off his résumé was "family man."

With her husband's future so uncertain, and with it his ability to provide, Anne Semmes had arranged to take her children

---

15 Spencer Semmes was living in Georgia and Oliver Semmes was attending West Point. The children at home were Electra, Katherine, and Raphael Jr.

to Cincinnati and live with her parents. As awkward as this would be with Raphael essentially committing treason against the United States, Anne had no other choice. Even so, despite previous strains, their parting was a difficult and heartfelt one. It would have been even more stressful if either Raphael or Anne had even imagined, let alone known, that they would not see each other again for over three years.

On March 5, 1861, Semmes boarded a train and resumed his secret mission. He toured manufacturing and military sites in New York, Connecticut, and Massachusetts. He did more than observe: He signed contracts to purchase munitions and other essential supplies. Astonishingly, perhaps because of the confusion of the change in presidential administrations, there was no prohibition against Southern representatives buying Northern products that would, very soon, be used against Northern forces.

One stop on his tour was more personally rewarding— Semmes traveled to West Point to visit his son Oliver. The twenty-one-year-old was in his third year there. The two had to have discussed the prospects of war and Semmes's resignation from the U.S. Navy, and Semmes possibly revealed his secret mission on behalf of the Confederacy. Oliver did not immediately join his father by switching sides, allowing for the possibility that should there be a war father and son could be fighting under different flags.[16]

After West Point, Semmes ventured to New York City and resumed his subversive activities, which included an unsuccessful search for ships that could be co-opted and sailed south to defend important Confederate ports. As the weeks passed, however, Semmes believed that his overtures to manufacturers and military supply officials had aroused suspicions. And with the

---

16 As it turned out, Oliver did quit the Academy later that year. He was offered a commission in a Confederate artillery regiment and rose to the rank of major during the war. He survived and became a very successful lawyer and judge. His older brother, Samuel Spencer, also joined the Confederate Army and was an officer of infantry with the rank of captain. He, too, survived the war and became a lawyer.

threats and other rhetoric between North and South becoming more heated, he had to consider his own safety. If war did indeed break out, what if he were arrested as a spy?

It was time to make his way home. Semmes booked passage on a steamship that took him to Savannah, then boarded a train to Montgomery. It was a relief to be back in Alabama and he was flattered to be met by the new Confederate secretary of the navy, Stephen Mallory.

The Trinidad-born forty-eight-year-old Mallory had served as chairman of the U.S. Senate's Committee on Naval Affairs and had pushed to update the American Navy so that it could better compete on the high seas. In January, the Florida senator reluctantly resigned from Congress when his state seceded. Confederate President Jefferson Davis was glad to take advantage of Mallory's nautical experience, which had begun in childhood when his family lived in the West Indies and then Key West.

After reporting on his activities and personally interacting with the secretary of the Confederate Navy, Semmes expected a high-level appointment in the department. He was disappointed. With what must have been teeth-grinding irony, Semmes accepted placement in the Confederate Lighthouse Bureau. The only uplifting news was that with only the lighthouses south of the Mason–Dixon line under his purview, his workload was cut in half. Semmes told Mallory, however, that he assumed this position was a temporary one and he would be better rewarded for his service thus far if war happened.

He did not have to wait long. On April 13, after being fired upon by Confederate batteries in Charleston Harbor, the Federal garrison at Fort Sumter surrendered. Semmes witnessed the cheerful celebrations in Montgomery. By now he fully supported the outbreak of hostilities, but more important to him personally, as was the case fifteen years earlier, war meant opportunity. He had been one of many young and ambitious lieutenants when the conflict with Mexico began; now he was an experienced of-

PHIL KEITH WITH TOM CLAVIN

ficer almost too old to return to a ship command. Semmes had to have a seagoing assignment and right away. He tried not to think of those hundreds of other officers who had left the U.S. Navy and were also anxious to fight for their young country.

He met with Secretary Mallory again. He pled that remaining ashore and overseeing lighthouses was really not suitable for his talents and experience. Fortunately, Mallory agreed. It had aided Semmes's argument that he strongly encouraged the attacking of oceangoing Union ships, but one of Mallory's concerns was the legality of such actions. Commerce raiders could be viewed as privateers, or worse, as pirates. The Confederate cabinet member did not care so much what the Union perspective on this tactic was as he did what England and France thought. The South's survival and possible success could be determined in London and Paris where the respective governments would be deliberating which side to support. Releasing a flock of pirates on the high seas could backfire.

Semmes's experience as an attorney and counselor came to the fore. He argued to Mallory that a privateer sailed a thin line to be sure, but a Confederate raider was not seeking plunder but was, in defense of its country, preventing its opponent from profiting and gaining an advantage. Semmes would not be a privateer or a pirate; he would be the captain of a Confederate States ship in a declared war engaging enemy vessels openly in international waters. Only Union ships would be prey while the ships of neutral countries could travel without fear.

That made sense to Mallory. But Semmes was only partway to receiving a commission. The next hurdle to overcome was finding a ship. The secretary handed Semmes documents on the paltry number of vessels available that could be seaworthy. One set of papers provided details about the government-owned *Havana*, a five-hundred-ton passenger steamer. Her biggest limitation was that she could travel only five days without refueling.

There were other drawbacks, including limited storage space and accommodations for only a handful of crew members.

However, Semmes was intrigued. Where Mallory saw deficiencies, Semmes saw potential. If he could have the *Havana*, he would find a way to bedevil the Yankees. As he would soon write to his daughter Electra about the expanding conflict, "The fierce and savage war which is being waged against us, by the fanatic and half-civilized hordes of the North, strikes a serious and an alarming blow at the principle of self-government—not only in these states but throughout the world." He tossed in "the rude, rough, unbridled, and corrupt North" for good measure.

And so, on Thursday, April 18, 1861—the same day Robert E. Lee turned down an offer from President Lincoln to command all Union troops—Raphael Semmes was appointed commander of a Confederate ship that would be the first to take the fight to the Union Navy on the high seas.

3

In the previous fifteen years the amount of American merchant traffic on the high seas had tripled. In that sphere, the United States now rivaled Great Britain. During this period that country and its European neighbors had found it increasingly difficult to compete with the younger nation's manufacturing expansion and its impact on the global economy. "European shippers looked on in dismay as swift and efficient American ships took over high-profit cargoes, leaving their own ships rotting in port or carrying bulk cargoes at reduced rates," observes the naval historian Chester G. Hearn. "With a strong commercial presence in virtually every port in the world, the American carrying trade in 1860 looked indestructible."

To add to the overall picture: In the years leading up to the Civil War, worldwide trade had increased 300 percent. And of that trade, 70 percent of it was conducted by American ships. In April 1861, almost all of them were Union ships.

When war broke out at Fort Sumter, the already beleaguered Confederate secretary Stephen Mallory could count only ten ships in his naval inventory. These were certainly not ships of the line because combined they carried only fifteen guns. One ship, the *Robert McClellan*, carried five of those guns.[17]

The list of what the Confederate States lacked to deploy a navy was much longer than what it had. Even if an effort to create a navy was supported enthusiastically by the Jefferson Davis administration, how could one be constructed? The manufacturing abilities of the South were dwarfed by those of the North. More specifically, there was at best a handful of shipbuilding facilities located in the new South. The Confederacy had an abundance of raw materials but turning them into ships that could outrun and outfight the Union naval forces would take a miracle. And even if facilities could be expanded and upgraded swiftly, how would the Confederacy pay for an ambitious shipbuilding program?

From the beginning, the South was strapped for cash. If classed as an independent nation, the area of the Confederate States would have ranked as the fourth-richest country of the world in 1860. But when the Union blockaded Confederate ports in the summer of 1861, exports of cotton fell 95 percent and the South had to restructure itself to emphasize the production of food and munitions for internal use. After losing control of its main rivers and ports, the Confederacy had to depend on a weak railroad system that, with few repairs being made, no new equipment, and destructive Federal raids, began crumbling away almost as soon as war was declared. The financial infrastructure collapsed during the war as inflation devastated Southern banks. The government seized needed supplies and livestock, paying with certificates that were to be redeemed after the war (they weren't, of course). Clearly, oceangoing warships were some-

17 Not to be confused with George McClellan, the soon-to-be-appointed general-in-chief of the Union Army, Robert McClellan of Livingston, New York, was elected as a Democrat to Congress in 1836. He served, with a one-term interruption, until 1843. His main achievement as a lawmaker was being chairman of the Committee on Patents. McClellan had died in Brooklyn in 1860 and was interred in Green-Wood Cemetery.

thing of a luxury. Mallory still argued that at least some sort of nautical force was a necessity.

Thanks to the resignations that had taken place in the U.S. Navy in the months since South Carolina had seceded, Mallory had a sizable pool of officer talent, with over three hundred officers pledging themselves to the Southern cause. There were more than enough experienced men to go around. Or more so, given the very few commands available. A plea issued by Mallory for separating U.S. officers with ship commands to bring their vessels with them fell on deaf ears—honorable men might turn in their uniforms, but they would not turn over ships which did not belong to them.

With Jefferson Davis not as supportive of a strong navy as was his presidential counterpart in the North, the South may have underestimated the impact of water-borne forces—inland and ocean—on the overall fight for independence. Early on, the Union blockade kept goods from Europe and elsewhere from getting into Southern ports, especially major ones like Charleston, Savannah, and New Orleans. The other primary purpose of the blockade was to prevent Southern ships from breaking out of their ports and sailing east with raw materials and other items that could be sold or traded.[18]

Secretary Mallory had to tackle the two-headed task of Rebel ships poking holes in the blockade to leave Southern ports with raw materials and successfully returning from the sea to bring finished goods onto the same docks. But he knew that blockade was, at most, only half of his navy's challenge. The other half was not allowing Union merchant ships to have free rein on the high seas, especially the Atlantic Ocean. With no seagoing Confederate Navy presence, Union ships and those leased by Northern companies could sail and steam back and forth to Europe and

---

18 The vexing blockade problem was never solved by the South. By the end of the Civil War, fifteen hundred rebel blockade runners had been destroyed or captured. This alone, with its effects on the Confederacy's economy and war effort, shines light on the often-overlooked accomplishments of the Union Navy.

the Caribbean with impunity. They could transport millions of tons of materials, making the Northern economy even more robust. To not be able to break or at least loosen the combined stranglehold of the Union blockade and leave unmolested Union ocean shipping could doom the Confederacy to an early death.

Though beginning the effort way too late, Mallory had to attempt to construct a Confederate Navy. A first step was to use captured vessels. After the fall of Fort Sumter Rebel troops moved on to take over the Gosport Navy Yard in Norfolk, Virginia. This proved to be a gold mine, first because it was the only shipyard in Southern hands with the machinery to build heavy warships, and second, docked there were three vessels undergoing repairs that Union forces left stranded when they hastily departed. Two were sloops of twenty guns each, the *Germantown* and the *Plymouth*.[19] The third was the twin-engine *Merrimack* which had the potential to be a formidable adversary for the Union Navy. It already was, with the 3200-ton *Merrimack* boasting forty guns. But Mallory wanted to go further, envisioning it as an ironclad warship.

Almost overnight, the Confederate States, with Gosport under its control, had doubled (or more) the strength of its Navy. Much more needed to be done, and quickly, but now Mallory had a functioning shipyard in Virginia and was cajoling and at times begging funds out of the Confederate Congress.

Where did the rather lowly *Havana* fit in the grand scheme? It was by no means a warship, but the *Havana* had been constructed only two years earlier and Semmes believed it was adaptable. Built at the Philadelphia shipyard of Birely & Lynn for the New Orleans & Havana Steam Navigation Company,

---

19 USS *Germantown*, a twenty-two-gun sloop of war, was completely functional and awaiting a crew when she was abandoned at Gosport. The U.S. Navy scuttled her at her pier. The Rebels raised her and commissioned her as a floating battery. Likewise, USS *Plymouth*, a four-gun sloop of war, was scuttled and partially burned in April 1861 at Gosport. She, too, was raised by the Confederates who intended to use her in the James River Squadron, but never did. She was rescuttled in 1862.

the *Havana* was powered by a four-hundred-horsepower engine made by Neafie, Levy & Co., also of Philadelphia, which drove a single propeller. She was also rigged for sail and measured about five hundred gross tons and had dimensions of 163 feet long, a 23-foot beam, and 12 feet of depth. When she was put to work as a mail carrier out of New Orleans, the *Havana* was considered a fast ship. The Confederate States government had just purchased her when the war began.

The repurposed *Havana* had two new things going for it. One was a lucky name. By the time Raphael Semmes arrived in New Orleans, where his new command was waiting, it was the end of April, and the *Havana* had a new signboard: It was then CSS *Sumter.* Cities throughout the South were still celebrating the Union's ignominious surrender in South Carolina, and a ship with such a name could only mean continued success.

Another advantage was a very motivated captain. Semmes was not content to simply make the most of a so-so ship. In her present condition she would not make much of a resolute raider. He ordered a work crew to get going immediately and was involved in every aspect of the renovation that turned the former passenger and mail steamer into a military machine. Cabins for officers and more storage space for drinking water and coal were added. Five guns were installed, and ammunition ordered. A cabin for the captain also had to be constructed.

"Everything had to be improvised," Semmes would later write, "from the manufacture of a water tank, to the kids [large iron cooking pots] and cans of the berth-deck messes, and from a gun carriage to a friction primer." Because the port at New Orleans had not previously outfitted a warship, "I had not only to devise all the alterations but to make plans, and drawings of them, before they could be comprehended."

As the work dragged on, one aspect of preparing the "new" ship turned out to go much smoother—the recruiting of a crew. There were plenty of experienced deckhands looking for wages to choose from because the blockade had dry-docked them. There were also former Union Navy sailors who had traded sides who wanted to sign on. Trained officers showed up including John McIntosh Kell—who Semmes had represented in court twelve years earlier. He appointed Kell the executive officer, his second in command, with the rank of first lieutenant.

No one would be more loyal to Semmes than his first mate. Kell had been born in 1823 to John and Margery Spalding Baillie Kell of Darien, Georgia. He spent his childhood at Laurel Grove Plantation and with his great-uncle Thomas Spalding, whose family owned a large part of Sapelo Island. Kell was seventeen when he was appointed a midshipman in the U.S. Navy on September 9, 1841. He had left the navy after the case in which Semmes defended him in 1849, then returned two years later after petitioning for reinstatement. He would serve in the Mexican War, was a member of the expedition of Commodore Matthew Perry to Japan in 1853, and was master of the flagship USS *Mississippi* on the cruise home. When Georgia seceded from the Union in early 1861, Lieutenant Kell resigned and was one of the first officers to offer his services to the Confederate States.

In April 1861, he commanded the Georgia state gunboat CSS *Savannah*, but only a month later Kell received a Confederate States Navy commission as first lieutenant. He was ordered to New Orleans where he received the invitation from Captain Semmes to join him on the *Sumter*.

Next in line was Second Lieutenant Robert Chapman from Alabama. The young officer had actually been the first selected to serve on the *Sumter*, as Semmes had met Chapman during his trip from Mobile to New Orleans and his intelligence and maturity had impressed the older man. Chosen as the third and fourth lieutenants aboard the *Sumter* were John Stribling from South Carolina and William Evans, fresh out of Annapolis.

Confederate warships also carried a contingent of marines. On the *Sumter* there would be twenty of them, commanded by

Lieutenant Becket Howell, who was the brother-in-law of Jefferson Davis. If having a relation of the Confederacy's president on his ship made things uncomfortable for the captain, he did not mention it.[20]

At last, Semmes's ship seemed ready. During a test run in June the *Sumter* managed to make close to ten knots. She certainly would not be the swiftest ship on the ocean, but she would be an efficient and, Semmes determined, well-handled one. And a fully manned one—the crew consisted of twenty-two officers and seventy-two seamen, plus the marines.

At the end of June, the transformed *Sumter* was poised for its first mission. However, it was almost stillborn. Understandably, the Union had included the mouth of the Mississippi River as one of its high-priority blockade points. Union forces were anticipating attempts at escape, and to make them more difficult, a small boat snuck ashore with a raiding party which put to the torch a telegraph station that was believed to be transmitting messages detailing the whereabouts and movements of Union ships. Not to be outdone, Semmes, the former lighthouse honcho, had the lights turned off in nearby lighthouses, making navigation at night more difficult for the Union Navy.

Finally, early in the morning of the 30th, the *Sumter* made a dash for it. The Union blockade ships took notice. The nearest one, the *Brooklyn*, was judged to be four miles distant when Semmes's ship crossed the bar into the Gulf of Mexico. The *Sumter* took off as best the wind filling all its sails and the steam emitting from its engine would allow. The Union ship was much larger than the *Sumter* and carried many more guns—several of them had begun firing—and it too was a fast runner in the open water. The *Brooklyn* gained on the *Sumter*.

The duel for speed between the two ships lasted for four hours.

---

20   Howell (1840–1882) was the brother of Varina Davis, wife of Jefferson Davis. He followed Semmes from the *Sumter* to the *Alabama*, and rose to the rank of Confederate Marine Corps captain.

Early on, when it appeared that his ship was not outpacing the *Brooklyn*, Semmes had the crew toss a field howitzer overboard, and it was soon followed by fifteen hundred gallons of fresh water. That still might not have been enough. Both ships entered a rain squall. Looking back after leaving it, Semmes saw the *Brooklyn* emerge closer than it had been before. Kell recalled his coolheaded captain observing that he "could not but admire the majesty of her appearance, with her broad flowing bows and clean, beautiful run, and her masts and yards as taut and square as those of an old-time sailing frigate."

But if Semmes did not want to observe the inside of a Union brig, more speed would have to be urged out of the *Sumter*. The beleaguered engine provided another half knot and there was now a stiff breeze that favored the Confederate ship. Mile by mile, the *Sumter* inched ahead. Finally, the frustrated captain of the *Brooklyn*, Charles Poor,[21] ordered his ship to turn around and return to its station.

With Raphael Semmes of Alabama at the helm, the CSS *Sumter* continued on into the open waters of the Gulf of Mexico and thus became the South's first seafaring raider.

---

21 Charles Henry Poor (1808–1882) commanded four Civil War ships and retired as commander of the North American Squadron and as a rear admiral in 1880.

4

Many people throughout history—especially before much was known about such celestial phenomena—viewed comets as omens. In the case of the crew of the *Sumter*, it was a very good omen indeed when on their first night in the Gulf of Mexico they observed what would be called the Great Comet of 1861.

How could the flickering flight of light not be good luck? It was one of the eight greatest comets of the nineteenth century and would be visible to the naked eye for three months. The comet had been discovered by John Tebbutt of Windsor, New South Wales, Australia, on May 13. It was not visible in the northern hemisphere until June 29, but it arrived there before word of the comet's discovery. On June 30, it would make its closest approach to the Earth at a distance of 12.3 million miles. As a result of forward scattering,[22] the comet could even cast shadows at night. It is believed the comet interacted with the Earth in an almost unprecedented way. For two days, when

---

22 Forward scattering can make a backlit comet appear significantly brighter because the dust and ice crystals are reflecting and enhancing the apparent brightness of the comet by scattering that light toward the observer.

PHIL KEITH WITH TOM CLAVIN

the comet was at its closest, the Earth was actually within the comet's tail and streams of cometary material converging toward the distant nucleus could be seen.[23]

Still, a comet, great or not, was not going to protect the *Sumter* from Union warships, so it was best not to dally. Captain Semmes had the ship formerly named *Havana* set sail for Cuba. The *Sumter* arrived in the waters off the Spanish colony on July 3. Fortune as well as the comet shone on the ship because that afternoon two sails were sighted, raising hopes of the Confederate cruiser's first raid. Semmes had a flag raised—a British one. Under maritime law at that time, it was perfectly legal for one ship to fly a false flag to chase an enemy ship or to try to escape, though it was universally agreed that immediately before an attack a vessel must fly her true national flag. It was not considered legal to lure a ship onto the rocks or otherwise to its destruction using a false flag, however.

The first ship complied with the command to halt and be boarded. There was general disappointment when she turned out to be a Spanish ship and thus immune from seizure. The *Sumter* quickly disengaged and went off in pursuit of the second ship. Drawing closer, it became clear to Semmes that she was an American vessel. This time he had the stars and bars of the Confederate States sent aloft. The prey strained to escape but the *Sumter* pursued her, and a shot across the bow ended the chase.

Semmes and several crewmen boarded the *Golden Rocket*, a Union merchant ship commanded by William Bailey. Understandably, Bailey was shocked to encounter a Confederate ship off the coast of Cuba, and then appalled when he was informed that Captain Semmes intended to set fire to his ship rather than take it as a prize. (Semmes intended to capture other ships and did not have the manpower to put prize crews on each of them.)

---

23 For those readers taking very good care of themselves, the Great Comet of 1861 has an orbital period of 409 years, meaning it should next be visible from Earth again in 2270.

And he was both mystified and irritated that the prize Semmes did claim for himself was Bailey's chronometer. It thus became the first of what would become an extensive collection that the Confederate captain would own.

It was fully dark by the time the forlorn captured crew as well as useful supplies had been transferred to the *Sumter*. The *Golden Rocket* was put to the torch. As they observed the merchant ship being devoured by flames that lit up the sky, Semmes and his crew were solemn. Destroying a ship of any kind was not usually a joyful enterprise, plus there was the crushing sadness of Captain Bailey watching his livelihood and probably his life savings go up in smoke. Sympathetic officers on the *Sumter* took up a collection which was presented to a crestfallen but grateful Bailey.[24]

While a few members may have been disappointed, the crew of the Confederate ship was not surprised the next day when Semmes ordered that there be no celebrations in honor of July Fourth. Such recognition could wait until the South was able to boast of its own Independence Day. And the *Sumter* could not be distracted from hunting. As it turned out, two more sails were spotted that afternoon, and both would become prizes.

The first was the aptly named *Cuba*, the second was the *Machias*. The hold of each contained sugar to be brought to Northern ports. With the crew of the *Golden Rocket* already squeezed aboard, the *Sumter* could not accommodate two more captured crews, so Semmes had the *Cuba* and *Machias*, with prize crews temporarily on them, follow his ship to Cienfuegos, a nearby Cuban port.

The small flotilla's arrival was delayed for two reasons—first a bad one, then a good one. As was often done, Semmes appointed

---

24 This would be the only time during their voyages that officers under Semmes's command displayed such generosity. While they did not lose their capacity for sympathy, so many Union ships were captured that the officers quickly would have become as destitute as their victims had they continued to take up collections for them.

midshipmen to head the prize crews of captured vessels. The one on the *Cuba* had apparently not taken the proper precautions because during the night the imprisoned crew took back the ship. With new prisoners, *Cuba* sailed away as fast as she could. Dawn revealed the missing ship. After a perfunctory search, Semmes resumed course with the *Machias* following docilely behind.

The good reason: more prizes. Late in the day of July 5, the *Sumter* sighted and ran down two more vessels. They too had holds full of sugar. The *Ben Dunning* and the *Albert Adams* were boarded, and prize crews took charge.

The next morning it became an embarrassment of riches for the *Sumter*. As the raider was approaching the Spanish port of Cienfuegos, the lookout announced there were three vessels leaving. All flew the American flag. As soon as they left Spanish waters, Semmes had the *Sumter* take them. Boarding parties made quick work of this chore. Predictably, the *West Wind*, *Louisa Kilham*, and *Naiad* all carried cargoes of sugar. After the haul of the past three days, Union citizens and soldiers with a sweet tooth were soon going to suffer.

The most opposition the *Sumter* was to face that day came from the small fort guarding Cienfuegos. Musket fire forced the ship to drop anchor. Semmes had Lieutenant Evans rowed ashore to ascertain the problem. After explaining Semmes and the *Sumter*, the red-faced Spanish officer in charge revealed he had never seen a Confederate flag before and had feared the multiple ships represented an attack by pirates.

The *Sumter* did not stay long in Cienfuegos—with more easy pickings no doubt waiting at sea, why should it? Semmes left the captured ships in the charge of a Spanish prize master, purchased coal and fresh provisions, and was back under sail by the night of July 7.

There had been one disappointment, however. Both the prize master and the governor of Cienfuegos indicated that while

Confederate ships could enter Spanish ports, Spain would not accept captured ships, nor allow any effort to turn them into cash to underwrite the South's efforts. Some or probably all of that sugar would find its way to Union consumers after all. If that was going to be the case, and there was little to no chance of realizing a profit from prizes, Semmes determined he would endeavor to bring captured crews to the nearest neutral port... after burning their ships.

The *Sumter* would prowl the seas for another six months and she would capture another ten ships, destroying six of them. There was a close call in November in Martinique. While the *Sumter* was at anchor in the harbor, the Union sloop *Iroquois* arrived. By this time word had spread from the crews of captured ships all the way to Washington, D.C., as well as throughout the Caribbean about the adventures of the Rebel raider, and to Commander James Palmer of the *Iroquois*, the *Sumter* would be a grand prize indeed. He waited for her to try to exit the harbor.

Semmes and his crew stayed put, though. For days the eight-gun *Iroquois* steamed back and forth just outside the harbor entrance. Semmes protested to the governor of the French territory that the Union vessel was inside the three-mile limit, but he was met with shrugs. However, it was a different story one night when crew members on watch saw the *Iroquois* enter the harbor and ease toward the *Sumter*. "He came along under low steam, but so steadily and aimed so directly for us that I could not doubt that it was his intention to board us," Semmes recorded in his diary.

The Confederate captain had his crew prepare for a fight, but the *Iroquois* veered off, moved away, then repeated the feint several times. By now, Semmes had gotten word to the governor of this aggressive violation of French waters. This time the Martinique official acted, ordering the French warship *Acheron* to weigh anchor and chase the Union interloper back out to sea.

That crisis was over, but the *Sumter* was still stuck in port. Worse, there were reports that more Union ships were on the way. Thankfully, the night of November 23 was dark enough to try to make a run for it. As silently as possible, the anchor was drawn up and the stern cable cut. The *Sumter* steamed slowly toward the harbor entrance. As dark as the night was, the outline of the *Iroquois* could still be viewed. The crewmen on watch on the *Acheron*, which remained ready to thwart further incursions, softly called good luck as the *Sumter* drifted past.

As the Confederate ship left the mouth of the harbor a lookout reported to Semmes that signals had been flashed from the shore to the *Iroquois*. He had to assume the message alerted his foe that the *Sumter* was escaping, but it was too late. By the time the Union gunboat had full steam and was in pursuit, Semmes had changed course twice, eluding his pursuer. At dawn, the adversaries were 150 miles apart. Presumably, Captain Palmer, with gritted teeth, had some explaining to do the next day when the USS *Dacotah* arrived in Martinique to aid in the capture of the *Sumter*.[25]

The last ship *Sumter*'s crew seized was taken on January 18, 1862.[26] The *Investigator* was a bark that had been built in Maine. However, the cargo of iron ore was registered to a company in Great Britain. The best Semmes could do was place the ship under ransom bond, which was probably a futile gesture. And he had the captured ship's captain hand over all the cash he had, which amounted to only $51. This might have smacked of pi-

25 When Gideon Welles, the Union secretary of the navy, read the report on the *Sumter*'s successful dash to freedom, he was so enraged he fired Palmer. It took Welles four months to cool down, then he reinstated the *Iroquois*'s captain. Palmer would later command the USS *Hartford* and the North Atlantic Squadron where he was promoted to rear admiral in 1865. He died of yellow fever in Saint Thomas in 1866.

26 The *Sumter* had overhauled more ships, but they had to be released when it was verified that they were owned by neutral countries.

racy but by this point Semmes was very low on funds to buy coal and other necessities for his ship.

By this time, the *Sumter* was on the other side of the Atlantic Ocean. With no other targets in sight and his ship in need of repairs as well as provisions, Semmes had the *Sumter* head for the British port of Gibraltar off the coast of Spain. An urgent message was sent to Confederate officials in London requesting funds. If he put to sea again without repairs, Semmes feared that soon the *Sumter* would be a toothless predator. As he waited for a response, the visiting captain and his officers enjoyed the hospitality of Sir William Codrington, the governor general of Gibraltar.

Over two weeks later, the funds for repairs arrived. Unfortunately, so too did two Union warships, the *Tuscarora* and the *Kearsarge*. The latter had recently been constructed and was captained by Charles Pickering. It and her companion vessel took turns anchoring in the Spain-owned Bay of Algeciras, keeping an eye on the *Sumter*. The Confederate ship was trapped. There would be no repeat of the daring Martinique escape—not with two warships carefully watching.

Still, to prepare for a miracle, Semmes lobbied British officials to allow local facilities to be used for repairs and to buy coal. In both pursuits, he was frustrated. February became March which became April. Stymied at every turn, including the continued blockade by the two Union ships, on the 7th Semmes used what funds he had left to pay off the crew and released them. Two conclusions can be drawn from the Lincoln administration allowing two warships to do nothing else but prevent the breakout of one Confederate ship: One, the *Sumter* had been effective enough that the deployment was worth it; two, on the high seas, at least, there were few other Southern ships to run down at that time.

Four days later, with a heavy heart, Semmes turned the *Sum-*

PHIL KEITH WITH TOM CLAVIN

ter over to Midshipman Richard Armstrong for safekeeping and temporary command.[27]

Semmes and Kell and the other senior officers departed. Who knew how long the war would last and it made no sense to sit it out on Gibraltar. The former CSS *Sumter* captain and his retinue would book passage on the next British vessel leaving for London and upon arrival see what could be arranged there to resume fighting for the Southern cause.

They would discover a brand-new ship to command that would ultimately dwarf the *Sumter*'s achievements.

---

27   The *Sumter* remained at anchor in Gibraltar with a caretaker crew for ten more months. In October, a midshipman who caught a master's mate stealing was shot. The killer was arrested but British authorities could not navigate the red tape to return him to the South for trial, so they released him. The *Sumter* was auctioned off in December for $19,500 to a British firm fronting for Confederate interests. Its crew remained vigilant, and the ship escaped Gibraltar in February 1863. It steamed west, where it joined other Confederate ships blockaded in the Wilmington, North Carolina, harbor. Unable to escape from this trap, the rechristened *Gibraltar* sat out the rest of the war there. The ship was put out of its misery during a storm in the North Sea in 1866.

5

Most of the credit for the construction of the next warship Raphael Semmes would command goes to James Dunwoody Bulloch.

Born in 1823 in Savannah, he was sixteen years old when he was appointed a midshipman on the U.S. frigate *United States*. During his service he graduated from the naval school in Philadelphia, and after fourteen years, Bulloch would seem bent on finishing his career in the navy. But like Semmes and many other junior officers at that time, there were very few opportunities, so in 1853 Bulloch resigned. His new career was with a New York company with a line of mail steamers operating between New York, Havana, and New Orleans. His experience as a commercial businessman as well as a mariner would make him especially valuable to the Confederate Navy.

When the war began, Bulloch was commander of the steamer *Bienville*, which was delivering to and collecting mail from New Orleans. He immediately offered his services to the South. Though pressured to exchange his ship's Stars and Stripes for the Stars and Bars, being a man of honor, Bulloch insisted on returning the *Bienville* to its home port of New York and its rightful owners. That mission completed, he left behind a wife and home (perhaps they were not covered by his code of honor) to journey to Montgomery in early May 1861, and on the 8th he presented himself to Stephen Mallory.[28]

The Confederate secretary of the navy decided that Bulloch's best service to the South would be as a purchasing agent. The Georgian not only knew how to command ships, but he also knew how they could be purchased and constructed. Bulloch was given the jaw-dropping sum of $1 million and instructions to sail to England and there negotiate for steamers that could be the foundation of an emerging Confederate Navy. He left without delay.

Bulloch's first foray when he arrived in June was to cast a discreet net to see if any existing hulls in several British ports could become warships. The possibilities were too few to pursue. Then the question was: How many ships could be built with $1 million?

But there turned out to be a more immediate question: Could ships destined to fight for the South even be built in England? Bulloch was aware of the Foreign Enlistment Act. It prohibited citizens of Great Britain from equipping or recruiting warships for use by any "belligerents," particularly the Union and the Confederacy. Looking ahead to probably having to get around that law, Bulloch set up a financial account through a London business firm and employed an attorney in Liverpool. He hoped to hide behind them long enough to get a few ships in the water bound for the South.

And then he remembered during his travels having met John Laird, the patriarch of a family that owned a shipbuilding firm

---

28 During his years in New York, Bulloch had been close to his half-sister Margaret and her family. Right before leaving for Montgomery he paid a visit, which included a farewell hug to his two-and-a-half-year-old nephew. The boy, Theodore Roosevelt, would always have a fuzzy memory of Uncle Jimmy.

in Birkenhead. The older man was serving in the British Parliament, but he kept a quiet hand in John Laird and Sons run by his two sons. The family may or may not have been supportive of the Southern cause, but more important was that the Foreign Enlistment Act was not broken. Through the fronts he had set up, Bulloch hired the firm to build a ship of which he was the sole owner and one that would be for private use only.

To that end, the ship would be constructed with wood and not of iron as was more often done in the early 1860s for vessels built for personal use. This would arouse fewer suspicions. But Bulloch was also thinking ahead to this ship roaming the globe and encountering ports where repairs to a wooden ship would be more available and more easily done than an iron-hulled vessel. When he arrived at the Laird and Sons construction facility, Bulloch turned over a design for a bark-rigged steamer with two engines. Its range would be almost limitless because of its ability to store up to 350 tons of coal. One innovative aspect in the design was a gear mechanism to lift the screw out of the water, which meant there would be less drag on the ship when it was under sail only. Condensers with a cooling tank to supply fresh water were also a critical part of the design: a roaming raider might not always have easy or instant access to supplies of fresh water.

These and other elements of the design were more than one's private ship would need for an enjoyable cruise. However, few questions were asked by the Laird family, and with the father in Parliament, few questions were asked of them. It helped that Bulloch was discreet enough to not include in the plans or conversations any mention of guns.

The construction cost would be close to fifty thousand pounds.[29] Bulloch paid the first of five installments and work began. The Lairds referred to the ship in progress as *"290."* This

---

29 In 1860 dollars, that would use up approximately one-quarter of Bulloch's $1 million purse.

was not really an attempt at secrecy—it was to be the 290th vessel constructed by the firm.

As the months passed in 1861, Bulloch followed the progress of the *290*, noting that the Laird builders were as good as their reputation. With other tasks underway, Bulloch decided he should meet with Secretary Mallory for further strategy discussions. This he did late in the year, first going to Bermuda and from there to Savannah—skirting the Union blockade—and then by train to Richmond, where the Davis administration had relocated. At least one of the discussions had a happy conclusion for Bulloch. By this time, the *290* was one of several ships being quietly constructed or refurbished for the Confederacy and Bulloch, to be commissioned a commander, was to become captain of one of them. His dream of commanding a ship of war was to be realized.[30]

Returning to Savannah, Bulloch intended to hurry back to England aboard the *Fingal*. The swift ship carried cotton to be sold to British merchants for much-needed cash. But it had to get out of the harbor first, and this time, a less-porous blockade prevented the *Fingal* from beginning its venture. Christmas found Bulloch still stuck in Savannah. As 1862 dawned, he was still there...and through January.

By this time the *Oreto*, a ship Bulloch had contracted to be built before work on *290* got underway, was ready to set sail, so Mallory switched commanders. The command was given to Lieutenant James North, who had the distinct advantage of already being in England. Bulloch, meanwhile, was faced with remaining in Georgia indefinitely if he couldn't find an escape. He heard of another ship, the *Annie Childs*, set to leave Wilmington, North Carolina, the first week of February that might do what the *Fingal* could not. Bulloch traveled north, got on

---

30   Mallory's orders had been that Bulloch would command the *Oreto*, which was expected to be ready to launch first, and then Lieutenant James North, Bulloch's assistant, would be captain of the *290*. The lieutenant acted as the Confederacy's naval agent in England during Bulloch's absence.

board, and waited. On the 5th, the *Annie Childs* got underway. Aided by a night filled with rain and fog, it managed to elude three Union gunboats and embark on an Atlantic crossing.

Back in England, Bulloch was confronted by a comedy of errors that for him, at least, did not generate laughs. Lieutenant North was still there as was the *Oreto*. Instead of enjoying this command, North coveted the *290*. While he dithered, and with the South desperately needing to expand its navy, the *Oreto* sailed away March 24…without North.[31] Instead, North busied himself complaining to Mallory that Bulloch had been unfairly given the *290*. Oddly imprecise, the navy secretary replied that North was to command the ship built by Bulloch. Mallory meant the *Oreto*. North insisted he meant the *290*. Believing Mallory had switched commanders again, Bulloch surrendered command of the *290* without ever setting foot on it.

Union officials in England, particularly Thomas Dudley, the U.S. consul in Liverpool, suspected that English authorities had let get away a ship bound for Confederate service (the *Oreto*). The Northerners turned their attention to the *290* as it neared completion at the Laird dock. If it could be proven that the *290* was intended for Southern service, a formal protest could be lodged with the British government that would stop not just the *290* but future construction projects as well. Spies were employed to keep an eye on the *290* and strike up conversations with workmen. So far, though, nothing definitive could be gleaned.

Meanwhile, Lieutenant North prepared himself to command as soon as the *290* was seaworthy…then Raphael Semmes showed up.[32]

When he and Kell arrived in London from Gibraltar, they

---

31 The *Oreto* was under the command of an English captain, James Duguid. The ship was to have many adventures—helmed by yet another captain—as the renamed *Florida*.

32 James Heyward North (1813–1893) never did get that elusive command he coveted, but he did very useful work in England for the Confederate Navy in Europe. He was promoted to captain and after the war settled back with his family in Virginia.

shared a two-bedroom apartment and met with James Mason, who was the chief representative of the Confederate States in the capital city. The men were kept busy seeing the sights and being feted. Word of the *Sumter*'s success on the high seas had reached London and Semmes was, easily, the most famous of the South's handful of naval commanders.

The captain also met with Bulloch and the ongoing construction of *290* was discussed. However, despite Semmes's achievements, no offer was extended to him to command the new ship. That was, of course, Mallory's decision to make, but more immediately, *290* already had a captain, maybe two, with both Bulloch and North still vying for the position. Semmes wished them good luck, enjoyed a bit more of the London society, and finally, in May, he arranged to sail home, accompanied by Kell and Dr. Francis Land Galt, who had been the *Sumter*'s surgeon.

The group of Confederate officers arrived on the island of Nassau on June 13. It was a beehive of activity as ships were loaded and then left the harbor with the hope of running the blockade and delivering goods, including weapons and ammunition, to Southern ports. Semmes was there only two days when he was told to turn around and sail back to London.

The reason was new instructions from Secretary Mallory who had changed his mind yet again and now wanted Semmes to take command of the *290*. With this direction came notice that he had been promoted to full captain. Without hesitation, Semmes wrote Mallory that he and Kell would be on their way immediately. He warned, though, that based on what he had observed on the other side of the ocean, "It will, doubtless, be a matter of some delicacy and tact to get the ship safely out of British waters, without suspicion."

Despite his eagerness, it was a month before they found a ship able to take them to England. During that time Semmes stayed at the Royal Victoria Hotel. One of the other guests was John Maffitt, who had also been considered as captain of CSS *Oreto* before that ship sailed. He and Semmes enjoyed each other's company, not expecting they would become the South's two most successful and famous naval officers.

Finally, Semmes and his small entourage left Nassau on the *Bahama* on July 13. It was not until August 8 that Semmes appeared at Bulloch's office in Liverpool and presented his orders. He was enormously disappointed to learn that the *290*—by then renamed the *Enrica*—had already departed.

After its boiler and engines had been installed, the ship had taken a trial run, which went well. Bulloch had arranged for another ship, the *Agrippina*, to be furtively loaded with cannon, other weapons, and munitions. The bark would have to meet the *Enrica* somewhere to be determined so that the brand-new ship could be armed for war. As those details were being worked out, in July 1862, the U.S. minister to Great Britain, Charles Francis Adams, confronted the British government with allegations and documents that purportedly revealed the true purpose of the new ship.

On July 26, word reached Bulloch that the British government might have no choice but to seize the *Enrica*, or at least prevent her from leaving Liverpool. The Confederate agent did not hesitate. He rushed to the Laird dock and arranged for the ship to go on another trial run. This time, however, it did not return but instead sailed to Moelfra Bay in Wales where its English captain, Matthew Butcher, had orders to remain. Meanwhile, Bulloch completed the work in progress of recruiting a crew. Three dozen men were sent in a separate boat to join the sailors already aboard the *Enrica*, along with further instructions to Captain Butcher: The ship's next stop was Terceira in the Azores.[33]

So it was that Raphael Semmes was in Liverpool, and the *Enrica* had been gone over a week. Bulloch told him that if he

---

33 The British government did indeed issue an order to detain the *Enrica*. However, the British official who was to convey the document to enforcement officers, Sir John Harding, suddenly went insane, and the telegram sent in its place arrived six hours after the ship sailed.

wanted to take command of the new ship, he would have to get back on the *Bahama* and catch up to the *Enrica* in the Azores. This Semmes did, and joining his entourage was Arthur Sinclair, an officer who had served on the *Sumter*. He also sent word to Midshipman Armstrong to leave the old *Sumter* in Gibraltar and make his way to the *Enrica*.

"She was, indeed, a beautiful thing to look upon," Semmes would record about his first full view of the *Enrica* when the *Bahama* arrived in the harbor of Porto Praya. He further praised her for having "the lightness and grace of a swan" and even referred to her as "my bride."

It had to be a heady moment for a captain who had already found success at sea with a salvaged and refurbished vessel to observe the brand-new warship that would presumably make him an even more formidable foe of the Union. Its keel length was 220 feet, and the beam was 31'8", and the weight was 1040 tons. She was larger than the *Oreto* and was expected to be able to outfight as well as outrun most of the ships she encountered.

The *Enrica*'s British-made ordnance consisted of six muzzle-loading, broadside, 32-pounder naval smoothbores—three firing to port and three firing to starboard—and two larger and more powerful pivot cannons. The pivot cannons were placed fore and aft of the main mast and positioned roughly amidships along the deck's centerline. From those positions, they could be rotated to fire across the port or starboard sides of the cruiser. The fore pivot cannon was a Blakely heavy long-range 100-pounder, with a 7-inch bore, rifled, and a muzzle-loader. The aft pivot cannon was a large 8-inch smoothbore, also muzzle loaded.

The new Confederate cruiser was powered by both sail and two three-hundred-horsepower horizontal steam engines to drive that single twin-bladed retractable brass screw. With the screw retracted (using the brass lifting gear mechanism), the ship could make up to 10 knots under sail alone. She could crank up

13.25 knots when her sail and steam power were used together. She would be one of the fastest ships on the ocean.

Also in Porto Praya was the *Agrippina*, and the crew of the *Enrica* labored to transfer stores from her and the *Bahama* into the hold of Semmes's new command. This process included, finally, the addition of the cannon and munitions. On the morning of Sunday, August 24, 1862, the ship officially became the CSS *Alabama*.

The ceremony took place just outside the three-mile limit, in international waters so as not to run afoul of Portuguese officials. The officers wore their best Confederate gray uniforms, and they and the undermanned crew stood at attention as William Breedlove Smith, Semmes's clerk, read out his commission as a Confederate Navy captain and then the orders from Secretary Mallory directing him to take command of the ship. A salute was fired, and the Confederate Stars and Bars replaced the British flag—which may have confused the sailors, most of whom were British. Then for most likely the first time their ears were subjected to a rendition of "Dixie" given by a makeshift band culled from the *Alabama* and the *Agrippina*.

There was one more important task to complete. If it went badly, the inaugural cruise of the *Alabama* could end before it fully got underway. The captain needed a crew. Semmes had plenty of potential crewmen, of course, made up of sailors from three ships, but that did not guarantee that enough of them would want to serve with the *Alabama*.

Making full use of his courtroom oratorical skills, Semmes had all the men assembled in front of him. He extolled the worthy cause of the South against the oppressors and invaders of the North. He warned that because the *Alabama* was a warship, there would be fighting, plus discipline had to be maintained at all times. Then he offered his most persuasive arguments: *Alabama* sailors would be paid twice as much as Royal Navy sailors, and in gold; plus, there was a good chance of prize money on top of that. Perhaps most enticing of all, the men could have a ration of grog twice a day.

Sailors from all the ships present lined up to give First Lieutenant John Kell their names and sign the ship's logbook. By day's end, the CSS *Alabama* was fully manned and equipped. She was ready to begin hunting.

A few hours later the *Alabama* sailed northeast and Captain Semmes repaired to his cabin for his first night at sea in his new command. He had hopes of enough success to play a significant role in the overall war effort of the South. He probably did not envision becoming the most feared sea captain of the Civil War.

ACT II:
THE HUNTER

*I wish to have no connection with any ship that does not sail fast;
for I intend to go in harm's way.*

John Paul Jones, Captain, U.S. Navy

6

As the booming guns of Fort Sumter finally fell silent on April 13, 1861, the Civil War had commenced in earnest and the U.S. Navy was beginning to take stock of its place within the grand scheme of things.

Newly appointed Secretary of the Navy Gideon Welles was a taciturn, driven Jacksonian Democrat lawyer who inherited a department woefully unprepared for the challenges immediately ahead. The senior officer then on duty was an eighty-three-year-old captain by the name of Charles Stewart who had fought in the War of 1812 and had commanded, at one time, the USS *Constitution*, "Old Ironsides," a revered relic commissioned in 1794. Although Stewart had been made "senior flag officer" by Congress in 1859, there was no rank in the U.S. Navy in 1861 higher than captain, the equivalent of an army colonel. The rank of admiral did not exist.

From the beginning it was clear to Welles that whatever the U.S. Navy would become, it would not be required to fight an opposing force of powerful warships. The South had no capital ships and was not expected to have much of a seagoing fighting force. Neither was it then understood how important a riverine force would become. Welles figured, correctly, that blockading Southern ports and support of army land operations would become the navy's primary tasks—and he began to organize and build a fleet to fulfill those roles.

After just one year in office, with every day feeling pushed by the demands of the war, Secretary Welles had the Navy Department humming. General recruitment was surging, officers were being commissioned by the hundreds, and Welles was building new ships or buying existing ones to convert at a dizzying pace. Before Welles was done, the navy would expand in population tenfold to 85,000 officers and men and the number of ships of all types would increase fifteenfold to 626 ships, 65 of which were ironclads. The navy budget went from a paltry $12 million to $123 million a year.

To accomplish all of this, Welles was ably assisted by an energetic and hardworking assistant secretary, Gustavus Fox. An ex-navy lieutenant who had served eighteen years on active duty, Fox was in the woolens business at the start of the Civil War. He immediately volunteered to serve the Union Navy, but after a brief period at sea, Welles plucked him from the fleet and made him his number two at the Navy Department. It was an inspired choice, as Fox worked just as hard as his boss and proved to be a very able administrator.

By the beginning of 1862 alone, the U.S. Navy fleet had jumped from 42 vessels to 212. By mid-1862, leadership of the at-sea service and all the ships afloat would fall on the navy's first-ever active-duty rear admiral, David Farragut. A daring and decisive officer, Farragut had first seen service as a midshipman in the War of 1812 when he was only twelve. By July of 1862, when Congress rewarded Farragut with admiral's rank, he had demolished the Confederate forts guarding New Orleans and had engineered the surrender of the city itself—a truly significant victory for the Union. His adopted brother,

David Dixon Porter, would become the navy's second admiral, and by the time the war ended, there would be thirty-seven Union admirals.

Farragut's victory at New Orleans was the premier example of how the navy would conduct one of the four main tasks Welles had assigned: tackling operations from seaward whenever the army could not. The other three tasks were blockading operations sufficient to cover over 3500 miles of coastline; support of army operations as required, primarily shore bombardment and transport; and, what would surprisingly become a high priority, chasing down Rebel commerce raiders at sea. It was this last task that would prove to be the most difficult.

By early 1863, tracking down the few but monumentally effective Confederate commerce raiders became essential to the survival of the American merchant fleet; that, plus, combating the skyrocketing insurance rates being forced upon ship owners. Some owners were even, if only temporarily, "selling" their ships to foreign owners so they could fly under flags other than the Stars and Stripes.

Secretary Welles, whom President Lincoln teased with the nickname "Father Neptune," began his building and buying spree immediately after taking office. The navy, however, had already begun a new *Mohican* class of warships in 1859. This was an all-new design officially described as a "sloop of war." The USS *Mohican* and the USS *Iroquois* led the class, soon followed by four more ships in 1861: The USS *Kearsarge*, USS *Oneida*, USS *Tuscarora*, and USS *Wachusett*. With extended hulls, narrow beams, swivel guns, internal steam engines, and retractable screw propellers, the navy would abandon the side-wheel steamers that had been favored in the 1840s and '50s.

The USS *Kearsarge*, named after a mountain in New Hampshire, was launched at Kittery, Maine, in September 1861, and

commissioned at Kittery in January 1862. Her first commanding officer was Captain Charles W. Pickering.[34]

The *Kearsarge* was not built to be a hunter-killer of commerce
raiders. Those terms did not even exist when her keel was laid
down. Rather, the five ships of the *Mohican* class were simply the
next step up in steamship design and were meant to incorporate
the many improvements coming along in warship construction.[35]

The dependence on sails was waning, but the U.S. Navy was
not ready to give them up entirely.[36] The advent of the steam-
driven engine, fired by coal-heated boilers, allowed the navy
to proceed without having to depend on the direction and ve-
locity of the fickle winds, but the steam engine could only take
the navy as far as coal supplies were available. Until fuel supplies
were readily at hand and abundant (and until coaling ships were
invented) sails would still be part of any warship's inventory.

The first steam warships were side steamers whose giant paddle wheels were connected directly to the engines. Sometimes
the paddle wheels were internal, sometimes external, but always
they took up enormous amounts of room. The external wheel
housings were also huge targets for enemy guns, and if hit or disabled, the ship was dead in the water. This challenge was solved
in the 1850s when shafts and propellers replaced paddle wheels.
A revolutionary and efficient four-bladed screw and a propeller

34 After *Kearsarge*, he would go on to command the USS *Housatonic*, another
    steam sloop of war, which was fated to be the first ship in history sunk by a
    submarine, the CSS *Hunley*, in February 1864.

35 After the first USS *Kearsarge* there have been three more ships so named.
    These vessels were not named after the New Hampshire mountain, however,
    but for the soon-to-be-famous ship. In 1896 the battleship USS *Kearsarge*
    (BB-5) was commissioned and was the only U.S. Navy battleship not named
    for a state. The next USS *Kearsarge* was CV-33, an Essex Class aircraft carrier
    (one of twenty-four in the same class) commissioned in 1946. She served in
    the 7th Fleet and the Far East for most of her career, including deployments
    in the Korea Conflict and the Vietnam War. CV-33 *Kearsarge* also picked
    up two *Mercury* astronauts during the early years of the space program. The
    fourth (and current) USS *Kearsarge*, LHD-3, was launched in 1990 and is still
    serving actively as a "landing helicopter dock" amphibious assault ship.

36 The U.S. Navy was far ahead of other nation-state navies of the time in adapt-
    ing to steam power, but Britain and France were rapidly catching up.

shaft gear box were designed into the *Mohican* class. The steam engines were two cylinder, and they drove horizontal pistons which kept their profile low and helped avoid engine damage from unfriendly guns.

The fifty-gun frigates that could throw 700 pounds of metal in a single broadside were also fading into obsolescence. The standard 32-pounder gun was being replaced with gigantic 9-inch and 11-inch Dahlgren guns and Parrot rifles. These powerful weapons, if well handled, could smash wooden hulls to smithereens at distances that were previously unimaginable. *Kearsarge*, with two 11-inch Dahlgren guns, firing shells of 133 pounds or solid shot of 166 pounds, equaled an entire broadside of the old 32-pounders. The *Kearsarge* also carried a 30-pound Parrot rifle in the forecastle. Operated by the ship's marines, the Parrot rifle was used mainly as a chase gun due to its long-range capabilities. Rounding out the *Kearsarge*'s ordnance inventory were four standard 32-pounders. The improved suite of guns also offered a tremendous weight savings which could be used for storing much more ammunition and powder.

The Dahlgrens, invented by the navy's John Adolphus Dahlgren, were the workhorse seagoing cannons of the Civil War.[37] Many of them were, like the guns on the *Kearsarge*, pivot guns or cannons capable of being swiveled, with pulleys and tackle, to point and fire from either side of the ship. This eliminated the necessity to have guns on both sides of a ship. When not being used, these pivot guns were stored in line with the centerline of the ship which greatly improved the stability of the vessel while underway.

The shape of the Dahlgrens was also unique. To handle the immense pressures of the explosive powder used to hurl the shells (or solid shot) from a muzzle-loading Dahlgren, the breech (or rear) of the gun was cast to be much wider and heavier than the

---

37 Dahlgren had established the U.S. Navy's Ordnance Department, and he would join the ranks of rear admirals in February 1863.

gun's muzzle. This produced a cannon that resembled a soda bottle, hefty on one end and slender at the mouth.

Each Dahlgren weighed nearly eight tons and could do incredible damage if handled properly by a well-drilled crew. Shells were favored over solid shot as they flew faster, more accurately, and packed an explosive punch when they landed. The solid shot was nothing more than a flying battering ram. The effective range of the shot or the shell was a little more than 3500 yards or a fraction under two miles. The guns were much more effective, however, at shorter ranges, a thousand yards or less was preferred.

The Parrot rifle on the forecastle could fire a 30-pound shell accurately out to almost five miles, depending on the elevation of the tube. It could, of course, be used at much shorter ranges, and a captain would not hesitate to fire it in close to a target.

The *Kearsarge* carried two 32-pounders port and two starboard, amidships, on the gun deck. Each of these weapons was on a trucked (wheeled) carriage and used a series of ropes and pulleys, manipulated by the gun's crew. First cast in the 1790s, the 32-pounder came in a number of different "weights"; that is, the heft of the individual shot as measured in "hundredweights" or "cwt." The greater the cwt, the straighter the ball would fly, and the harder it would strike. For example, the *Alabama*'s 32-pounders were 57 cwt, and the *Kearsarge*'s 32 cwt. The range for all 32-pounders was in the vicinity of a mile, but they were much more effective at about five-hundred yards. Of course, no seafaring Civil War gun was any more useful than the crew behind it. Drill and practice were the most important factors in a successful outcome for any gun crew.

Made from sturdy New England pine and oak and cross-braced with iron "knees," the *Mohican* class ships were cut down to a single gun deck below the main deck and shaped to be long and slender. The *Kearsarge* was as close to a knife slicing through the water as the naval constructors of the day could make her.

When she slid down the ways at Kittery there were no other ships in the world of her size and armament that could compete with her and her sister ships.

Reducing the number of decks, adding fewer but more powerful guns, and blending steam with sail reduced the manpower needs of the Civil War sloops of war. For example, the USS *St. Lawrence* needed 500 men and fifty guns to sling as much iron at the enemy as the USS *Kearsarge* could do with 162 men and seven guns. And although the hull was thinner, it was longer and with the reduced manpower needs each sailor had more living space.

As a warship, the *Kearsarge* could be the best of her day…if she had the right captain.

7

The life of John Ancrum Winslow was almost a very short one. He and his year-older brother, Edward, were avid habitués of the docks along the shores of Wilmington, North Carolina's busiest harbor. Both boys had developed an early fascination with ships and the sea, and when the brothers were not engaged in their studies they could often be found ogling the vessels of all nations tied up along the quays, and they would eagerly chat up any sailors who wandered by them.

These ramblings always worried the boys' mother, Sara, who had familiarity with such things thanks to her ancestors, several of whom had been ship captains or naval officers of note. She was always afraid that an unscrupulous ship's master, in need of cabin boys, would scoop up her sons and sail off before anyone was the wiser.

One summer afternoon in June 1821, the brothers undertook an adventure that could have turned out even worse than getting shanghaied. Stuffing a sack full of apples, bread, and cheese, plus two bottles of water, the lads "liberated" a dinghy tied up between two abandoned piers. With a greasy tarp they found in the bottom of the eight-foot-long boat, they soon rigged a sail, and they were off, skittering across the light chop of Wilmington Harbor.

This was great fun, indeed, and gave the boys a whole new perspective on the ship traffic coming and going. The rocking of the boat, the warm summer sunshine, and the filling lunch soon had the young sailors napping soundly in the bottom of the dinghy. Unbeknownst to either youngster, the tides, current, and steady breeze were pushing them rapidly beyond the harbor and out to sea. Only the most fortunate of circumstances avoided catastrophe and the need for history to find another captain for the future USS *Kearsarge* and its date with destiny.

An alert sailor in the crow's nest of an inbound coastal schooner spotted the dinghy and its occupants. The schooner's captain ordered the helmsman to come about. The dinghy and its startled crew were taken under tow and pulled back into Wilmington. A bustling scene greeted the incoming schooner as dozens of people seemed to be searching the docks. A few men were even dragging the waters near the docks with nets. As the rescuing schooner tied up, a frantic Sara Winslow came running. Equal parts angry and frightened, she had assumed that her sons had been tossed in the bay by thugs or had been kidnapped and were already halfway to China.

John Winslow's father, Edward, was a prosperous freight broker and a direct descendant of the famous Winslows of *Mayflower*, Plymouth, and Massachusetts Bay Colony renown. John had a great-grandfather, William Rhett, who had successfully defended Wilmington, North Carolina, from a Franco-Spanish invasion in 1704 and in 1718 captured the infamous pirate Stede Bonnet, who had an alliance with the even more famous pirate "Blackbeard" (Edward Teach). Swashbuckling, seafaring, and daring were literally in John Winslow's blood.

Nonetheless, John's father hoped he would follow him into

the family business, but with the call of the sea too strong, Edward Winslow's good friend, Daniel Webster, who was then a senator from Massachusetts, arranged an appointment for John Winslow to become a midshipman in the U.S. Navy, beginning February 1, 1827.

The education of midshipmen was nearly 100 percent on-the-job in those days, and John Winslow was taught the seagoing skills he needed in that fashion. After collecting his uniforms and sea bag, he was assigned to the USS *Falmouth*. This sloop of war with twenty-four guns had just been commissioned, and in November 1827 she sailed from her home port of Boston with a crew of 190 officers and men, including the eager and ambitious new recruit.

The *Falmouth*'s first assignment was to the West Indies Squadron. For the next three years she and her crew would be engaged in hunting down pirates menacing American trade in the Caribbean. During those three years Midshipman Winslow would learn much he needed to know—and then some—about the seagoing trade. There were times when he was placed in charge of raiding parties and he and his men captured several miscreants. It was, perhaps, the perfect assignment for the new officer, who was already following in the footsteps of his great-grandfather, old Admiral Rhett, the "pirate hunter."

The *Falmouth* returned to Boston in 1830. For the tanned and fit Midshipman Winslow there was not much time for shore leave and visits, however, as the *Falmouth* was given a quick turnabout and sent hurriedly to the Pacific, around Cape Horn. This was highly unusual. Although the *Falmouth* was a new ship, years at sea without at least one serious overhaul might set her up for considerable damage from ship worms, barnacles, and other biologics, plus the stress and strain on her hull and masts. No reason has surfaced for her being rushed to the Pacific, other than protection of American shipping, but she seemed to survive the cruise without major deterioration. The *Falmouth*, in fact, served for thirty-two years, a wooden ship in an age turning to iron. She was decommissioned in 1859, on the cusp of the Civil War, becoming one of the "laid-up" hulls inherited by the pre–Civil War Union Navy.

The Pacific cruise lasted another three years, after which the *Falmouth* returned to Boston again. Winslow's captain was impressed enough with his maturing midshipman that he recommended he take the exams for passed midshipman. Winslow did so and succeeded. In the U.S. Navy of the nineteenth century, a passed midshipman was usually counted as an officer who had completed all the examinations for a lieutenant's position but was waiting for a lieutenant's appointment to become available. The term went out of use when the rank of ensign was created in 1862.

Winslow spent several months at the Boston Navy Yard awaiting his next assignment. It finally came in June 1834, when he was ordered to the USS *Erie*, sailing to join the Brazilian Squadron. The months in Boston also changed Winslow's life in that his attentions turned in a very serious way toward his first cousin, Catherine Amelia Winslow, daughter of his uncle Benjamin Winslow of Boston. At this point, John was twenty-two years old, and Catherine twenty. Amorous relationships between first cousins were not taboo, but neither were they encouraged. With Winslow facing another long tour at sea, and in South America no less, family members were reputed to be hopeful that whatever romance might have blossomed between the cousins would not last.

The USS *Erie* was a sloop of war of twenty-two guns built in 1813 and the Brazilian Station was a posting created in 1826 to protect the rights of U.S. citizens and American commerce in and around Brazil and Argentina, countries often in conflict with one another. While on this assignment, Winslow briefly served aboard a sister ship to *Erie*, USS *Ontario*, to fill in for a lieutenant who had fallen seriously ill and been sent home. It gave Winslow some practical experience in performing in a lieutenant's billet.

Winslow returned once again to Boston in the early autumn of 1837 with another successful cruise under his belt. He had not forgotten cousin Catherine, nor she, him. They were married on October 18, and took up residence in Roxbury, Massachusetts, a growing suburb of Boston. They were reportedly quite smitten with each other and remained so throughout the rest of their lives. The union produced seven children in ten years between 1839 and 1849.[38]

For the next two years, Winslow was able to stay on shore duty at the Boston Navy Yard, which pleased both him and his bride. However, in 1839, he was finally promoted to lieutenant and with that advancement came a set of orders to go to sea again. It would be back to the Brazilian Station, this time aboard the USS *Enterprise*.[39]

Winslow's *Enterprise* was a ten-gun schooner built in 1831, specifically to serve on the Brazilian Station, although she did serve in other capacities until she was decommissioned and sold in 1844. Unfortunately, the experience did not pan out well for the new lieutenant. Several months after arriving on station, Winslow fell ill with mysterious repeating fevers. No one seemed to know if it was malaria or some other tropical malady, but Winslow weakened rapidly and was often unable to perform his duties. He was sent back to Boston on a packet ship to recuperate. In an amazingly short amount of time, under his wife's ministrations, he recovered completely.

Next for Winslow was being assigned to the Receiving Station in Boston, which was part recruiting duty, part riding herd

---

38 Of the five boys and two girls, two males also became naval officers: William (1844–1869) was a paymaster who died of scarlet fever at age twenty-five; and Herbert (1849–1914) went to Annapolis and rose to the rank of rear admiral.

39 This *Enterprise* was number four of the nine U.S. Navy ships that have borne the name. The first was commissioned in 1775 and the ninth and latest, CVN-80, will likely enter service in 2028.

on the sailors awaiting assignment, and part waiting around for a new set of orders for himself. He did not expect much action, but he had plenty to handle on October 27, 1841, when Winslow and others rushed to the Receiving Station dock where the civilian mail ship RMS *Britannia* was temporarily moored. This new Cunard freight and passenger steamship experienced a fire in the engine spaces that could have easily doomed it. Thanks to Winslow's excellent coordination of the numerous volunteers, the fire was snuffed out quickly with minimal damage. His efforts so impressed the ship's captain and the owners that several months later Winslow was presented with a pair of new epaulettes and a commemorative sword as gifts from Queen Victoria.

The following summer, Winslow was finally given new orders, this time to the newly commissioned USS *Missouri*. To Winslow, this seemed to be a very fortuitous posting. The USS *Missouri* was the pride of the fleet, a radical new design in both steam and sail. She housed two complete, coal-fired, six-hundred-horsepower engines, each driving one of the side paddle wheels which together could propel the warship through the waves at an astonishing (for those times) speed of ten knots. She was also furnished with a complete set of masts, spars, rigging, and sails and could easily cruise along on wind power alone when the engines were idle.

The U.S. Navy was about to send the *Missouri* on a "show the flag" cruise which was more of a "show off the ship" cruise. The *Missouri* was the first of her type in the navy and a harbinger for the end of the age of sail. She was also equipped with two 10-inch guns, the largest and heaviest then afloat, and eight 8-inch guns; all in all, more raw firepower than any ship afloat. The Navy Department had combed through all the officers and men available and handpicked the best of them to form the crew of this formidable treasure of a ship, said to have cost $600,000 to build (or about $18 million in today's dollars). To be in this company would be good for Winslow's career and recognition that he, too, was held in high regard by the Navy Department.

The commander of the USS *Missouri* was Captain John Thomas Newton, a solid veteran who had been born in 1794, made a midshipman in 1809 (two years before Winslow's birth), and had fought heroically aboard the USS *Hornet* in the War of 1812. In 1829, Newton was the captain of the USS *Fulton*, the very first steamship in the U.S. Navy. This rather unique ship, designed by Robert Fulton and launched just before his death in 1815, spent exactly one day on active duty as a U.S. warship ferrying President James Madison around New York Harbor before being deactivated and turned into a training ship for new sailors. It was a moored platform, permanently tied to the dock, its engine removed, when Captain Newton assumed command.

For training purposes, the *Fulton* still had cannon aboard, and as such needed a munitions locker. On June 4, 1829, for reasons that almost defy logic, an experienced navy gunner went into the locker, where loose gunpowder was stored, looking for something. He was carrying a lamp with an open flame. Seconds later, the gunner and forty-six of his shipmates were blown to bits. Captain Newton was nearby, off the ship, having his dinner. Fortunately for Newton, he was not fixed with any blame, which would not be the case in today's navy.[40]

In October 1842, the *Missouri*, having finished an extensive tour of East Coast ports, was finally sent on a mission of substance. Beginning at Norfolk where she picked up a courier with dispatches for Veracruz, she stopped next at Savannah, Georgia, then moved on to Pensacola, Florida, and Havana, Cuba.

In Havana, many of the officers of the crew were invited to a formal dinner with the Spanish governor general, Jeronimo Valdes. Lieutenant Winslow was impressed with the twenty-two

---

40 Just ask the captain of the USS *Cole*, which was bombed in Aden in 2000: Commander Kirk Lippold was relieved of his command and barred from further promotion for a terrorist attack that came out of nowhere and killed sixteen of his crew.

courses served and being personally handed a cup of coffee and a fine Cuban cigar by the governor general himself. In a letter he sent to his wife, Winslow described the dinner and his conversation with one of the other guests, an American named Moreland. It seems that Mr. Moreland had been in Cuba for twenty years and engaged in the slave trade. According to Winslow, he had made quite a fortune and returned to Boston, but had recently "lost it all, and was obliged to return here in his old age and go to work again. It is said he invested it all with a slave dealer; if such is the case he deserved to lose it all."

Although a native of North Carolina, it seems that Winslow inherited the abolitionist attitudes of his numerous New England forebears. His extended shore duties in Boston no doubt also influenced his feelings on slavery.[41]

Anxious to further prove the value of its newest warship, especially to the European navies, the Navy Department selected the USS *Missouri*, in June 1843, to steam to Gibraltar, then on to Alexandria, Egypt. The ostensible mission was to convey the newly appointed U.S. minister to China, Caleb Cushing, as far as Alexandria, after which he would sail on, by commercial ship, to Peking. A secondary mission was to try and beat the record for an Atlantic crossing by a warship, which with her combination of steam and sail, the *Missouri* should easily be able to do. It would be a big feather in the cap for Captain Newton and practically guarantee him prizes and an even greater command, perhaps even a squadron.

USS *Missouri* left Norfolk on August 2 under full steam. Although equipped with both steam power and sails, both means of propulsion would not likely be used at the same time although they could be, depending on wind conditions. The thirty-foot stack spewed smoke and cinders. It would not take long for the

---

41 Massachusetts, at that time, was the center of the Abolitionist Movement and Boston the hotbed of agitation against slavery. Winslow attended many antislavery lectures and rallies and subscribed to the movement wholeheartedly.

sails to turn black with coal smoke or be shot through with holes as hot cinders hit the canvas. The *Missouri* was an eager consumer of coal. Only so many tons could be stored aboard, and if used too quickly it would rapidly diminish the ship's ability to steam. Captain Newton would likely use his sail power when the winds were strong and favorable. The ship would switch to steam power only when poor wind conditions existed.

The *Missouri* had an uneventful and speedy crossing, but the copper boilers had been used more than anticipated, so the ship was running low on coal. Captain Newton's engineering officers persuaded him to stop at Fayal, in the Azores, for more fuel instead of pressing on straight to Gibraltar. Lieutenant Winslow had a few hours to get off the ship and stretch his legs. "The island is like one great flower garden, beautifully cultivated; never before have I seen such a variety of plants from every clime," he wrote his wife. "The splendid magnolia and japonica trees are here as common as lilacs with us." This short stop in the Azores was a preview to an important time in Winslow's future.

The USS *Missouri* left Fayal on August 21 and sighted Gibraltar four days later. The spectacle of this mighty warship chugging up to The Rock, maneuvering smartly with nary a sail aloft, caused many a jaw to drop that day at Gibraltar—even more so since her arrival was a complete surprise. At anchor were numerous ships from all over the Mediterranean and, indeed, the ocean-trading world. Also present was a Danish Navy contingent and several warships of the Royal Navy. The British squadron was commanded by Admiral Sir George Sartorius[42] who was flying his flag in the HMS *Malabar*, a seventy-four-gun ship of the line.

The next two days would be eventful, to say the least, for the USS *Missouri*, her crew, and Lieutenant Winslow. According to an account given later by the purser Rodman M. Price, the crew "took immense pride in their ship. Under steam, she

---

42 Sartorius (1790–1885) would become naval aide to Queen Victoria and a future admiral of the fleet.

skimmed across the harbor waters without the slightest effort, trailing only a slight cloud of light gray smoke. Her wooden decks were holystoned to a smoothness that would rival silk. Her brass gleamed and smelled of the tangy polish. Her handrails, ladders, doors, and window frames shone with wax; her glass windows sparkled clean in the bright Mediterranean sun. Her sails had been scrubbed and freshly washed, taking on the appearance of bright white linen, then smartly lashed down to the spars. The rigging was unfrayed and taut, blocks and winches oiled. Even her cannons had a fresh coat of paint, and all the rods, rammers, spongers, and firelocks were cleaned and placed in their proper racks. Every member of the crew not working the coal bins and oily engines had a freshly washed and pressed uniform, buttons gleaming. Captain Newton smiled to himself believing that in that place, on that day, no finer, better-manned, more handsome ship existed anywhere in any fleet in the world." He may have been correct.

The only piece slightly amiss was the freewheeling form of "Bess," the ship's mascot, who had the run of the ship. Bess was a small cinnamon bear that one of the sailors had picked up in a port-side bar somewhere along the way, probably as a prize after a drunken game of cards.[43] Mostly, she curled up in the ship's galley, always looking for scraps. On smooth sailing days, however, she could often be found in the rigging, somewhere high above the deck, soaking up fresh air and sunshine. The crew loved their pet and considered her a good luck charm.

As soon as the *Missouri* was safely anchored, ten feet of water beneath her keel and under the shadow of the looming form of The Rock, the visitors swept in, coming by small boats. One of the first guests to come aboard was Admiral Sartorius, who marveled at the ship's construction, her intriguing engine de-

---

43   Cinnamon bears are a subset of the North American black bear family: great climbers and excellent swimmers. If you have to have a bear aboard ship, this might be a good one to have!

TO THE UTTERMOST ENDS OF THE EARTH

sign, and the massive guns. A spirited trade commenced with the officers and sailors of the ship swapping all sorts of trinkets and personal items for fruit, sweetmeats, treats, and souvenirs of Gibraltar to stow away and bring home. By dusk, the visitors were shooed off the ship and the very tired crew could begin to settle down for the night.

For Captain Newton, history was about to repeat itself. That Sunday evening, he, Ambassador Cushing, Purser Price, Lieutenant Winslow, and several of the other officers were enjoying a dinner at the home of the American consul in Gibraltar, Horatio Sprague. As the wine flowed ashore, a small group of enlisted engineers back aboard the *Missouri* were working hard to complete essential boiler repairs so the *Missouri* could put to sea again. Darkness was nigh and two small globe lanterns attached to the bulkhead were giving off only dim light for two of the sailors wrestling to complete a critical pipe fitting. A third crewman retrieved a kerosene lantern to supply more illumination.

One deck above the compartment where the repair crew was struggling another crew member was doing an assigned chore. He needed a beam scale to measure coal, and as he reached for it, he knocked a large metal wrench off a shelf. The wrench fell on top of what was described as a "demijohn of turpentine," a bulbous, narrow-necked glass bottle containing anywhere from three to ten gallons of liquid. The wrench shattered the demijohns and several gallons of turpentine began seeping through the floorboards straight down into the compartment below where the enginemen were working—with their open-flame kerosene lamp. In seconds, the starboard engine room erupted in flames. Smoke began to curl up from below and find its way through the main deck. The engineers scrambled out of the compartment, dashing for safety. A marine on guard duty noticed the smoke right away and began shouting, "Fire! Fire! Ring the bell!"

The ship's bell began clanging away, and the *Missouri*'s drum-

91

mer boy started beating a loud and frantic tattoo. Soon, however, the forward part of the vessel was being consumed by the fire. Flames licked away at the rigging and began creeping up the foremast. Meanwhile, over the sounds of dinner and several spirited conversations going at once, Lieutenant Winslow thought he heard shouting outside of Consul Sprague's home. He got up from the table and went to a window. Even his rudimentary Spanish picked out the words *el frigate Americano* and *fuego*.

A mad scramble of breaking glass and crashing plates sent all the American officers out the door and racing the mile and a half to the waterfront. Fortunately, the senior officer left behind aboard the *Missouri* had been thinking clearly enough to send the captain's gig to pick up the officers ashore. By the time the ship hove into view the flames were halfway down the length of the ship and licking at the side-wheel housings. The fore and main masts were giant candlesticks poking into the quarter-moon sky.

The *Missouri* had two fire pumps, one fore and one aft, and the crew had held frequent fire drills. They had not prepared for anything like this, though, and no one had anticipated just how much the gallons of paint, wax, turpentine, and other flammable liquids aboard the ship could contribute to a fire. Moreover, the ship was wood, after all, and had just been loaded with tons of coal. The pumps and hose turned out to be thoroughly inadequate to the demands. Undaunted, the crew formed bucket brigades.

Marines were sent below to retrieve Mr. Cushing's important papers and personal items, including gifts for the Emperor of China. His impeccably tailored new ambassador's uniform was lost, however. So too was poor Bess the bear. She proved to be too scared to jump off the ship, so she ran for her favorite spot in the rigging high above, but she never made it.

After valiantly fighting the fire with the bucket brigade team, Lieutenant Winslow made a mad dash for his quarters to try and save some letters and personal items. He was blocked by a wall of smoke and fire and barely managed to wriggle out a porthole and drop into the harbor. His magnificent sword from Queen Victoria and his special epaulettes became victims of the conflagration.

After three frantic hours fighting the flames the crew and Captain Newton knew the battle was lost. All knew, too, that the fire was creeping ever closer to the forward magazine where tons of powder and shot were stored. If those munitions went off, many lives could be lost. Reluctantly, Newton ordered the ship's Kingston valves opened. These internally operated valves, along the keel of the ship, would allow seawater to rush in and scuttle the vessel. The *Missouri* was in shallow water, and if she could be sunk quickly, it might be possible to put out the fire, save some of the ship, and flood the magazine. Newtown also ordered all hands to "save themselves."

No sooner had all hands left the ship when the magazine exploded, blowing off the bow and toppling all the masts into the water. Remarkably, not a single hand was lost (if you exclude the bear) and that was in no small measure due to the numerous ships, large and small, including boats from the *Malabar*, who came to the rescue and pulled the crew from the harbor. The blackened hulk of what was left of the proud *Missouri* settled to the bottom, and the fires went out.

Lieutenant Winslow had the sad duty of being selected to bring the bad news to the secretary of the navy. With a uniform loaned from a British officer and a few new pieces of clothing and necessary toiletries, he was loaded down with dispatches and letters, plus the captain's official report. A Channel boat took Winslow to England where he was to find the fastest ship to America. He caught a steamer headed to Boston which allowed him a quick overnight visit with his wife before heading to Washington. He arrived in D.C. on October 5.

His report was not well received by the Navy Department nor the secretary nor President Tyler. A large chunk of the navy's budget lay at the bottom of Gibraltar Harbor, to say nothing of a huge piece of the navy's pride. Winslow was given terse orders to hand deliver to the snake-bitten Captain Newton, which amounted to "salvage what you can, then report back to the Navy Department for court-martial." Winslow raced back to England via mail ship, then Lisbon, and on to Cádiz, arriving at Gibraltar on November 11.

Captain Newton had not been idle. He had chartered an American ship to take most of the *Missouri*'s crew back to the States. He had kept a few engineers and several officers to help with salvaging the hulk. An attempt was made to raise what remained of the *Missouri*, but it could not be accomplished. Instead, she was cut into pieces and hauled up so as not to create a hazard to navigation in the busy and important harbor. Captain Newton and the remainder of his crew sailed to England in January 1844, then took a Cunard steamer back to America.

Lieutenant Winslow was able to find an assignment ashore in Boston to await orders. Nothing came to him during the spring and summer of '44. In October he was needed in Washington as a witness in the court-martial of Captain Newton and his chief engineer. Newton was convicted, on several counts, of unnecessarily hazarding his ship and received a two-year suspension from duty. He did not serve the full term, however. President Tyler, in one of his last acts before stepping down in March 1845, remitted the remainder of Newton's suspension. What was left of his career included commanding the U.S. Home Squadron and a couple of shipyards. At the age of sixty-five, in 1857, while serving as a member of a court of enquiry on someone else for a change, Captain John Thomas Newton died of apoplexy.

8

During the winter of 1844 and the spring of 1845, the seemingly fragile Lieutenant John Winslow was struck down with a serious case of erysipelas. The disease is a bacterial infection of the upper layers of the skin that causes fevers, chills, rashes, blisters, and swollen glands. It can be treated today with very standard antibiotics, but these medicines were not available in Winslow's time, so he suffered, and greatly, for months until the disease ran its course.

One might wonder what happened to officers like Winslow who were often ill or "laid up" for long periods of time. Given the rigors of the profession, bad food, long cruises, harsh conditions, frequent illnesses within ships' crews, and more, it was not that uncommon for officers to become frail, indisposed, or despondent. If such was the case with any officer, it was necessary to get a navy surgeon or medical board to declare the officer "unfit for active duty." The officer was retained on the rolls if the surgeon considered it was possible for a complete recovery, but the man was suspended in rank and reduced to half pay. Such was the case with Lieutenant Winslow. Going back on active duty meant getting a certificate of fitness from a navy surgeon or medical board, which Winslow finally obtained in November 1845.

The following month, Winslow was ordered to the USS *Cumberland* as a watch and division officer. This was a heavily armed fifty-gun frigate. She was originally laid down in 1824 but because of budget squabbles in the Quincy Adams, Jackson, and Van Buren administrations she was not finished until eighteen years later. The *Cumberland* would have a storied career as a command ship, flagship, pirate hunter, scourge of slave traders, and participant in the Mexican War. It would be in the Civil War that she would achieve her greatest fame, but not in a good way: She was destined to become the first ship in history to be attacked and sunk ("torpedoed") by an ironclad ship, CSS *Virginia*.

By 1845 Lieutenant Winslow had been a commissioned officer in the navy for eighteen years. He had been off-and-on ill or placed on shore duty for almost half that time. His progress toward higher rank was, in a word, "average." He was neither the best nor the worst and, like everyone else, was shackled to an advancement system that was glacially slow and rarely based on merit. Survival and seniority were the names of the game and only on the rarest of occasions was an officer "jumped" up the list. Still, there were a few men of Winslow's seniority who were the next rank up, commander, and some lieutenants of Winslow's year group, give or take a couple of years, who had been ship captains, albeit of small ships, usually ten guns or less. On the other hand, some officers finished their careers as lieutenants after forty years of service. Said in another, and more congenial way, Winslow was a middle-of-the-roader—solid, dependable, efficient, brave, and loyal, but not exceptional—at least not thus far.

The *Cumberland*, with Winslow aboard, was ordered to join the Mediterranean Squadron in early 1846, but tensions between the United States and Mexico started taking a turn for the worse at the same time. On February 3, the *Cumberland* hauled up her anchors in Nantasket Roads (near Boston) and pointed her bow not east but south, her orders changed from the Med to Veracruz, Mexico.

Winslow, though, was still ill, his erysipelas having returned though not as fierce as before. On the way to Mexico, he seems to have spent several days in his cabin and unable to stand his watches. The closer the ship got to Veracruz, though, the "war talk" became more intense, and the excitement and possibilities seemed to have acted as a tonic for Winslow. By the time the *Cumberland* arrived in early March, Winslow was fit for duty and eager to fight, if need be.

The two-year Mexican War was primarily a land-based conflict. Mexico had no navy to speak of and its merchant shipping capability was practically nonexistent. There was almost nothing for the U.S. Navy to do, and only rare naval officers, like Raphael Semmes, found adventure away from his ship. Nonetheless, blockades of key ports were put in place and the navy was employed in moving troops as well as carrying diplomats back and forth with dispatches.

USS *Cumberland* was flagship to the squadron of navy ships at Veracruz and the commodore commanding, as noted previously, was fifty-four-year-old David E. Connor. Known as the Home Squadron, the group consisted of eleven vessels: frigates, sloops, and steamers. The title of commodore was an honorary one as the U.S. Navy had yet to have any official rank higher than captain. Connor was regarded as a solid officer having fought in the War of 1812 and later, in 1841–1842, had become the navy's first chief of construction, equipment, and repair.

The *Cumberland* spent most of its time at Anton Lizardo, a harbor formed by several low-lying islands that stuck up above the sea by no more than two or three feet. The islands were small and completely barren except for seagrass and a few shrubs.

The monotony began to wear on Winslow and his fellow officers, as evidenced by a portion of this letter to Catherine during June 1846:

> We looked forth from our ships as from a prison, upon the glittering specks of sand, glowing like so many furnaces beneath a tropical sun, day after day, without other variation than the occasional arrival of one of the blockading squadron, to fill up with water and provisions, and depart again on her cruise... We juniors chafed somewhat under the curb that was placed on our ambition of emulating the army in its glorious achievements.

Winslow was soon thereafter partially relieved of his constant boredom by the arrival of a new officer that Commodore Connor had hired for his staff. The lieutenant, two years Winslow's senior, would share Winslow's cabin and become a pal to light cigars with at sunset as they leaned over the taffrail and gabbed about the war. His name was Raphael Semmes.

Discontent with Connor began spreading from ship to ship. The army, under Generals Zachary Taylor and Winfield Scott, were racking up victory after victory (albeit at a steep cost in American lives) and the newspapers back home were singing the praises of the brave American soldiers. Little to nothing was being said about the navy—nothing positive anyway. The sailors were itching for some action, anything, to break the monotony. Yet day after sweltering day, the proud vessels swung at anchor or periodically ran up one of the local rivers to obtain fresh water and provisions.

In fairness to Connor there was little for him to do without a viable opponent. He could have sent out small expeditions or amphibious landing parties to harass the Mexicans, but he did not. It would have been great practice and a viable way for the men to blow off some steam, but he deemed it too dangerous and likely to incur unnecessary casualties.

The Navy Department, egged on by the press, began to fret about Connor's inaction too. Something needed to be done. The navy decided to send down a more aggressive commodore to become Connor's deputy: Captain Matthew C. Perry. The theory went that it would be an unnecessary disgrace for Connor to be relieved, especially since his term as commodore of the Home Squadron was nearly completed. Perry would be sent to Veracruz to see what he might do to stir things up and would also be on-site to take over when the time was right. Perry arrived in early October and was given command of the steamships in the squadron.

A hero of the War of 1812, Matthew Perry was brother to Oliver Hazard Perry, the hero of Lake Erie during the same war. Gruff, hard-charging, and hard-drinking, Matthew Perry had become an outstanding advocate of modernizing the navy as well as properly training its young officers and sailors. Having spearheaded the development of the steam navy, and having commanded the first USS *Fulton*, it seemed quite logical that he would direct the steamships of the Home Squadron as he waited for Connor to vacate his post.

Before that would happen, however, the naval situation in Mexico began to change. As soon as Perry shifted his flag to the USS *Mississippi*, a ten-gun steam frigate, on October 8, 1846, General Scott began his march on Mexico City. He wanted no distractions from Mexican outposts he would pass along the way, especially any along the coast that could be used to resupply the Mexican Army. Neither did Scott want any groups of Mexican soldiers left on his flank that could circle around behind his large, ponderous force and cause trouble in his rear. The navy was (finally!) tasked with executing landings against these nagging targets and eliminating them as Scott moved forward.

Tampico became a prime focus. Connor released Perry and

his steamships to capture and invest the city on October 28. The USS *Vixen*, a side-wheel steamboat small enough to get over and beyond the sandbars of the Tabasco River, was sent forward with two hundred U.S. Marines under the command of Captain Alvin Edson. Relishing being part of the mission was Lieutenant Winslow with a contingent of about seventy sailors from the USS *Mississippi*.

Perry was also aboard the *Vixen* and sent a deputation to meet with the town leaders of Tampico. The negotiators were to try and secure a bloodless surrender, but the town leaders refused. The *Vixen* soon thereafter began a bombardment using her three guns and the marines were sent ashore. Winslow and his men were landed farther upstream, at Tabasco, to outflank the defenders.

In Winslow's many letters to his wife during this period he constantly wonders how he would handle himself under fire—will he prove adequate? On October 29, 1846, Winslow began to find answers to his concerns.

In short, he proves to be—somewhat surprisingly—a fierce warrior. The embedded correspondent for the *New York Journal of Commerce*, writing days after the Tampico battle, sent off this dispatch:

Lieutenant Winslow, occupying the wing of the force up the river, perceived a number of Mexicans firing from the roofs of their houses. [He] gained permission to dislodge the Mexicans…which was done with a few men; and once adrift from the main force Lieutenant Winslow manifested no disposition to return, but commenced skirmishing further up the street, with some musketeers who had opened up on him further in advance, until following up with his men, who were imbibing all the spirit of their leader he finally reached one of the corners of a square from which he had been fired upon.

To go further into the city would exceed his orders, so Winslow left his men in place and dashed back, through enemy fire, to get that permission from Captain Edson, who was in command of the expedition at that juncture. Winslow "begged permission to cross the plaza and 'drive the rascals,' as he said," the correspondent reported. But Edson would not, and could not, give Winslow the permission he sought. The town officials had finally agreed to surrender, and the American landing force had already been ordered to withdraw by Perry.

Winslow had proved to be cool under fire, gallant, and aggressive. He was also understated and does not even brag about himself to his wife. Instead, in the next letter he pens to her, he simply says, "I have just returned from an expedition to Tabasco of which the papers will give you all the information."

His courage was not unnoticed, however. Edson reported the lieutenant's conduct to Perry, who in turn publicly complimented the young officer. The commodore's actions were extremely important for Winslow. There were, at that time, no medals or decorations authorized for the U.S. Navy (or the army for that matter). The War and Navy Departments favored a completely egalitarian approach to service. Unlike some of their foreign counterparts (especially the French and the Russians), where uniforms could be completely covered with gaudy badges of honor, sashes, medals, and other gewgaws, American frock coats or tunics would be simple, bare, and clean. It was important, however, to be recognized by a senior commander, which could also get one bumped up a few spaces for promotion. The honors from Perry would forever be a mark of valor and recognition for Winslow.

Though it amounted to very little of significance strategically, the dustup at Tabasco resulted in Winslow being given his first independent command. The *Laura Virginia* was a two-gun, 112-foot-long schooner that had been captured from the Mexicans. Immediately after the Tabasco skirmish the ship had been renamed USS *Morris*, in honor of Charles Morris, a navy lieutenant who had been mortally wounded during the Tampico Expedition by a bullet to the throat. Morris was a friend of Winslow's and the son of Commodore Charles Morris, another hero of the War of 1812.

The *Morris* might not sound as if it was much of a ship, but dispatch boats were crucial to naval operations. These were the days before radio, of course, or even effective long-range semaphore devices, so messages, orders, papers, and commands that needed to be sent over more than sight distance were conveyed by the fleet's little dispatch boats. They were also used to swap personnel, convey prisoners, and transfer funds.

Winslow took command of the USS *Morris* on or about December 2, 1846. He was ill with fever but did not let it show to his crew. His new ship was being caulked and made ready for its first adventures at sea. Winslow was desperately trying to find the equipment he needed, especially charts and navigation devices, which, in the Caribbean in the middle of the hurricane season, could prove crucial to survival. Good news was the *Morris* proved to be a sprightly little vessel that could slice through the waves at a respectable eight knots. The new caulking was keeping the ship's interior nice and dry and all in all Captain Winslow was quite happy with his new command.[44]

Unhappily, on December 16, everything would change. A powerful storm with howling winds and lashing rains of deluge proportions blew up out of the southern latitudes. It was, indeed, a hurricane but in those days, no one could predict them, and without a barometer to track the falling air pressure, Winslow was clueless as to what was facing the *Morris*.

USS *John Adams*, a thirty-gun sail frigate, was acting as temporary lighthouse ship for vessels in the area. Built in 1799, she was one of the oldest U.S. Navy ships on active duty. As the

---

44 Even though still a lieutenant, Winslow was given the honorific of "captain" in recognition of his being in command.

beacon ship, *John Adams* was to maintain a bright light aloft during the storm for other ships to use as a navigational aid. It was the only navigational marker in the area. If Winslow could see the beacon, and hold his position, he might be able to weather the powerful storm.

Providence would not favor Winslow that night. The winds and rain were too much even for the *John Adams*. Despite strong anchor chains laid out, the *John Adams* was dragged across the sea bottom, and as her position changed, so did Winslow, thinking he was keeping station successfully.

The sickening sounds of rock crushing stout wooden beams soon told Winslow he was on one of the many reefs in the vicinity. Water began pouring into the hold. The crew of the *Morris* tried one of the only measures available to them. They tossed their anchors over the side, manned the capstans, and slowly began to wind themselves off the rocks. The cacophony of cracking oak and splintering beams told Winslow they were probably creating more damage than the ship could stand. He then tried to raise some sail hoping the enormous winds would blow and drag them off the rocks, but the chains he had relied on were doing the job too well, pinning the faltering hull to the jagged corals beneath them. No amount of pounding and smashing by the crew could break the chains.

A massive wall of roiling water rose out of the dark and took aim at the little *Morris*. The ship was turned on its side and angry waves poured over the gunwales. The masts cracked, the sails shredded, and men and material were tossed into the ocean. The *Morris* was doomed. The men begged Winslow to abandon ship. He told them to do so if they wished but he would stay. The crew manned the one surviving longboat or grabbed anything that would float and pulled away from the *Morris*, which was now smashing itself to kindling. Winslow's heroic (if foolish) determination to go down with his ship was soon thwarted as another gigantic breaker grabbed him in its maw and yanked him from the wreck.

Fortunately, the *John Adams*, which was certainly having enough trouble of her own, observed the fate of the *Morris* and pulled away to try and rescue the survivors. Miraculously, not one of the crew was lost including her water-logged captain. The navy convened a perfunctory court of inquiry into the loss of the *Morris*. Given the storm, lack of navigational aids, and heroic efforts to save the ship, Winslow was completely exonerated.

Winslow was transferred from the *John Adams* to the steamer USS *Raritan*. His spirits were lower than the keel of the ship he rode. He was suffering from yellow fever, the destruction of his first command, the loss of all his uniforms and personal effects, he couldn't get any quality rest from the mosquitoes that plagued him in swarms and penetrated all forms of netting, and he slept in a bed from which he rose each morning to discover a mattress strewn with fleas. He blamed all his misfortunes on Commodore Connor, who "knowing well that it was shameful in him to send me to sea without the least means of navigation in a sea so liable to heavy tempests," he complained in a letter to his wife.

The only lightness in his life was that which irony thrust upon him: his friend Raphael Semmes ended up, once again, sharing his mosquito-infested, flea-strewn cabin. Even more ironic, Semmes, too, had inherited command of a ship while in Veracruz, the ill-starred USS *Somers*, which capsized and sank in a squall while chasing a Mexican blockade runner on December 6. These situations led to endless rounds of cigars and banter with Winslow saying, "Captain Semmes, they are going to send you out to learn to take care of ships in blockade." To which Semmes would reply, "Captain Winslow, they are going to send you out to learn the bearing of reefs."

In April 1847, after finally recovering from his various ailments and back in the U.S., Winslow was given orders to assume the post of ordnance officer at the Boston Navy Yard. Nothing could have pleased him more because he was growing tired of the long separations from his family as well as the illnesses. This assignment should have been good for at least three years. He and Catherine and their growing family settled into quarters in the Navy Yard, temporarily vacating their permanent home in Roxbury.

But barely a year went by and Winslow received orders to report to the sloop of war USS *Saratoga*, twenty-two guns, built in 1842, and one of the last sail-only capital ships built for the U.S. Navy. As disappointing as this news was to Winslow regarding having more time with his family, the appointment was a propitious one. He was ordered aboard as executive officer or number two in the chain of command. It was a significant upgrade for Winslow in terms of responsibility and an assignment that was preparation for his eventual promotion to commander. He could not have turned it down and still expect a profitable career in the navy.

Winslow reported aboard on April 8, 1848, and met his new commander, Captain W. C. Nicholson,[45] and the 210 other officers and crewmen. Winslow was attached to the *Saratoga* until September 1849. During those seventeen months, the ship spent most of its time in the West Indies and had a few stops in and around the Yucatán, Veracruz, and Tampico, places familiar to Lieutenant Winslow from his combat adventures. Although the Mexican War was over, there were still plenty of U.S. troops in Mexico and various pieces of unfinished business that needed to be concluded. The navy was on station to make sure treaty conditions were complied with and to keep an eye on the Mexicans, whom very few Americans trusted to keep their word.

At one point in late November, Winslow writes the following to Catherine:

---

45   Nicholson (1790–1872) rose to the rank of commodore before retiring in 1862.

I must say there is little heard in a mess which will bear repetition—stale jokes and conversations which have little charm for me. So you may think I am not the most popular person in the world—not that I am ever in dispute—but I don't think my retired ways and habits of thinking suit the officers, in other words I am not "hail fellow well met." I am more pleased in discovering traits of character in the men, with a view of exerting a healthy influence over those who seem capable of being improved.

The role of executive officer (XO) is unique. He can often be the loneliest person on the ship. If something happens to the captain, the "exec" needs to be trained, prepared, and ready to take over. The XO is also the chief morale officer, executor of the captain's orders, head of discipline, and the meanest "badass" on the ship (when required). The captain has total control and the final say, but the XO must make it all happen and pull everything together the way the captain wants it done while at the same time making the crew do it right. The best XOs eventually become captains. The bad XOs reveal themselves quickly and the navy has a chance to pull them out of line before they become captains and make mistakes that could be fatal to the ship or crew. (Little has changed since 1848.)

Winslow turned out to be a good executive officer, and he was rewarded with shore duty back in Boston that lasted until Christmastime in 1851. Then the navy called him back to sea. His next assignment was to the USS *St. Lawrence*, a fifty-gun frigate with nearly five hundred officers and enlisted sailors. She was a behemoth for her day, one of the largest and most powerful sailing ships ever built for the U.S. Navy.

In a ship of this size and complement, Winslow would not be senior enough to be an executive officer, so it was back to being a division officer, but as the ordnance head, he had the most important divisional command on the ship. All fifty guns and the gun crews that manned them were his responsibility. However, except for firing a few salutes and signals, Winslow and his men never fired a round in anger for the next three and a half years.

When the *St. Lawrence* cleared New York Harbor in December 1851, she was headed to take up duties as the flagship for the Pacific Squadron, loosely headquartered in and around San Francisco Bay. There being no Panama Canal yet, the *St. Lawrence* would have to sail around Cape Horn and through the treacherous Strait of Magellan to reach the Pacific Ocean. On her travels she would touch at some of the most strategically important and beautiful ports in the world: Rio de Janeiro, Brazil; Valparaíso, Chile; Honolulu, Hawaii; San Francisco; Callao, Peru; and Acapulco, Mexico.

For Winslow, however, it was the cruise from hell. Nothing much happened. The tedium and hard duty weighed on him. Forty-two months was a long time to be away from home; longer, in fact, than many of the whaling ship voyages of the day. There was personal tragedy to deal with, as well: In February 1853, while at Valparaíso, he learned of the death of his youngest child, whom he had never seen because the little boy had been born shortly after his departure from New York.

Winslow could now add grief to being tired, lonely, bored, and worried about the pitiful pay of a navy lieutenant and whether it would be sufficient to provide for his family. He was a bit distracted too. In his spare time (of which there seemed to be plenty), he had toyed around with some ship models and in the process invented what he called a "camel steam tug." This ingenious design for a powerful tugboat, using the newly harnessed power of steam, and "strong as a camel," could be used to pull much larger vessels over the numerous sand bars that shifted in and around many of the major ports of the southern United States. Winslow was aiming to get the device patented as soon as he could get back to home base (which he eventually did) and then go out and sell it and make a fortune. He might have, but he never quite got around to building a full-scale, actual tug, although he demonstrated his little models quite successfully. Had he pursued the contraption, as he often said he wished to do, his life could have been very different.

Off the coast of Mexico and in Callao, Peru, there were American vessels to rescue. The postwar, in-and-out, resident of Mexico, Santa Anna, was constantly playing politics and issuing threats to American shipping. In October 1853, the *St. Lawrence* sailed into Acapulco and escorted a dozen U.S. ships safely to sea that Santa Anna had impounded for one ridiculous reason or another. The same sort of business occurred in January 1854, in Callao, with the compounding factor that Peru had just gone through yet another nasty revolution. In both cases, however, neither Mexico nor Peru had any appetite whatsoever for tangling with a fifty-gun frigate.

There were challenges in San Francisco, too, but of a different sort. Gold had been discovered in 1848 at Sutter's Mill north of San Francisco, and in August 1852, the "gold fever" was still rampant as the *St. Lawrence* pulled into port. "We are on duty every moment," Winslow informed his wife. "Our men are infected with the gold fever to such a degree that we have to keep all the [M]arine muskets loaded for service, sentries posted everywhere, and a brace of pistols for the officer of the deck. Five of our men have deserted today."

The *St. Lawrence* sailed into Callao again at the beginning of summer 1854. Winslow's state of mind was obvious in a letter he sent to his wife on June 11: "Your letter with accounts of home made me homesick. It requires great self-denial to be away from you all. I have missed my profession; I am not fit to remain away. There are many who like this life, but I cannot believe that anyone who is of a domestic turn of mind can receive pleasure away from those he loves."

Finally, Captain Nicholson received notice from the Navy Department that as soon as the ship returned to the U.S. it would be decommissioned. The *St. Lawrence* had had the inconvenience of losing its active status twice before, in 1850 and 1851, which was a way of cutting budget for very big and very expensive ships like her.[46] Finally, on February 7, 1855, the *Independence* arrived in Valparaíso to relieve the *St. Lawrence*. The entire crew broke into rousing cheers as soon as the sails of the *Independence* broke the horizon outside Valparaíso Harbor. It meant they were finally going home.

A happy family reunion took place at the Winslow homestead in Roxbury at the end of April 1855. A few days later he was placed in command of the navy recruiting office in Boston, an excellent assignment which would keep him at home for five more years. More happy news arrived in September when he received word that he had been promoted to commander. In December 1860 Commander Winslow was ordered to the post of inspector of the 2nd Lighthouse District, also headquartered in Boston. The man who signed Winslow's new orders as inspector was none other than the secretary of the Lighthouse Board, Commander Raphael Semmes.

---

46 It would, in fact, happen three more times before she was sold in 1875.

9

The *Sumter* had found success beyond the early expectations for her, but it had not been the only Confederate ship to challenge the Union on the seas. Initially, the South's naval efforts were focused on breaking the blockade of its most important ports. Not having nearly the manufacturing might of the North, the new nation's economy would depend on being able to get cotton and other raw goods out and to get weapons and other manufactured goods in. These early efforts, however, had mixed results at best.

Hopes were pinned on the *Merrimack*. The steam frigate had been burned and scuttled as Union forces abandoned the Gosport Navy Yard near Norfolk, Virginia. However, navy secretary Mallory was not inclined to give up on her. The newly appointed commander of the Gosport base, French Forrest, contracted on May 18, 1861, to salvage the wreck of the frigate. This was completed just twelve days later, and the *Merrimack* was towed into the shipyard's only dry dock. The wreck was surveyed, and her lower hull and machinery were discovered to be undamaged.

Mallory decided to convert the *Merrimack* into an ironclad, since she was the only large ship with intact engines available in the Chesapeake Bay area. Preliminary designs were submitted. The one selected showed the bow and stern portions submerged. Workers at the shipyard got busy. The hull's burned timbers were cut down past the vessel's original waterline, leaving just enough clearance to accommodate her large twin-bladed screw propeller. A new fantail and armored casemate were built atop a new main deck, and a V-shaped bulwark was added to her bow, which attached to the armored casemate. This forward and aft main deck and fantail were designed to stay submerged and were covered in four-inch-thick iron plate, built up in two layers. The casemate was built of twenty-four inches of oak and pine in several layers, topped with two two-inch layers of iron plating oriented perpendicular to each other, and angled at thirty-six degrees from horizontal to deflect fired enemy shells.

There was a sense of urgency because the Confederate designers were aware of the Union plans to also build an ironclad. Since they assumed their similar ordnance would be unable to do much serious damage to such a ship it was decided to equip the Confederate ironclad with a ram, an anachronism on a nineteenth-century warship. The *Merrimack*'s steam engines were in poor working order, having been slated for replacement when the decision was made to abandon the Norfolk Navy Yard. Having been scuttled in the salty Elizabeth River water didn't help much either. The addition of tons of iron armor and pig iron ballast only added to her engines' propulsion issues. When completed, the *Merrimack* would have a turning radius of about one mile and require forty-five minutes to complete a full circle, so the ship would certainly not be very nimble.

There was another significant change to the ship—its name. It was determined that *Virginia* was a much more palatable name than one derived from a river in New England.

The emerging ironclad's casemate had fourteen gun ports, three each in the bow and stern, one firing directly along the ship's centerline, the two others angled at forty-five degrees from the centerline. The six bow and stern gun ports had exterior iron shutters installed to protect their cannon. There were four gun ports on each side, but there would not be enough time to install their protective iron shutters. *Virginia's* battery consisted of four muzzle-loading single-banded Brooke rifles and six smoothbore 9-inch Dahlgren guns salvaged from the old *Merrimack*. Two of the rifles, the bow and stern pivot guns, were 7-inch caliber and weighed 14,500 pounds each. They fired a 104-pound shell. The other two were 6.4-inch cannon of about 9,100 pounds, one on each side. The 9-inch Dahlgrens were mounted three to a side and both amidships Dahlgrens nearest the boiler furnaces were fitted out to fire heated shot. On her upper casemate deck were positioned two 12-pounder howitzers.

There was no time for trial runs and simple sorties. Under the command of Captain Franklin Buchanan,[47] CSS *Virginia* set out—with workmen still aboard—to take on the blockading Union fleet. Her very first action became known as the Battle of Hampton Roads, which began on March 8, 1862. She took on the all-wood, sail-powered USS *Cumberland* (Winslow's former ship during the Mexican War). The Union vessel was first crippled during a furious cannon exchange then rammed in her forward starboard bow by the *Virginia*. As the *Cumberland* began to sink, the port-side half of *Virginia's* iron ram was broken off, causing a bow leak in the ironclad. Seeing what had happened to the *Cumberland*, the captain of a second Union ship, USS *Congress*, ordered his frigate to escape into shallower water. However, she was soon grounded. *Congress* and *Virginia* traded cannon fire for an hour, after which the badly damaged *Congress* finally surrendered.

While the surviving crewmen of *Congress* were being ferried off the ship, a Union battery on the north shore opened fire on *Virginia*. Outraged at such a breach of war protocol, an angry

---

47 Buchanan (1800–1874) served forty-five years in the U.S. Navy before defecting to the Confederate Navy. He became the CSA's only full admiral.

Buchanan gave the order to open fire with heated shot on the surrendered *Congress*. Set ablaze by the retaliatory shelling, the *Congress* burned for many hours into the night, a symbol of Confederate naval power and a costly wake-up call for the all-wood Union blockading squadron.

Though victorious, the *Virginia* had wounds to tend. Her hanging port-side anchor was lost after ramming *Cumberland* and the bow was leaking. Shot from *Cumberland*, *Congress*, and the shore-based Union batteries had riddled her smokestack, reducing her boilers' draft and already slow speed. The damage also put two of her broadside cannons out of commission and both of *Virginia*'s twenty-two-foot cutters had been shot away. Even so, Buchanan, who had been injured during the fight, ordered an attack on the USS *Minnesota*, which had also run aground on a sandbar trying to escape. Because of the ironclad's twenty-two-foot draft, she was unable to get close enough to do any significant damage to the *Minnesota*. It being late in the day, *Virginia* retired from the conflict with the expectation of returning the next day and completing the destruction of the remaining Union blockaders.

But the Union Navy had a surprise sailing into the fray. Later that night, the USS *Monitor* arrived at Union-held Fort Monroe. She had been rushed there, still not quite complete, all the way from the Brooklyn Navy Yard, in hopes of defending the force of wooden ships and preventing the CSS *Virginia* from further threatening the Union's blockading fleet and nearby cities, especially Washington. While under tow, she had nearly foundered twice during heavy storms on her voyage south. She arrived in Hampton Roads by the bright firelight from the still-burning triumph of the *Virginia*'s day of destruction.

Thus, it was on March 9 that the world's first battle between ironclads took place. The smaller and faster *Monitor* was able to outmaneuver the larger, slower *Virginia*, but neither ship proved able to do any severe damage to the other, despite numerous shells launched by both combatants, many fired at virtually point-blank range. *Monitor* had a much lower freeboard with only its single rotating, two-cannon gun turret and forward pilothouse sitting above her deck, and thus was much harder to hit with the *Virginia*'s heavy cannon. *Monitor* finally had to retreat into shallower water after a direct shell hit to her armored pilothouse. While looking through the pilothouse's narrow horizontal viewing slits, the captain, Lieutenant John Worden, had taken a direct gunpowder explosion to his face and eyes, blinding him.[48]

The *Monitor* remained in the shallows, but as it was late in the day, the *Virginia* steamed for her home port, the battle ending without a clear victor. The *Virginia* remained in dry dock for repairs until April 4, then sallied forth again. However, she was unsuccessful in her attempts to break the Union blockade, which had been bolstered by the hastily ram-fitted paddle steamer *Vanderbilt* and other ships. The *Virginia* made several sorties back over to Hampton Roads hoping to draw the *Monitor* into battle, but the Union ironclad was under strict orders not to reengage.

The following week, the Confederate Navy sent the paddle side-wheeler *Jamestown*, along with the *Virginia* and five other ships in full view of the Union squadron, to entice them to fight. When it became clear that Union Navy ships were unwilling to engage, the Confederate squadron moved in and captured three merchant ships. As they were towed back to Norfolk their Union flags were hoisted upside down to further taunt the Union Navy into a fight. That tactic did not succeed either.

All of this became moot on May 10 when advancing Union troops occupied Norfolk. The *Virginia* faced the prospect of being no more than a steam-powered heavy battery and she was judged unseaworthy for entering the Atlantic. She was also unable to retreat farther up the James River due to her deep

---

48 Worden recovered and continued in what would turn out to be a long career in the U.S. Navy, including commanding the European Squadron in the late 1870s. He retired as an admiral in 1886.

draft. Still, in an attempt to help her escape, supplies and coal were dumped overboard but this was still not enough to make a difference. Without a home port and no place to go, the *Virginia*'s destruction was ordered to keep the ironclad from being captured. Early on the morning of May 11, off Craney Island, powder trails reached the magazine, and the *Virginia* was destroyed by a great explosion. What remained of the ship settled to the bottom of the harbor.[49]

There was also a rather inglorious end to the USS *Monitor*. On the last day of 1862, she was swamped by high waves in a violent storm while under tow off Cape Hatteras, North Carolina. Sixteen of her sixty-two-member crew were either lost overboard or went down with the ironclad, while many others were saved by lifeboats sent from the tugboat. The wreckage was not located until years later when the *Monitor* was found on the floor of the Atlantic Ocean about sixteen nautical miles southeast of Cape Hatteras. Her upside-down turret was raised from beneath the capsized wreck years later with the remains of two of her crew still aboard. They were eventually buried with full military honors in March 2013 at Arlington National Cemetery.

The brevity of the CSS *Virginia*'s success indicated to the Jefferson Davis administration that a strategy to break the Union blockade was not feasible. The Confederacy had too few naval resources and, as 1862 progressed, it became apparent that the Union already had many more vessels and it would only add to that as Gideon Welles had more hulls refurbished and modernized as well as constructed. If the Union Navy was not sufficiently vulnerable, the next best target was the Union's merchant ships.

The North's manufacturing plants as well as its much larger population needed raw materials and some goods only available

---

49 CSS *Virginia*'s Stars and Bars battle ensign was saved from destruction. Today it resides in the collection of the Chicago History Museum, minus three of its thirteen original stars. Only a few remnants of the Confederate ironclad have been recovered for preservation in museums because the wreck was heavily salvaged following the war.

in Europe. Putting enough pressure on that maritime pipeline would weaken the enemy's overall war effort and at least gain the South valuable time. The longer the South lasted as a viable foe, the better the chance Great Britain and/or France would declare support. The South could not possibly blockade Northern ports, but it could attack shipping on the high seas.

The early achievements of Raphael Semmes and the *Sumter* had shown the way…but there would have to be other birds of prey. While the *Sumter* was still roaming, the CSS *Nashville* began its voyages. It actually had the distinction of being the first Confederate Navy warship to put in at a European port.

The *Nashville* and by extension the Confederacy benefitted from good timing. The 1200-ton wooden side-wheeler had been constructed as a passenger vessel in 1853 and eight years later had a thorough upgrade including new boilers. As it happened, she steamed into Charleston in April 1861 as the Civil War began. She was soon acquired by Secretary Mallory and received more upgrades to make her a faster ship. By the end of September, the *Nashville* was ready to undertake its first mission under its commander, Lieutenant Robert Pegram.[50] But it was a month before she was able to slip through the Union blockade.

On the other side of a stormy crossing of the North Atlantic, the *Nashville* found its first prize. Off the west coast of Ireland, it crossed paths with the *Harvey Birch*, a clipper ship bound for New York. Though the *Nashville* was not heavily armed, the merchant ship would be no match for it in a battle. Its captain lowered the American flag and he and his crew were taken prisoner. Pegram set fire to the *Harvey Birch* and down she went.

The *Sumter* had been operating in southern waters so when the *Nashville* arrived in the English port of Southampton to drop off its prisoners, word spread fast of a Confederate raider in the

---

50   Pegram (1811–1894) was a U.S. Navy officer from 1829 to 1861 when he "went South" for his home state of Virginia. He rose to the rank of captain before the war ended.

North Atlantic. And then there was more sensational news: An American warship had boarded a British steamer and removed passengers. Might this be an act of war? It had to at least be good news for the Confederacy. "Bitter anti-Union feeling erupted across Great Britain at the thought of the upstart United States violating the sanctity of its vessels," writes the naval historian Chester Hearn. "The press raged at the affront, demanding an immediate apology from the Lincoln administration."

Here's what had happened: Jefferson Davis had dispatched two Confederate commissioners, John Slidell and James Mason, to persuade the governments in France and Great Britain to become proponents of Southern independence. The ship carrying the two men eluded the blockade and brought them to Cuba where, in Havana, they boarded the British ship *Trent*. Soon after the *Trent* got underway it was stopped by the *San Jacinto*, a Union ship commanded by Charles Wilkes.[51] American marines boarded the *Trent*, training guns on the British crew and other passengers, and removed Slidell and Mason and their secretaries. Bidding adieu, Wilkes set a course for Boston.

The two Confederate commissioners were released and apologetic overtures were sent to Great Britain, but until that happened, in January 1862, the *Nashville* enjoyed a special status. Then Union warships arrived and bottled it up in port. Still stung by the *Trent* affair, the British government ordered that the *Nashville* could leave Southampton and could not be followed for twenty-four hours. This was more than enough time for the speedy Confederate ship to escape. It kept going, back across the Atlantic, and on February 26, off the Carolinas, it captured the *Robert Gilfillan*, a schooner out of Philadelphia. It too was set ablaze.

---

51   Wilkes (1798–1877) was one of the more intriguing officers in the U.S. Navy in the nineteenth century. He was one of the first explorers of the Antarctic. He commanded a round-the-world expedition of discovery from 1838 to 1842 and he was captain of the USS *San Jacinto* during the infamous Trent Affair of 1861. He was court-martialed twice and constantly argued with Secretary Welles. Despite all this, he still managed to attain promotion to rear admiral before retiring in 1866.

That, however, concluded the decidedly modest career of this Confederate raider. The *Nashville* put in at Beaufort, North Carolina, in late February, and except for a few abbreviated decoy runs, she remained there. She was renamed the *Thomas L. Wragg* and then in November received yet another name, *Rattlesnake*. This proved to be bad luck for the steamer because later that month the ship ran aground and was destroyed by the guns of the ironclad monitor USS *Montauk*.

But the voyages of the *Nashville* and the *Sumter* and the destruction of Northbound cargos convinced the Davis administration that seagoing hunters could make a difference. Certainly, that would be true of the *Alabama*. What the South needed was more ships like it.

Initially viewed as the Confederacy's best seagoing weapon was the *Florida*. This was the ship originally known as the *Oreto*, which had left England on its maiden voyage in March 1862, bound for the Bahamas. To avoid suspicions that she was destined for Confederate service, the ship was loaded with only enough coal to reach Nassau. However, once there she planned to meet with a Confederate ship, take on a portion of that ship's coal, and use the additional fuel to steam to the nearest Confederate port.

This plan went awry quickly. Suspicions that the ship had been constructed for the Confederate Navy followed the *Oreto* to Nassau where the British governor prevented her from attempting a rendezvous with her planned tender. Plan B was having the *Oreto* met by two ships near the more isolated Green Cay. There, stores, armaments, and coal were taken aboard. While anchored off Green Cay, she was officially commissioned into the Confederate States Navy as CSS *Florida* on August 17, with Lieutenant John Newland Maffitt[52] in command.

---

52 Maffitt (1819–1886) was a lieutenant in the U.S. Navy before switching sides in 1861. He was naval aide to General Robert E. Lee before being given command of the CSS *Florida*. He was forced to give up *Florida* because of illness in 1864. After recovery he became a successful blockade runner in South Carolina until the war's end.

The warship's prospects got worse, however. During her out-fitting, yellow fever raged among her crew. After five days, her effective crew was reduced to one fireman and four deckhands. The *Florida* made a desperate dash to Cuba. In Cárdenas, the captain too was stricken with the disease. Amazingly, the intrepid Maffitt managed to direct his ship from Cárdenas to Mobile. It braved a hail of projectiles from the Union blockade vessels and raced through them to anchor beneath the guns of Fort Morgan in Mobile Bay, where she was received with a hero's welcome. That all the *Florida* had done thus far was survive was enough for the population to cheer her. The ship took on additional supplies and a healthy crew. The Union blockade was thwarted again in January 1863 when the *Florida* escaped to sea, with its recovered commander having been promoted to captain.

Citizens in the North were outraged by the *Florida*'s fast getaway. The Congress even condemned Gideon Welles for incompetence. During the remainder of the year, as reports arrived about the *Florida*'s conquests, it became more difficult for the secretary of the navy to excuse the blunders made in Mobile Bay.

Including the *Alabama*, *Florida*, and *Nashville* there would be eight Confederate warships which set off to prey on Union shipping. The others were the *Alexandra*, *Tallahassee*, *Chickamauga*, *Georgia*, and *Rappahannock*. None, however, approached the success of the *Alabama* in disrupting Union shipping psychologically as well as physically. There were CSS *Alabama* sightings everywhere—most of them false—and Raphael Semmes became a larger-than-life figure.

No wonder the North spared no expense in assigning ships to hunt *Alabama* down and consign her to Davy Jones and his immortal locker.

10

As a North Carolinian by birth, John Winslow might have gone with the South. However, his deep New England roots, a home in Boston, a Northern wife, and strong feelings about abolition keep him solidly with the North.

As soon as hostilities commenced with the shelling of Fort Sumter, Winslow dutifully requested relief from his peaceful but unexciting duties as a lighthouse inspector. He expected to go back to sea, and most likely aboard one of the frigates being pressed into blockade duty along the southern and Gulf coasts. That was not quite the way it worked out.

Unbeknownst to Winslow, his presence was already being requested—and not upon blue waters but way up the "muddy Mississippi." An ambitious, dedicated, hard-charging captain by the name of Andrew H. Foote sent a telegram to the Navy Department in September 1861, specifically asking for his "friend" Commander Winslow. It is not exactly clear how, when, and where Foote and Winslow became pals. They never served on the same ship, same shore duty, or in similar assignments together. Foote was five years older and had attended West Point for a brief period before switching to the navy. Foote missed participating in the Mexican War which did so much to anneal Winslow to military service. The U.S. Navy was, however, a small circle, especially among the commissioned officers, so it is entirely likely the two men had at least met and had gotten to know one another somewhere along the way.

There was also their shared hatred of slavery. From 1849 to 1851 Foote had commanded the USS *Perry* and spent most of those two years sailing up and down the African west coast suppressing the slave trade. He even wrote a book about those experiences, published in 1854 and titled *Africa and the American Flag.* Foote was probably the most outspoken naval officer of his day regarding the abolition of slavery. He even gave lectures on abolition while on active duty. Winslow, too, was noted among his fellow officers for his antislavery views, although he did not take the usual step of getting on the lecture circuit. In calling for Winslow to join him on the Mississippi River, Foote could have been looking for a kindred spirit. In any case, Winslow was given orders to join Foote's staff, then based in St. Louis. Foote's task was to build a "brown water navy" and Winslow was to be his principal deputy.

The proximity of powerful Confederate cannons along the Mississippi's riverbanks made the use of high-profile, slab-sided frigates common to the navy virtually useless. They would be blasted to pieces by big guns that could hardly miss at those close ranges. Warfare afloat along the Mississippi and its tributaries would be the province of ungainly low profile, mud-hugging gunboats. Most would be built of iron, some of wood or stout timbers. Their guns would be internalized behind iron or logs, and they would be propelled by steam boilers tucked inside the gunboat hulls. They were slow, stubborn, hard to maneuver, and often plowed into sandbars, each other, and mud banks thrown up by the meandering Father of Waters. They did, however, as events would prove, get the job done of wresting control of the river from the Rebels.

Nine gunboats were contracted initially—seven new hulls and two conversions of existing side-wheel steamers. Each ship would sport fifteen guns of very heavy caliber: mostly 9-inch and 24-pounders. The steering mechanisms were placed amidships behind the inclined sides of the gunboat. The gunboat captains expected to take direct hits—many of them. Survival depended on the slanted sides of the hulls, the ability of their own crews to give as good as they got, and the avoidance of those lucky shots that could send shrapnel through a crack in the plating or glance off a sheet of metal and fly through an open gun port. Most of the gunboats resembled giant tortoises and moved at about the same speed—or sometimes hardly at all if they were going against the river's current.

In the convoluted command structures of the early war, the gunboats were commanded, manned, and operated by the navy, but they were under the operational control and ownership of the army. Captain Foote (soon to be promoted to the new navy rank of rear admiral) reported at first to Major General John C. Fremont, who was soon replaced (due to incompetence) by Brigadier General Ulysses S. Grant. The constructor of the first gunboats, James Buchanan Eads, was a civilian under contract to the navy building ships to army and navy specifications. A situation as complicated and unwieldy as this was ripe for confusion and chaos, but the competing interests somehow made it work. Fortunately, Foote got along splendidly with Grant and the two formed a very effective partnership. Winslow worked well with Foote, and Eads coordinated easily with all three.

Winslow's first task was finding crews for the gunboats. Each ship would require approximately 120 to 170 officers and men. To find enough "sailors," Winslow went to Cleveland for ten days on a recruiting trip. He was accompanied by his wife who rarely joined her husband on any of his assignments. Winslow scooped up volunteers, sailors the navy would call "landsmen" until they got their basic training and "sea legs," or in this case, "river legs." He cast about for veterans and former merchant seamen. He was free to pick off any army soldiers who wanted to volunteer and hundreds of men came forward, curious about the opportunity. Would life on the river be better than thirty-mile marches slogging through mud with sixty-pound packs? Between Cleveland and St. Louis Winslow found plenty of volunteers—and his wife found plenty of shops and mercantile boutiques to explore in the bustling streets of both cities.

Eads, meantime, was working his employees at a blistering pace and his factories boomed twenty-four hours a day. He and his crews would convert the steamer *New Era* into USS *Essex* and build another five gunboats from the keel up in just three months. In addition, Eads took one of his river salvage ships, *Submarine No. 7*, and converted it into the ironclad USS *Benton*. The *Benton* would be the biggest and most powerfully armed of the Eads gunboats.

In early December 1861, Foote and Grant sought to move the new squadron downriver to Cairo, Illinois, to be ready to support land operations planned for early spring 1862. Foote gave Winslow the assignment of squadron commander and the task of moving the ships. Rather than sail all at once, Winslow wisely decided to split the eight gunboats into two sections. Section 1 would execute a trial run to ensure the boats could successfully navigate the currents and sandbars of the fickle Mississippi.

Ice was beginning to form on the river as the first gunboats cast off and slipped into the current. Cairo was about 150 miles north of St. Louis and the river was straight between these two points. All the gunboats sailed off smartly and the trip went off without a hitch. Winslow happily turned over Section 1 to Grant's safekeeping, then took passage back up the river on a commercial steamboat to round up Section 2.

USS *Benton*, part of Section 2, had been designated flagship of the entire flotilla due to her size and firepower. A true behemoth as far as the river was concerned, she was over two hundred feet long and weighed over 660 tons. Most problematic for the Mississippi, however, was that she drew nine feet of water. The river, between St. Louis and Cairo, then averaged between nine and thirty feet deep, depending on the season. Shifting sandbars and mudflats were constantly changing the river's configuration—and depth.

Winslow decided to take personal command of the flagship. To assist him getting down the river to Cairo, Foote assigned Eads to accompany Winslow. The voyage started well enough, but soon thereafter, about thirty miles south, the *Benton* grounded hard onto a mud bank. With the engines in full reverse and the boat shuddering, nothing happened. Winslow ordered an anchor set out astern and the engines thrown in full reverse against the anchor to get the gunboat out of the mud. The efforts went on all night while the river dropped another nine inches. By morning, Winslow was growing more and more frustrated. At that point Eads stepped forward and offered an alternative.

Eads suggested that several stout hawsers be thrown over, rowed to the opposite bank of the river, roped to sturdy tree trunks, and tied to the three steam capstans on the ship. It worked, but not without nearly tragic result.

As the ropes and heavy chains took the strain and began slowly easing the *Benton* out of the mud, a one-inch-thick metal link snapped. That chain fairly exploded into three pieces. One piece was found later over five hundred feet away. Another piece ricocheted off the iron plating but not before punching a deep hole into the iron. A third, short piece of a couple of links struck Winslow, tearing through his coat and ripping away most of the muscle and flesh just below the elbow of his left arm. It was an extremely ugly and painful wound and potentially life threatening for loss of blood, but had the flying iron struck him in the face, head, or chest, it likely would have killed him.

Five days later, on December 13, the *Benton* pulled into Cairo. Winslow was suffering mightily. The doctor on board the *Benton* had managed to reattach most of the muscle and sew up the jagged gash. Fortunately, the bones were not broken. Had they been it would have surely resulted in amputation of the arm.

Providence smiled on Winslow once he got to Cairo: It turned out that one of his sons, William, was stationed there as a U.S. Navy paymaster. William took charge of his father's care and got him back to Roxbury to convalesce.

The wound healed sufficiently well that Winslow was able to return to his Mississippi Squadron by May 1862. Unfortunately, he was suffering from "swamp fevers," which could have been anything from dysentery to malaria. Also, there was some pain behind his right eye, his vision began to cloud, and he suffered from what seemed to be a continuing, weepy infection in that orb that would not go away. Winslow was not a well man, overall, and complained about it constantly to his wife. To his credit, however, his various maladies did not seem to keep him from performing his duties, nor did he complain of them to or in front of his men. He also had a bad habit of ignoring most of his ailments in terms of seeking medical help for them. This would later prove disastrous to his afflicted eye as well as his general health and constitution.

While Winslow was away recuperating, he missed the crucial battles of Fort Henry, Fort Donelson, and Shiloh (Pittsburgh Landing), all of which involved Admiral Foote, General Grant, and the gunboats.

When he resumed his duties, Winslow was immediately given command of a section of gunboats, with the USS *Cincinnati* as his flagship. *Cincinnati* was one of the original Eads ironclads and although it was ponderously slow (four knots, maximum) it was slathered in metal plating and bristling with guns. Winslow was on scene in time to witness and participate in the river battle of Fort Pillow. A gaggle of Confederate armed steamers surprised and jumped on seven Union gunboats chugging downriver, headed for Memphis. A sharp fight ensued, and both the gunboats *Cincinnati* and *Mound City* were rammed, badly damaged, and in danger of sinking. The Union craft were able to slip into shallow waters where the deeper-draft Confederate ships could not go. Nonetheless, both *Cincinnati* and *Mound City*[53] ended up settling into the mud.

The flotilla soon recovered from this near disaster and proceeded downriver to Memphis. On June 6, the Federal forces, consisting of five gunboats and four rams, engaged the Confederate River Defense Fleet, composed of eight rams. The resulting battle was likely one of the most lopsided naval victories of the war. In less than two hours the Union ships blasted, crushed, or sank all but one of the Rebel boats. The city of Memphis, many of whose citizens had been watching the river battle from the bluffs above, surrendered shortly after the last gun was fired. There was only one Union casualty. Confederate losses were considerable, but no one ever bothered to tally them.

This resounding Union victory was led by Captain Charles Henry Davis, who was standing in for Flag Officer Foote, who had been wounded, ironically, in the foot at Fort Donelson. Foote requested leave to recover, which was granted, and he left command of the growing Western Flotilla on June 17. Sadly, Foote, a gifted and extraordinarily capable officer, would never return. In July, he was formally promoted to the new rank of rear admiral and given the Thanks of Congress. His promotion also came with a new assignment as chief of the Bureau of Equipment and Recruiting. As important as this command was to the navy and the war effort, it was not to Foote's liking or his combat temperament. A year later he was finally able to talk the navy into a seagoing posting, this time as commander of the South Atlantic Blockading Squadron. To the shock of all, however, while on his way to assume his new duties, he was

---

53 Both ships were subsequently salvaged and soon placed back in service.

stricken with Bright's disease (severe kidney failure). He died very soon after in New York City on June 26, 1863.

After Foote's departure from the flotilla, Captain Davis was appointed overall commander and promoted to temporary flag officer. Winslow remained at his rank of commander. On June 29, Davis split his forces, taking half the gunboats and rams downriver to Vicksburg, leaving the other half under the command of Winslow at Memphis. Winslow was soon thereafter happily surprised when he was notified, in July, of his promotion to captain.

All was amiable between the two commanders, though Winslow never enjoyed the harmony he had with Flag Officer Foote. The situation turned worse, however, when Davis was given new orders in October to become chief of the Bureau of Navigation, one of the navy's most powerful fiefdoms. To replace Davis, Secretary of the Navy Gideon Welles nominated Commander David Dixon Porter.

The Porter family had been prominent in the U.S. Navy from the service's very inception, back to the early days of the Revolutionary War. David Dixon Porter's father, also David, had been a hero of the War of 1812. Young David's foster brother, adopted by his parents, was the soon-to-be admiral David Glasgow Farragut. Porter had all the right connections and had punched all the right tickets on the way up the U.S. Navy gangplank. Two years younger than Winslow, he had first been a midshipman in the Mexican Navy at the age of twelve.

Mexican Navy? His father had resigned from the U.S. Navy in 1826 after being court-martialed for conducting an unauthorized raid to rescue a fellow officer from jail in Puerto Rico. The government of Mexico made the elder Porter an immediate offer to command the entire Mexican Navy, which he accepted, taking two of his sons, Thomas and David, with him. Both boys were made Mexican Navy midshipmen, but poor Thomas, only ten, died of yellow fever soon after arrival in Mexico. The elder

Porter commanded the Mexican Navy until 1829, after which he entered the U.S. Foreign Service and was appointed minister to the Barbary States. Young David petitioned for a midshipman's appointment in the U.S. Navy and was accepted.

Young Porter's career was steady and took many of the same twists and turns as Winslow faced, including combat in the Mexican War. He was promoted to lieutenant in 1841 and commander in 1861. In April of 1862, his adopted brother, Captain Farragut, was finishing his plans to storm past the Mississippi River forts defending New Orleans and then capture the city itself. He gave Porter command of the twenty-one mortar schooners that had been assigned. Between Farragut's frigates and gunboats and Porter's mortars, the Confederate fleet defending New Orleans was wrecked. The forts also took a pounding, and after Farragut's death-defying charge past them, the battle was over. Porter's mortars lobbed almost three thousand shells into the forts and the city itself, and the city finally surrendered on April 28. Farragut's stock skyrocketed, and Porter, who had a fair hand in the action, found favor as well.

Meanwhile, Winslow sat idle, his gunboats tied to the docks in Memphis. He knew the overall plan was for Farragut's ships and Porter's schooners to get on up the river and begin to harass Vicksburg, the last remaining obstacle to freeing the Mississippi River and getting its entire length back in Union hands. Winslow did not yet know what part he would play, if any. He sat and chafed at the uncertainty.

Captain Winslow had his new stripes sewn to his coat in August, then sat and waited some more. With Captain Davis's transfer to Washington, Secretary Welles had a choice to make: Who should replace Davis? Under the navy's new and evolving command structure the commander of the Western Flotilla had become a rear admiral's billet. Welles looked around to see what captains might be available for promotion and assignment. It is unknown whether Welles ever considered Winslow for the job—he certainly did have the experience on the river that would be necessary. But Welles did something radical and almost unthinkable: He promoted Porter directly from commander to rear admiral and gave him the job. By doing so, he passed over all his captains, including Winslow. Welles knew that Porter was his own best lobbyist (Secretary of War Edwin Stanton once called Porter a "gasbag") and a fast-talking promoter, but he was also aggressive, demanding, energetic, and fearless.

This was a bridge too far for Winslow. To not have gotten the posting—and the further promotion—was bad enough but combined with then having to serve under someone who was junior to him was yet another insult. The unwritten rule in situations like this had always been that the "aggrieved" party could request another assignment as opposed to the indignity of taking orders from a junior officer. On October 10, 1862, Winslow submitted a request to Secretary Welles for "further assignment."

Complicating Winslow's predicament, he had unwisely spoken to at least one reporter, possibly a group of reporters, soon after General John Pope's disastrous defeat at Second Bull Run in August. He was highly critical of both Pope and the man who appointed him—President Lincoln. The *Baltimore American* soon thereafter ran a front-page story in which Winslow was quoted as having said, "I'm glad of it. I wish the Rebs would bag Old Abe too." Winslow also called the President a "chowderhead," not a term of respect or endearment.

Secretary Welles and President Lincoln saw the article. Welles was furious. Lincoln laughed it off, as he often did when stories popped up that were uncomplimentary. Lincoln reportedly told Welles, "Just wait. Give him enough rope and he'll hang himself."

If this indiscretion were not enough, another report reached Welles within days that Winslow had apparently given a captured Confederate officer a tour of one of his gunboats, the *Baron de*

Kalb, and had treated the officer courteously before he was sent off to be exchanged. Welles exploded again.

In a short but blistering note to Winslow on October 22, Welles essentially fired Winslow and sent him packing. He was placed on "furlough" which was tantamount to tossing Winslow on the beach. There would be no further assignments and Winslow would languish at home on half pay until some official mercifully retired him.

Winslow was shocked—although he should not have been. In a letter full of indignation and pique, but salted with some remorse, Winslow explained to Welles that the reporter had taken his remarks out of context. Yes, he admitted, he had said those things about Mr. Lincoln, but he also said that he made the comments to "arouse Washington" that a solid, steady policy was needed in order to successfully prosecute the war. Winslow also explained that the Confederate officer he treated so well was actually an old shipmate from his days aboard the USS *Missouri*, and he had given the officer a tour to show him that deficiencies in the gunboat's original design had been corrected so that the Rebels would have a tougher time attacking them in future.

In the same missive Winslow included a second letter from the officers of the *Baron de Kalb*. Signed by every one of them, it was full of praise for Winslow's qualities as a commander, their appreciation for his skills and talents, and that the navy would certainly not benefit from him being placed on the "furlough" list.

The veiled apology and the strong letter of support from his wardroom seemed to have done the trick. Only four days later Winslow received the following letter from Welles: "Sir: your letter of the 1st instant, explanatory of your previous one requesting to be detached from the Mississippi Squadron has been received and which is satisfactory to the Department. You are hereby relieved from Furlough and you will regard yourself as awaiting orders. I am, respectfully—Gideon Welles."

Winslow made his way home from Mississippi to await those

orders. When he arrived in Roxbury, he was a physical and mental wreck. His swift and arbitrary dismissal still weighed heavily on his mind, and although he had been reinstated, his future in the navy was far from clear. His right eye was painfully swollen and his vision fading rapidly. He still had "Mississippi swamp fevers" and as soon as he got home, to cold and chilly Massachusetts, his erysipelas (neuralgia) returned. He took to his bed immediately.

It took the Navy Department and Secretary Welles less than a month to find a new assignment for Winslow. As far as Welles was concerned, Winslow still had one foot in purgatory, so he decided to give him a challenge, an important one, but a posting slightly less than his seniority deserved. Welles wanted to see what Winslow could do, and if he could do it, there might be redemption and better, brighter days ahead.

Welles gave Winslow command of the USS *Kearsarge*.

11

Captain John Winslow's doctor advised him to turn down the *Kearsarge* assignment, but he would not hear of it and dragged himself out of bed to begin packing.

Winslow was ordered to proceed to New York City to board the USS *Vanderbilt*, departing for the Azores. It was expected that the USS *Kearsarge* would soon pull into port at Fayal, where Winslow would take over command from Captain Charles Pickering. Accompanied by one of his sons, Winslow pulled himself aboard a train from Boston to New York. He almost did not make it to the *Vanderbilt* in time.

A severe winter snowstorm derailed the locomotive outside of Springfield, Massachusetts, and the flailing engine dragged three cars off the tracks with it—including Winslow's. Winslow was so out of it with fever and neuralgia he did not even notice. Miraculously, thanks to his son, he made it on time and slipped aboard the *Vanderbilt*, took to his berth, and barely moved for the two weeks it took to get to the Azores.

Once in Fayal, Winslow began to recover, albeit slowly. The felicitous climate no doubt helped, but so did the *Kearsarge*—

inadvertently, because she was nowhere in sight. The ship was, in fact, in Cádiz, Spain, where she had limped into port with a bent propeller shaft and badly damaged screw. The beating she had taken in a recent hurricane had done the damage. The repairs, such as they were, delayed the ship for four months.

Captain Pickering fumed every day. He wanted off the *Kearsarge* as much as Winslow wanted on. Pickering was tired of the frustrating duty of chasing shadows hither and yon with no result. The crew was coming unglued, too, resulting in bad discipline and a poor work ethic. Several deserted the ship as soon as she steamed into Cádiz. Pickering was anxious to move on to his next command, a large frigate, USS *Housatonic*, anchored in Charleston Harbor and assigned to blockade duty. He would come to regret this new assignment, though, as we shall learn.

On April 5, 1863, Winslow was, as he had most days since arriving, pacing up and down the pathways of Fayal Harbor, a brass telescope tucked under his arm. The three-month interval ashore amidst fragrant blooms, daily exercise, good food, and pleasant weather had done much to better his health—except for his pesky eye infection. On that score, he had consulted an oculist and two medical doctors who had applied several concoctions to the eye, but there had been no improvement. The pain and swelling were less, but the vision continued to wane.

Midstride on a high trail above the harbor a slight smudge of smoke broke the horizon. Winslow lifted his glass to his good left eye. The crosstrees and masts of a large vessel soon came into view. As soon as a smokestack appeared, he smiled. He knew his long-awaited command was finally sailing toward him.

By nightfall on the next day Winslow was secure in the captain's cabin of the *Kearsarge*. Pickering had turned over command and left the ship at noon, smiling broadly. A single glass of madeira at hand, Winslow began, at long last, a cheerful letter to his wife.

When he finally had a chance to set his (good) eye on his

crew, he saw a dispirited bunch. Little wonder: they had been dashing all over the vast Atlantic and the North Sea in search of commerce raiders, with a special focus on the CSS *Alabama*. The near impossible logistics of communicating with ships at sea meant that captains like Pickering and Winslow were essentially on their own in terms of strategy and tactics. Resupply, monetary transactions, crew departures, replacements, repairs, and everything associated with keeping the *Kearsarge* at sea, steaming, and chasing the foe, was in the captain's hands.

Pickering had adopted a strategy of always chasing days-old or weeks-old sightings and trying to make logical guesses as to where the enemy would turn up next. It was an utter failure, and one that wasted resources, exhausted the crew for no gain, and used up the ship. Additionally, when the CSS *Alabama* was out of the Atlantic Ocean or even far below the equator in South America, she was essentially safe, since Union frigates rarely ventured into those waters during the conflict. When the *Alabama* was in the Atlantic the chances of her heaving into view of the *Kearsarge* were infinitesimally small. If it were to happen it would only be by the most incredible gift of luck given the vast spaces that each ship prowled. It took a while for Winslow to figure this out, but once he did the situation—and the odds—were to improve considerably.

He also ascertained that the *Kearsarge* had a first-rate executive officer in Lieutenant Commander (a new Navy rank between lieutenant and full commander) James Shepard Thornton. New Hampshire born and raised (and no doubt familiar with Mt. Kearsarge), Thornton was a great-grandson of a signer of the Declaration of Independence, Dr. Matthew Thornton. In addition, Dr. Thornton had drafted the constitution for the State of New Hampshire, became the first Speaker of the New Hampshire House, and even served, for a time, on the state's Superior Court.

Young James Thornton's father, also James, was ambassador

to Peru in the Van Buren administration (1838) but died of fever in Peru at the very young age of thirty-seven. James S., born in 1827, was taken in by the family of future president Franklin Pierce (the only president from New Hampshire) who had been good friends with Thornton's father. With the backing of New Hampshire Congressman Charles G. Atherton, Thornton received an appointment as a midshipman in 1841, when he was just fourteen years old.

Over the next five years Thornton saw service aboard three different frigates and in 1846 was sent to the new U.S. Naval School at Annapolis, successfully completed all his courses, and was promoted to passed midshipman in 1847. He served at sea during the Mexican War aboard the storeship USS *Relief* and then in 1850 transferred to the USS *Ewing* for coastal geodetic work along the California coast. A mysterious dispute with his captain caused Thornton to resign from the navy in 1850. He pursued survey work in the California and Utah gold fields but came back to the navy in 1854, once again assigned to the USS *Relief.*

Never one to shy away from a fight, Thornton got into a duel with one of his fellow officers in 1857, was severely wounded (but killed his opponent), and was sent home to recuperate. While on leave, in New Hampshire, he (like his future commander, Captain Winslow) married his first cousin Ellen Thornton Wood. The duel did not seem to stunt Thornton's career prospects. He was sent back to the USS *Relief* in 1858 but with the new rank of lieutenant.

Finally relieved from the *Relief* in early 1860, Thornton was briefly stationed ashore at the Receiving Station in Boston before being ordered to the frigate USS *Bainbridge*, on blockade duty in the Gulf of Mexico. While aboard *Bainbridge* he got one of the big breaks of his naval career: assignment as executive officer of the steam frigate USS *Hartford*, whose aggressive, talented squadron commander was David Farragut.

During Farragut's famous 1862 dash up the Mississippi to capture the New Orleans forts and the city itself, with Farragut lashed to the mainmast for stability, the *Hartford* took a pounding from the shore guns, her captain was killed, she was nearly crushed by the Confederate ram CSS *Manassas*, and suffered a near disaster from a fireship that was slipped alongside by the Rebels. *Hartford* ran aground near Confederate Fort St. Philip and was directly under the guns of the fort. Without some fast thinking by Lieutenant Thornton and extraordinary skill getting *Hartford* refloated, she would have been pounded into kindling. The executive officer scrambled a section of the crew to drag out all the ship's excess chains. He had the men drape the chains over the side of the ship facing the Confederate guns. This tactic provided some instant iron "plating" for the ship. The cannonballs began bouncing off the hull, giving time for the engineers to back the ship off the sandbar and get to safety.

For his quick and heroic actions, Thornton would be promoted to lieutenant commander and given orders as the executive officer of the USS *Kearsarge*, to which he reported at almost the same time Winslow took over as captain. The two officers would make an excellent team.

In addition to Winslow and Thornton, the USS *Kearsarge*, on her date with destiny, would be served by sixteen other officers: one passed midshipman, three acting masters, two masters mates, a surgeon, five engineers, a lead boatswain, the head gunner, an assistant paymaster, and a quartermaster. The lone midshipman was Edward E. Preble, grandson of the famous Revolutionary War Commodore Edward Preble, one-time captain of "Old Ironsides," USS *Constitution*. Preble would serve as a navigator aboard the *Kearsarge*.

John M. Browne was assigned as ship's surgeon. Doctors were treated as officers in terms of status, berthing, and wardroom privileges but they held what was called "relative rank" (until 1918). As a designated surgeon, Browne was equal to the rank of lieutenant commander. Another New Hampshire native, Browne was born in 1831, graduated from Harvard Medical School in 1852, and was appointed an assistant surgeon in the U.S. Navy in 1853. By the time he reported to the *Kearsarge*, Dr. Browne had also served aboard the USS *Warren* (a twenty-gun sloop of war), USS *Dolphin* (a brig and antislave ship), and USS *Constellation*.

William Cushman was chief engineer, and he supervised four assistant engineers. He was equal to a line commander in rank.

The enlisted crew aboard the USS *Kearsarge* consisted of thirty-one petty officers (senior enlisted men) of various specialties. Also aboard were three "ship's boys." These were male juveniles, usually age twelve to sixteen, most hoping to become midshipmen. They ran errands for the ship's officers, cleaned and swept cabins, became "powder monkeys" in combat (hauling ammunition and powder to the guns), and sometimes served as assistants to the surgeons or the cooks.

The majority of the crew were ordinary seamen, men one step up from complete novices. They may have had some experience aboard ships elsewhere, probably a whaling or merchant ship. They knew their way around a vessel and may have had some familiarity with sails, armament, or basic shipboard duties. The next step up was that of seaman, or an experienced hand. They often trained the ordinary seamen and the handful of greenhorn landsmen and were on the cusp, if they were any good, of qualifying as a petty officer.

The bottom rung of the ladder was occupied by the "landsmen." These crewmen were the "lubbers" with no experience and very little training (or in a couple of cases, seamen who had been "busted down" because of disciplinary problems or court-martials). The engineering department equivalent crew were "coal heavers," or men with just enough experience to pick up a shovel and toss coal into a furnace.

Almost all of the members of the *Kearsarge* were native-born American citizens, volunteers, and favorable to the Union cause.

Typical of the many young men who volunteered for service in the navy and ended up on the *Kearsarge* was nineteen-year-old John Fairfield Bickford of Bass Harbor, Maine. Bickford was one of nine children of a seafaring and fishing family, so it was no wonder he gravitated to the navy when President Lincoln called for volunteers. He enlisted on January 4, 1862, and was rated a seaman. He would more than ably serve during the entire three-year first cruise of the *Kearsarge*, steadily advancing in rank until he was rated an acting master's mate in early 1864. Unlike most of the crew, there is not a single black mark on his record for any infraction, including drunkenness, which seemed to be an endemic problem every time the ship entered a port.

Bickford would later tell a tale of picking up on the fact that Captain Winslow was desperate for information on the CSS *Rappahannock*, especially after she escaped across the Channel in November 1863 to end up under repairs in Calais. Bickford decided to do something about this lack of knowledge and hopefully please his captain.

The next time the *Kearsarge* pulled into Dover for mail, newspapers, and fuel, Bickford requested shore leave. Due to his excellent record, Winslow let him have it. Donning civilian clothes, Bickford walked down to the Dover packet ferry and paid for a ride to Calais. The next morning, he appeared aboard the *Rappahannock* and volunteered for service. Claiming truthfully that he had experience at sea, he was immediately enlisted, paid $50 in gold coin, and made part of the crew. Bickford spent a whole day aboard carefully inspecting the ship. The next day, claiming he needed to retrieve his clothes and personal effects, he was granted a pass to get off the ship. He headed straight for the Dover ferry and bought a ticket to return.

Bickford claimed that if anyone on the *Rappahannock* figured out he was a spy and tried to chase him down, he had a pistol loaded and handy underneath his coat. He even stood close to the packet's captain in case someone signaled for him to turn back. Fortunately, he made good his escape.

Bickford returned to the *Kearsarge* and reported immediately to Lieutenant Commander Thornton. The executive officer was dumbfounded. He took Bickford to Winslow's cabin and made him repeat the story. Winslow was equally shocked—though very glad to have Bickford's information. According to Bickford, Winslow "took his facts" but informed him there could be no recognition for his surreptitious mission because it was "irregularly done, without authority, and by breaking leave." Bickford was not punished and Winslow no doubt marked the young man as someone to watch, in a good sense.

Perhaps much more typical of the rest of the sailors was William Gowin, an ordinary seaman from Michigan. Like Bickford, he had joined the *Kearsarge* as part of its original commissioning crew in early 1862. Unlike Bickford, he was one of the rowdiest members of the deck gang. When granted liberty Gowin could be counted on to find the nearest pub and dive right in. He was constantly in irons for drunkenness or returning late from leave. He did have a saving grace, however: he was an accomplished musician and could play several instruments. He was also a bit of a clown and free spirit. When sober, he could work hard and both Pickering and Winslow seemed to have a soft spot for Gowin since he did so much to keep the crew entertained with his music and his jokes. Although his foibles would prevent him from advancing any higher than his initial rank, he was well-liked among the men and he pulled his weight when needed.

There were fifteen "coloreds" or Black crewmen, which was not all that uncommon on U.S. Navy ships of the Civil War. Two of the Black men aboard were cooks, two were stewards, two were ship's "boys," eight were landsmen, and one—and only one—was a rated seaman. Five of the men were coal heavers, often stripped to the waist, sweating, and feeding the ship's boilers with the fuel they devoured constantly.

Among the Black men aboard, the one rated seaman was Joaquin Pease. Some records have incorrectly credited Pease to Long Island, New York. That is likely due to a misinterpretation of his original enlistment papers. He enlisted in the U.S. Navy on January 13, 1862, and whoever transcribed the record—in longhand, in ink—wrote sloppily enough that his birthplace could be read as "Long" Island instead of the correct spot of "Fogo" Island. Sleuthing done by the Naval History and Heritage Command did find, indeed, one "Joaquin Pease" in the 1842 birth records of Fogo Island, a part of the Cape Verde Islands, which lie off the West Coast of Africa.[54]

Nineteenth-century whaling ships, especially from Massachusetts and Sag Harbor, New York, made frequent stops in the Cape Verde Islands and it was on Fogo Island, apparently, that a fifteen-year-old Black youth standing five feet six and one-half inches tall signed aboard the whaler *Kensington*, home port, New Bedford, on October 20, 1857. The *Kensington* would roam the Pacific and Indian Oceans and the Sea of Okhotsk until returning home on August 27, 1861. While aboard the *Kensington*, Pease would learn more than enough seamanship to qualify him to enlist in the navy as an ordinary seaman in early 1862. He was immediately assigned to the newly commissioned USS *Kearsarge*. Pease was later promoted to seaman and served as a loader for a 32-pounder, designated Number 1 gun, located on the gun deck, one deck below the main deck. His boss would have been Acting Master Sumner.

Two of the ship's permanent cooks were Black, including George Williams, more commonly known to his shipmates as "Ham Fat." Williams was, indeed, quite "portly" and of only

---

54 Research on Seaman Pease should be credited to Danny Stevens and Jennie Ashton, "The Search for Seaman Joaquin Pease," Naval History and Heritage Command, Washington, D.C.; Feb. 18, 2020.

medium height, but he was called Ham Fat because he was constantly humming or singing an old minstrel tune by the same title. Williams was Captain Winslow's personal cook, and apparently quite a good one, as he kept that job all through the cruise. He was also the ship's drummer and called upon whenever official drum rolls (such as the proverbial "beating to quarters") was required. His nickname was also appropriate in that he was also a "ham" when it came to entertaining the crew. He was a frequent organizer of informal concerts on the fantail, impromptu dances and sing-alongs during otherwise quiet evenings in port or at sea. And he was a belt-it-out baritone whenever a song was required.

Under Winslow's steady hand, the crew's spirits rebounded. They would follow their captain as the USS *Kearsarge* set off on its quest to, as Secretary Welles had put it, hunt the CSS *Alabama* "to the uttermost ends of the earth." Along the way, as they heard more reports, the officers and crew of the Union warship came to appreciate that they were on the trail of the most formidable foe on the high seas.

ACT III:
THE PURSUIT

We must all either wear out or rust out, every one of us. My choice is to wear out.

Theodore Roosevelt

12

Captain Raphael Semmes not only had as fine a warship to command as the Confederates States could provide, he also had the most elite group of officers the South could supply. This could only guarantee success on the high seas and, perhaps, that would be enough to tilt the war in the Confederacy's favor.

His first officer, First Lieutenant John McIntosh Kell, came aboard with others Semmes had brought over from the *Sumter* including the second officer, Richard Armstrong; the third officer, Joseph Wilson; the chief engineer, Miles Freeman; and the surgeon, Francis Galt. Kell and Freeman went as far back as when the *Havana* had been converted to the *Sumter*. Also returning to sea with Semmes was Becket Howell, the lieutenant in charge of the small contingent of marines.

With Stephen Mallory's help, Semmes had added several more officers. They included Arthur Sinclair Jr. as fourth officer, his brother William (a midshipman who later transferred to the CSS *Tuscaloosa*), Eugene Maffitt, the son of the commander of the CSS *Florida*, and Irvine Bulloch, the half-brother of the man who had been the driving force behind the construction of the original *290*.

According to the naval historian Chester Hearn, Semmes's officers "were bright young men who fought a different war and believed deeply in the principles for which they were fighting. Their crew, on the other hand, was mainly English, Irish, and Scottish—few having been trained for service on a man-of-war. Under the officers of a new nation, these men developed into an effective fighting force."

What the CSS *Alabama* had to do was get involved in the fighting. In this case, that meant hunt down, capture, and burn ships, wherever in the world they might be, carrying cargo bound for Northern destinations. That the Confederate raider did without delay.

Still, the *Alabama*'s mission did not begin auspiciously. During the first few days of hunting in the Azores, into the first week of September, it caught three ships but had to release them because two were registered to French owners and the third was Portuguese. Finally, the *Alabama* encountered a ship occupied with cutting up a sperm whale. After the British flag was raised, the whaler answered with the Stars and Stripes. Immediately, Semmes had a boat dropped into the water manned by a boarding party. And the Confederate flag was raised.

The unfortunate whaler was the *Ocmulgee* out of Massachusetts and its captain was Abraham Osborn. He and his ownership papers were rowed back to the *Alabama* where he was escorted to the captain's cabin. Semmes stood to greet him and examine the papers. They confirmed the *Ocmulgee* was a Union ship. With some sympathy, Semmes informed Osborn that he and his crew were now prisoners of the Confederate States of America and his ship would be burned.

The flabbergasted whaling captain was rowed back across the water. Once on board the *Ocmulgee*, he told the nonplussed crew to collect their personal belongings and that they would soon be enjoying the *Alabama*'s hospitality. Meanwhile, members of the Southern ship went to transfer any useful supplies and discovered a motherlode. The whaler had provisioned for a voyage of three years, and having left Martha's Vineyard only two months prior, the *Ocmulgee*'s hold was bursting with barrels of meat and other seaworthy staples. The *Alabama* took in as much as it could contain.

When Captain Osborn returned to the *Alabama*, he transferred to it one more item—his chronometer. Resuming his previous practice, Semmes placed this trophy in his cabin. He gave one of his officers, Arthur Sinclair, the task of winding the clocks regularly.

When darkness fell, Semmes postponed putting the *Ocmulgee* to the torch. No sense attracting attention with a blazing fire at night that could be seen for miles. At dawn, however, time ran out for the whaler, which was soon consumed by flames. Osborn remained below on the *Alabama*, unable to bring himself to watch his ship and his financial future in ruins.

The *Ocmulgee* had had a crew of just thirty-seven men but that still caused crowded conditions on the *Alabama*. Semmes searched for an opportunity to unload his prisoners. He sailed close to Flores, an island at the western edge of the Azores. There he had Osborn and his crew climb into their own whaleboats, which had not been burned. Carrying provisions to tide them over, the crew rowed toward the shore.

There was no time for Semmes to observe if the *Ocmulgee*'s men arrived safely. A shout came down from his lookout and telescopes revealed a sail. The *Starlight*, a schooner, attempted to run but the *Alabama* chased her down. The boarding crew found she was an American ship. Its captain and crew of seven were welcomed aboard. There was not much cargo to transfer but the *Starlight* burned just as brightly as the previously captured ship.

After its slow start, September 1862 turned into a very successful month for the *Alabama*. Within a short time, the captain and crew of the raider established an effective routine. At all times a sharp-eyed sailor was aloft to scan the horizon. The shout of "Sail ho!" galvanized everyone into action. Semmes and Kell produced telescopes and peered through them in the direction the excited sailor was pointing. If it was indeed a sail—or a wisp of smoke indicating a steamship—a decision had to be made: Go for it or hesitate? The reason to hesitate was that the sail could belong to a Union warship. Those odds were low, however, so if there was no other indication of danger Semmes would order the *Alabama* in pursuit, flying a British or Union flag. In most instances, his ship was faster and better handled than the other captain's vessel and the prize was his.

Well, sometimes. The other captain might think he could outrun the *Alabama* and a chase could last for hours. A persuasive action was the firing of a blank shot from the Confederate ship's forward pivot gun, and if that was not enough, a live shell came next. With very few merchant ships armed, their captains soon reasoned further resistance was suicidal. The captured vessel hove to and prepared to be boarded as its crew watched the Stars and Bars being raised on the approaching warship.

Through the 18th, there was hardly a day when the *Alabama*, with gleeful determination, did not take and destroy a Union ship. After the *Starlight* there was the *Ocean Rover, Alert, Weather Gauge, Altamaha, Benjamin Tucker, Courser, Virginia,* and *Elisha Dunbar.* The Azores were fertile ground indeed, and more captured crews rowed away from the *Alabama* toward Flores. To break up the routine and for necessary practice, the *Courser* was used as a target for the Alabama's gunners...then set on fire.

What Semmes could only assume was true: As the formerly imprisoned sailors arrived in Flores and from there fanned out, some signing aboard other ships, tales of the Confederate predator began to spread. The stories of the relentless raider and its "pirate" captain appeared in newspapers, eventually American ones read by Union officials and, of course, Gideon Welles.

These would be just the early days of the navy secretary's frustration as goods costing hundreds of thousands of dollars were lost.

The *Alabama* hit a dry spell the third week in September and Semmes, feeling confident and wanting to stick a knife even deeper into Union commerce, sailed north toward Newfoundland. Two hundred miles south of it, the captain's intuition was confirmed when not one, but two ships became prizes.

The first, taken on October 3, was the *Brilliant*. Its 839 tons included a hold full of flour and grain. Just this one ship was valued at $164,000, the most expensive loss to the *Alabama* thus far. It became little more than a very costly candle when the torch was put to her.

The fate of the *Emily Farnum*, the second ship captured, was different—she became the first ship not destroyed by the *Alabama*. The commander of the merchant vessel produced papers showing that her cargo was owned by merchants in a neutral country. If Semmes had truly been a pirate, he would have tossed the documents overboard and emptied the *Emily Farnum* out, but instead, the ship was released on bond. She did not get away scot-free, though—the *Alabama* still had prisoners from the *Virginia* and *Elisha Dunbar* as well as the *Brilliant*, and they were transferred to the *Emily Farnum*. Its captain promised to take the men with him to his intended destination of Liverpool.

Captain N. P. Simes of the *Emily Farnum* broke his promise as soon as the *Alabama* sailed away. The bonded ship sailed to Boston, where word spread rapidly of the Confederate raider preying in Northern waters. Officials and the press angrily denounced the depredations of the *Alabama* and its captain who, preferably, would soon be hunted down and hanged. The commander of a ship lost to the *Alabama* who had made his way back to New York told the *New York Herald*: "His whole appearance is that of a corsair, and the transformation appears to be complete from Commander Raphael Semmes, United States Navy, to a combination of Lafitte and Kidd."

Over time, as more ships were captured, Semmes made a point of asking for any newspapers which had been brought aboard. He read accounts of the *Alabama*'s adventures with a mixture of pride and anger. He was pleased that his ship's exploits were causing such an uproar in the North and wreaking economic havoc on the Union war effort but labeling him a privateer or pirate was quite unfair. He followed the law of the sea and nothing he did was for personal gain…except, perhaps, his expanding collection of chronometers.[55]

As the *Alabama* ran down and captured more ships in its fertile northern hunting grounds—eleven total in the month of October, with nine of them burned—Semmes had to realize the North would react with fury and its navy would be turned loose to hunt him. For all he knew, every week another Union ship was being launched and not all of them would be relegated to blockade duty. He had to assume there were warships looking for him and quite possibly the *Alabama*'s next engagement could be with one of them. Semmes's crew had to be ready.

That might not be easy. "Semmes viewed all sailors in much the same light: lazy, morally corrupt, incapable of any lasting loyalty, and totally unable to handle alcohol," writes the military historian John M. Taylor. "Under the right leadership, however, something could be made of this unpromising material. He considered the *Alabama*'s first months at sea, removed from the temptations of port, as his one chance to whip his wharf rats into some kind of fighting unit, for Semmes had no intention of limiting his war against the North entirely to merchantmen."

Semmes and his officers kept the crew busy because they believed idleness threatened discipline, but now they stepped up their preparations for battle. Every day a quarter of the sailors exercised the guns so they could become both fast and accu-

---

55 Pleasure would have turned to delight if Semmes knew that on October 18 Gideon Welles had written in his diary, "The ravages by the roving steamer *290*, alias *Alabama*, are enormous."

rate. The sight of a sail could now mean a military ship as well as a merchantman. Given the speed and armaments of the *Alabama*, it would be hard to defeat if the crew was in top shape, ready for action.

And, indeed, the Union Navy was paying more attention to the *Alabama*. Before her activities in New England waters were revealed, word had reached Washington of its presence in the Azores. USS *Tuscarora* had been dispatched to find and capture or destroy the *Alabama*. USS *Kearsarge* was already there but its captain, Pickering, was writing messages advising there had been no *Alabama* sightings of late and she may have left those waters. As would become routine, Semmes remained one step ahead of his pursuers.

Of the eleven ships run down and boarded by the *Alabama* in October 1862, one capture was of particular interest. On the 9th, the captain of the 1300-ton *Tonawanda* struck his colors. Its hold was full of grain and, ordinarily, with no documentation of the cargo being neutral, the *Tonawanda* would have been set ablaze. However, it also carried seventy-five passengers, thirty of them women and children. Semmes could not release the ship to continue on its way to Liverpool, but he could not accommodate all those people either—especially putting his crew and the women in close quarters. Another wrinkle: One of the passengers had brought with him his slave, a man named David White.

Of course, a major reason why the Confederate States of America, which Semmes represented on the ocean, existed was to preserve the right to own slaves. But the captain thought it hypocritical that a passenger from the North, which sought to take that right away, could legally own a slave. On the *Alabama*, there was no higher law than Semmes. He declared that David White was free and signed him up as a member of the crew. In a short time, he became an assistant to the ship's surgeon, Dr. Galt.

About the passengers in general, Semmes had no choice but to keep the torch away from the *Tonawanda*. But this dilemma

of having a sort of caboose follow the *Alabama* was soon re-
solved. Two days later, the *Alabama* captured the *Manchester*. She
was on her way to Liverpool and her hold was also full of grain.
The *Alabama*'s crew added what grain could be fit from the
Tonawanda and set fire to the *Manchester*. Its crew and passengers
were placed on the *Tonawanda*, that vessel's captain pledged an
$80,000 bond, and with Semmes's blessing the *Tonawanda* re-
sumed her own journey to Liverpool.

Ten more ships were taken by the Alabama during what
was left of 1862—the *Lamplighter, Lafayette, Crenshaw, Lauretta,
Baron de Castine, Levi Starbuck, Thomas B. Wales, Parker Cook,
Union,* and *Ariel.* The latter was a particularly interesting and,
for Semmes, gratifying capture. Not only did she carry 140
U.S. Marines among the 700 passengers, but she was owned by
the tycoon Cornelius Vanderbilt. When the *Alabama*'s boarding
crew arrived, they found the marines lined up for battle. However, their commander realized muskets could not triumph over
cannon, plus the loss of innocent lives in such a battle could be
horrific. After all the troops surrendered and signed paroles,[56]
the *Alabama* was richer by 124 muskets, 16 swords, and a 12-
pound cannon with ammunition.[57]

One reason for the diminishing number of merchantmen
taken was that fewer ships were plying northern waters at that
time of year. Another was the increasingly violent autumn
weather off the Grand Banks. The worst of it was a hurricane
that almost swept the *Alabama* off the map.

---

56 Paroles during the Civil War were mostly "matters of honor" more than
actual obligations. Typically, a paroled soldier or sailor was to go home and
agree not to take up arms again until an opposite of similar rank from the
other side was also paroled. Early in the war many actual prisoners of war
were swapped the same way. Soon, however, the vast numbers of prisoners
taken by both sides made swaps onerous. General Grant, in 1864, stopped the
practice and POW camps sprang up everywhere.

57 As Semmes expected, the Vanderbilt connection caused headlines. The one on
the front page of the *New York Times* blared, "THE PIRATE *ALABAMA*.;
The Vanderbilt Steamship Ariel Captured by Her. She is Released Under
Bonds, After Three Days' Detention."

It had begun for Semmes's ship on the morning of October 15 when the wind increased so dramatically that it carried away the main yard and ripped apart the main topsail and the fore staysail. Having previously lost a ship in a storm, the captain could only wonder if history was about to repeat itself. But the *Alabama* was a larger and much sturdier ship than the *Somers* had been.

Still, it was a close call. Quick and risky work by a crewman cut the fore-topmast staysail away before the ship was pulled down into the sea. Officers ordered crewmen lashed against the weather bulwark so they would not be tossed overboard when the ship rolled. Spray blinded dozens of eyes. It was recorded that the barometer sank as low as 28.64 inches ("normal" being 30 inches). There was a brief respite when the *Alabama* entered the eye of the hurricane, but then the tempest resumed. Many prayers were answered—including those of the devout Catholic captain—when the wind and waves began to subside.

The next two days were spent on urgent repairs and, once the sun revealed itself, determining where they were. The damage inflicted by the mighty storm forced Semmes to cancel what he viewed as being his most daring raid—on New York City. He had concocted a plan to dash into the harbor, set fire to ships docked there, and hurry away, leaving a conflagration in the *Alabama*'s wake. However, after surviving the hurricane, there were too many repairs to make, and Semmes realized if he did not replenish his supply of coal his ship would not be dashing anywhere.

Though denied the command of a ship, James Bulloch continued his yeoman efforts on behalf of the far-flung Confederate Navy. He had arranged for the *Agrippina* to rendezvous with the *Alabama* in Martinique. No doubt when Semmes arrived, he had to have thought about having been there with the *Sumter* and how much had transpired since that time a year ago. However, after only a short time in port, Semmes decided not to take on coal there. He learned that Captain McQueen, skipper of the *Agrippina*, had spent too much of the week waiting for the *Ala-*

bama by frequenting the Port Royal saloons. Though the phrase would not become popular until decades later, the fear was that in this case loose lips could indeed sink a ship. McQueen had been boasting of the achievements of the *Alabama* and foretelling its imminent arrival.

The Confederate raider could not afford to wait and see if this intelligence had found its way to a Union official (it had). Semmes ordered a hungover McQueen and his supply ship to a new rendezvous, La Blanquilla, an island owned by Venezuela. The *Alabama* would leave the next day, after taking on some supplies. But what also arrived with the morning was the *San Jacinto*, a Union warship with eleven guns.

Another memory for Semmes: Would the *Alabama* be trapped like the *Sumter* had been in Gibraltar? Not necessarily, as the commander had also escaped warships too. That night, the *Alabama* did just that. With the guns run out in case there was a confrontation, the Confederate ship quietly eased out of the harbor, the night dark and rainy. It was a clean getaway, and on November 21 she was once more keeping company with the *Agrippina*. A few days later, its coal bunker full, the *Alabama* returned to hunting prey in the Caribbean.

During the weeks remaining in the year, Raphael Semmes had to consider 1862 mostly a success. The completion of a full year of war saw the South as still strong and defiant, though it had suffered several setbacks, such as at Antietam during its invasion of Semmes's birth state of Maryland in September. The year had begun with Semmes at the helm of the feared *Sumter* and ended with him the commander of the even more feared and successful *Alabama*. The next year, he believed, would see the South as an independent nation.

13

Captain Semmes and his crew had spent a quiet but pleasant Christmas Day. The *Alabama* had drifted along the Yucatan Peninsula and then on December 23 had anchored off one of the tiny islands in the Arcas Keys. This was not a good hunting ground but at the same time Semmes felt safely hidden from Union ships. The *Agrippina* was there too, and once more the raider's coal bunker was replenished. On the 25th, members of the crew went ashore where using nets they caught turtles and fish in the lagoon. The change in diet was very much welcomed.

When Semmes himself set foot on land, it was the first time he had done so in almost five months, when he had left Liverpool. Here he was on the other side of the world in what many people would view as a tropical paradise. During those five months among the crew there had been a few desertions and court-martials for bad behavior and disputes and illnesses and close calls but for the most part the *Alabama* by now had a solid, veteran, and well-trained contingent of sailors. And to some of them it mattered that they served on what could well be the most famous ship in the world.

Some of the sailors could read, and a few of them could read well enough to make use of the captured newspapers once the officers were done with them. The crew learned that their ship was a newsmaker. The crew, of course, already grasped that having pursued and captured twenty-six ships—destroying twenty-one of them—since her christening. The *Alabama* had a remarkable record of success for any ship. Some Northern editorial writers and lawmakers were apoplectic about the seemingly effortless conquests and the millions of dollars' worth of ships and goods lost. The Lincoln administration and Gideon Welles in particular were blamed because of the inability of the so far hapless and intimidated Union Navy to rid the seas of the ghostly Confederate warrior. The crewmen of the *Alabama* may have grumbled a bit about the dearth of prize money promised to them months earlier, but here at year's end pride helped fill up their otherwise empty pockets.

Then there was the commander of the famous vessel to consider. With his prominent and well-waxed mustache—behind his back he was called "Old Beeswax"—and graying hair and formal demeanor, Raphael Semmes was not a warm and personable captain. He was a stern disciplinarian, but this was not necessarily seen as a negative, especially by his officers. A ship on the ocean was its own nation, the captain its head of state. Anarchy and insurrection meant doom. A trained crew that maintained discipline and worked together efficiently, overseen by competent officers loyal to their commander greatly increased the chance of a successful voyage, whether it be a ship of war or a merchantman. A captain who was hundreds or possibly thousands of miles from a friendly port had to be in firm control.

He rarely mixed with the crew and was a bit aloof even from his officers, including the steadfast Lieutenant Kell. He was a fair man, though, and sometimes displayed a sense of humor, which coupled with the raiding success of the *Alabama* earned him the respect and loyalty of a rather diverse crew.

Was Semmes a pirate? Certainly, he was portrayed that way in the North. His pride and integrity were wounded by what he viewed as prejudiced and sensational portrayals of him in the press. In a letter to his wife, Anne, he decried "the false and malicious reports that you see in the Northern newspapers. You know the kind and humane disposition of your husband too well to believe he can be the heartless tyrant he is represented." He added, "I make war according to civilized rules, and with far more mercy than my enemies."

Clearly, he did not capture ships for his own gain. And Semmes was a lawyer well versed in maritime law and he believed that he stuck to it. He fought for his country, what he hoped in 1863 would be an independent one, cleaved from the mother country as America had separated from Great Britain eighty years earlier. For the most part he treated captured captains courteously (albeit confiscating their chronometers) and he was a Southern gentleman in the eyes of civilians he had to accommodate on the *Alabama* for brief periods of time. In the Confederacy, Semmes was not a pirate at all but a hero at times mentioned in the same breath as Robert E. Lee, Stonewall Jackson, and even the dashing Jeb Stuart. While the bookish Semmes was anything but dashing, his actions on the high seas defined him.

When the new year began the *Alabama* and *Agrippina* continued to share the small harbor and the beauty of their surroundings. It was not all lazing about, however, as the *Alabama* needed as many repairs as it could manage without being drydocked. The ships weathered a southeast storm, then on January 5 it was time to resume the war against the Union. The *Alabama* weighed anchor and sailed north, into the Gulf of Mexico. Semmes had decided to see what trouble he could stir up off the coast of Texas.

His intention was actually more focused than that. He rued having missed the opportunity the invasion of New York Harbor had represented to sow fear in the North. Let the Yankees believe nowhere was safe from the Confederacy's boldest and best raider. They were already rattled enough that attempts to catch the *Alabama* had been fruitless and panicked reports had her appearing several places around the globe at once. It was time to intensify that fear by instead of running from the Union Navy, attacking it.

One of the advantages of reading confiscated Northern newspapers was they carried military news. Semmes had read in December about a force being assembled in New York by Nathaniel Banks. In the 1850s, Banks had served as Speaker of the House of Representatives and then been elected governor of Massachusetts. He was a powerful political figure when the Civil War began and President Lincoln made him a major general—alas, without determining first if Banks had any military skills. He didn't. His shortcomings became evident early in 1862 when he had been defeated by Stonewall Jackson in the Shenandoah Valley campaign. He was later relieved of his command.

But in November, Banks was back. The loyal—and politically savvy—Lincoln had appointed him commander of the Army of the Gulf. The first challenge was to raise such an army, and Banks did recruit thirty thousand troops from New England and New York. They left from the latter in transports with the destination being Galveston, Texas. Semmes aimed to surprise what he predicted would be a perfunctory Union Navy escort, blow some of those transports out of the water, and flee with the Confederate flag flapping in triumph.

Ironically, a Confederate victory spoiled that plan. Forces under General John Bankhead Magruder had taken Galveston back on the first day of 1863. When the *Alabama* neared the city on January 11, not only had the Banks expedition ended its journey in Louisiana but six Union vessels had gathered to serve as blockade ships. The Confederate warship was spotted, and a signal was flashed to the Union squadron. One of the six gunboats, the *Hatteras*, was ordered to run down and capture or sink the newcomer—and thus did Semmes have his opportunity to take on the Union Navy.

The *Hatteras*, captained by Lieutenant Commander Homer Blake,[58] was an 1126-ton iron-hulled side-wheel steamer which had been successful in capturing several blockade runners. She took off in pursuit of the unknown ship at about 3:00 p.m. that afternoon and for the next four hours followed her as she ventured closer and closer to shore. Finally, as dusk was falling, *Hatteras* came within hailing distance of the square-rigged ship. Blake demanded her identity. "Her Britannic Majesty's Ship *Petrel*," came the reply. Still suspicious, Blake ordered one of *Hatteras*'s boats to inspect the visitor.

Scarcely had the longboat pulled away from *Hatteras* than a new reply to Blake's question rang through the night, as Kell called through a speaking horn, "We are CSS *Alabama*!" With this, Semmes had the Union Jack taken down and replaced with the Stars and Bars. The *Alabama* began raking the *Hatteras* with her heavy cannon. Through the gloom, for about twenty minutes, the two ships exchanged broadsides at distances ranging from twenty-five to two hundred yards. The flashes of the guns and their rumbling were heard in the Union squadron sixteen miles away, and a ship familiar to Semmes, the *Brooklyn*, was dispatched to investigate and render aid if needed.

The Union warship arrived too late. The *Hatteras* had already been badly holed in two places and was on fire and beginning to sink. Captain Blake ordered the magazines flooded to prevent an explosion and reluctantly fired a single bow gun, indicating surrender and a need for assistance. Semmes sent boats to help remove *Hatteras*'s crew and her wounded.

The last boatload of men had barely pulled away when the Union steamer sank. Of the *Hatteras*'s crew of 126, two had been killed and five wounded. Six escaped back to the squadron in

---

58 Blake (1822–1880) commanded several ships after *Hatteras* and retired as a
    commodore in 1880 shortly before his death from malaria.

the boat originally sent out to board and investigate "HMS *Petrel*," and the remainder, including Captain Blake, were taken to Port Royal, Jamaica, and from there paroled back to the United States. The *Alabama* suffered only two wounded, though there had been a few scary moments, including two cannonballs that flew through the captain's cabin.

When the *Brooklyn* reached the site of the battle early the following morning, she found the hulk of the *Hatteras* upright on the shallow bottom of the bay about twenty miles south of Galveston. Only the *Hatteras*'s masts poked out of the water, and from the topmast the U.S. Navy commissioning pennant was still waving in the breeze. Even after surrendering, she had not struck her colors.[59]

By the 20th, the *Alabama*, its officers and crew still reveling in their victory over a Union gunboat, was nearing the coast of Jamaica. Seeing it enter the harbor, the band on the British warship *Greyhound* started playing "Dixie." Thus began a warm but delicate reception for the now internationally famous Captain Raphael Semmes.

Once the *Alabama* was secure at its berth in Port Royal, captains of several British ships docked there came aboard to pay their respects. Such displays toward the Confederate captain and his ship put the British government in an awkward position because its officers were certainly not displaying much neutrality.

Semmes gave permission for some members of the crew to explore the pleasures of Port Royal while others remained to be supervised by Lieutenant Kell as supplies and coal were brought aboard. The captain visited officials in Kingston where a crowd prevailed upon Semmes to give a short speech. Welles and other members of the Lincoln administration would not be pleased when they later heard of the fawning over the Rebel raider.

---

59 To this day, the hull of the *Hatteras* rests in approximately sixty feet of water twenty miles off Galveston and is buried under three feet of sand. Her steam engine and two iron paddle wheels remain on the ocean bottom.

Top: John Winslow, captain of
the USS *Kearsarge*.

Left: Raphael Semmes, captain
of the CSS *Alabama*.

Top Right: Stephen Mallory was the Secretary of the Navy of the Confederate States of America.

Photo courtesy of Naval History and Heritage Command.

Bottom Right: Secretary of the Navy Gideon Welles, sometimes called "Father Neptune," guided the Union's efforts against the Confederate raiders.

Photo courtesy of Naval History and Heritage Command.

Top Left: At the end of June 1861, the CSS *Sumter* escaped the Union blockade and began to prey on Union shipping.

Photo courtesy of the Library of Congress.

Middle: The commission letter signed by Jefferson Davis on June 22, 1862, authorized Raphael Semmes to command the CSS *Alabama*.

Photo courtesy of Naval History and Heritage Command.

President of the Confederate States of America,

TO ALL unto these Presents shall come, Send Greetings-

Know Ye, That we have granted, and by these Presents do grant, License and Authority to *Raphael Semmes Captain*, Commander of the *Steam Barque* called the *Alabama* of the Burden of Tons *1200* or thereabout, and mounting *ten* Guns to fit out and set forth the said *barque* in a warlike Manner, and by and with the said *barque* and the crew thereof, by Force of Arms, to attack, subdue, scuttle, and take all ships belonging to the United States of America or any vessel carrying Soldiers, Arms, Gunpowder, Ammunition, Provisions, or any other goods of a military nature to any of the Army of the United States or Ships of War employed against the Confederate States of America in a hostile manner. And to take by force if necessary any vessel, barge, or floating transporter belonging to said United States or persons loyal to the same, including Tackle, Apparel, Ladings, Cargoes, and Furniture on the High Seas or between high and low water mark, Rivers and Inlets accepted. (the Ships and Vessels belonging to Inhabitants of Bermuda, the Bahama Islands, and Great Britain and other persons with Intent to settle or serve the cause of the Confederate States of America you shall suffer to pass unmolested, the Commanders thereof permitting a peaceable Search and after giving satisfactory account of Ladings and Destination) And that said Ships or Vessels apprehended as aforesaid, and the Prize taken, to carry to a Port or Harbor within the Domaine of any Neutral State willing to admit the same or any port of the Confederate States, in Order that the Courts therein instituted to hear such claims may Judge in such cases at the Port or in the State where the same shall be impounded. The sufficient securities, bonds and sureties having been given by the owners that they nor any person in command of this vessel shall not exceed or transfer the Powers and Authorities contained in this commission. And We will and require all Officers whatsoever in the Service of the Confederate States to give assistance to the said *Captain* in the Premises. This Commission shall remain active and in Force until this Government of the United Confederate States of America shall issue Orders to the contrary.

By order of the President of the

Confederate States of America

Port of.........................

C.S. Navy Ship

Given under my hand this *22 nd* of *June* 186*2* at *Richmond*

President

Jefferson Davis

Bottom Left: With few exceptions, a ship captured by the *Alabama* was doomed to be destroyed by fire.

Photo courtesy of Naval History and Heritage Command.

OPPOSITE PAGE:

Top Left: In a fierce battle off the coast of Texas in January 1863, the *Alabama* sank the Union gunboat *Hatteras*.
Photo courtesy of Naval History and Heritage Command.

Bottom Left: John Newland Maffitt was another successful Confederate raider as captain of the CSS *Florida*.
Photo courtesy of Naval History and Heritage Command.

Bottom Right: Arthur Sinclair and Richard Armstrong (leaning against a 32-pound gun), two of the officers during the long voyage of the *Alabama*.
Photo courtesy of Naval History and Heritage Command.

THIS PAGE:

Top Left: James Thornton was second-in-command under Capt. Winslow on the *Kearsarge*.
Photo courtesy of Naval History and Heritage Command.

Bottom: Raphael Semmes is shown on the deck of the *Alabama* and behind him is his ever-loyal first officer, John McIntosh Kell, standing by the ship's wheel.
Photo courtesy of Naval History and Heritage Command.

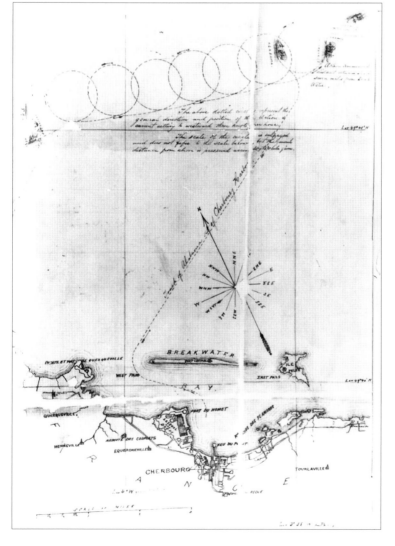

Top: Blow after blow from the *Kearsarge*'s guns have mortally wounded the *Alabama*, and word spreads that the legendary Confederate raider has surrendered.

Photo courtesy of Naval History and Heritage Command.

Middle: As water surges through holes in the ship's hull, the *Alabama* begins to sink beneath the waves.

Photo courtesy of Naval History and Heritage Command.

Bottom Left: A 56-pound shell from the *Alabama* lodged in the sternpost of the *Kearsarge*. It would have been a crippling blow, if it had exploded.

Photo courtesy of Naval History and Heritage Command.

Bottom Right: Over a century later, this bronze, 10-inch-tall bell was recovered from the wreckage of the *Alabama* off the coast of France.

Photo courtesy of Naval History and Heritage Command.

An event involving Clarence Yonge, the paymaster of the *Alabama*, would also have far-reaching repercussions on the Confederate Navy. If Semmes had known what a rascal the Georgia native was, the captain would not have entrusted Yonge with a penny let alone the ship's treasury. Yonge had already written a letter of resignation when he had been sent ashore with $400 to pay for what was being delivered to the *Alabama*. The money instead underwrote a lengthy binge for Yonge and drinks for whoever happened to be his companions. Some of them turned out to be Americans who were not only entertained by Yonge's stories about his ship's origins and adventures but eager to pass them along to the U.S. consul in Kingston.

When Kell determined the paymaster was missing and probably in the act of deserting, he headed a search party. The inebriated Yonge was dragged back aboard the *Alabama*. His court-martial began when he was sober, which took a few days. Yonge was charged with neglect of his duties "and behaving in a most disreputable manner by talking to the enemy." Within a half hour he was found guilty. After refusing Semmes's offer to remain on board, confined to his room, until the *Alabama* reached a Confederate port, Yonge was deprived of his sword and sent ashore in disgrace. If that had been the end of the Yonge-*Alabama* connection, little damage would have been done.

However, for several weeks after the *Alabama* departed Port Royal, Yonge resided at a local lodging house run by a young biracial widow and her mother. Deciding to move on, he first married the widow, ignoring the fact that he had left a wife behind in Savannah. Yonge convinced his new wife to sell the lodging house and all property to her name. Along with his wife, her two teenage children, and mother-in-law, Yonge traveled to Liverpool, arriving on March 22. They lodged for a while at the Angel Hotel before Yonge abandoned them all on the streets with barely enough money to survive.

The miscreant next sought refuge in Lancaster before moving to London on April 1, on advice from Thomas Dudley, the American consul in Liverpool. There he called on the U.S. minister, Charles Francis Adams. He informed Adams about his duties as "private secretary" to James Bulloch and about his brief service aboard the *Alabama*, which he later agreed to put down in the form of an affidavit. Yonge did not stop there. He became one of a number of paid informers of the U.S. minister and was dispatched to Liverpool on April 5 in search of evidence of the building of the two Confederate steam ironclads, *294* and *295*. Yonge found them to be under construction in the south part of the Laird yards. The following day, at the Liverpool Customs House, he signed another affidavit over what he had seen at the Laird yards as well as witnessing the plans, drawings, and specifications of the designs the previous year. This would prove instrumental in destroying Bulloch's chances of purchasing the ships for the Confederate government.

With those warships scuttled before they were ever completed, Yonge was recalled to London. There, persuaded by various promises, he revealed more about Bulloch's supposed secret machinations on behalf of the Jefferson Davis administration and Stephen Mallory in particular. Some of this was in the form of testimony in a court of inquiry. Yonge was glad to oblige. But his downfall was a defense attorney describing Yonge as "this specimen of humanity—a man who commenced his career by abandoning his wife and child in his native country, who betrayed every one of his friends and fellow officers in the cause of the country to which he had promised allegiance, and who tricked a young widow into marriage in order that he could ruin and plunder her property. And then brought her to Liverpool, where he turned her adrift penniless in the streets before hurrying up to London to pour into the ear of Mr. Adams, the American minister, his tale of treachery."

The jury proceeded to discount most of what Yonge had said. Suddenly, England was not nearly as welcoming to the former

Alabama paymaster as before. Maybe the Union would be more friendly. Yonge slipped out of England and wound up in New York, where he enlisted in the 25th Regiment of New York Cavalry. He lasted in the regiment only a short time before being discharged. He sat out the rest of the war in Poughkeepsie.[60]

For the *Alabama*, it was time to return to the war. The ship left Port Royal and quickly made two captures, the *Golden Rule* and the *Chastelaine*. After prisoners and passengers were rowed over to the *Alabama*, to be greeted cordially by the captain, both ships were set on fire. The captives were soon dropped off at Santo Domingo, but the *Alabama* did not linger there. It made sense to Semmes that word was circulating swiftly in the Caribbean of his ship's whereabouts, so even though he would have preferred to put in at a friendly port for much-needed maintenance and repairs, the raider had to keep moving.

The beginning of February found the *Alabama* well out in the Atlantic Ocean. One ship had been taken along the way, a schooner out of Maine, but otherwise there were no sails to see. This dry spell ended rather dramatically on the 21st when not one but four sails were sighted. The *Alabama* managed to run down two of them. Semmes relieved the first ship, the *Golden Eagle*, of some supplies—and, of course, a chronometer—before burning her, but the cargo of the *Olive Jane* he left on board untouched because she was filled with liquor. His thirsty crew was especially sad to see this prize perish in flames.

There were more ocean conquests in March, then an especially welcome one came on April 4. The hold of the *Louisa Hatch* was full of coal from Cardiff. As much as could fit was crammed into the *Alabama* when she and the *Louisa Hatch* were in the harbor of Fernando de Noronha, an island near Brazil. It was against the rules to do this but none of the local officials

---

60   Yonge later worked as a clerk in the U.S. Department of the Interior. He disappears from the historical record after 1880.

were versed in maritime law, and Semmes did not volunteer his legal services.

When the coaling process was completed, the *Alabama* resumed her hunt. It produced good results the rest of the month. Two of the captures were particularly satisfying. The *Dorcas Prince* was en route from New York to Shanghai with coal for U.S. warships in the Pacific fleet—fuel that would never arrive, as the ship was burned on the 26th. Then on May 3 the *Alabama* chased down the *Sea Lark*, and Kell estimated that when she and another capture, the *Union Jack*, were burned together that evening, it cost the Union over $600,000 in cargo and vessels.

Raphael Semmes believed in his bones that his ship and officers and crew had given the North a lot of aggravation as well as financial grief. He knew that too from reading newspapers taken from captured ships before they were set aflame. From them, it seemed that the South was still holding its own, valiantly fighting a larger and better-equipped enemy. To keep doing so might mean the North would want to cut its losses and give the Confederacy its independence.

But it was also a wearying war of attrition for both sides. The South could not replace its dead and wounded in anything like the numbers the North could. New weapons to supply the Army of the Potomac, then commanded by Major General "Fighting Joe" Hooker, were being manufactured at an astonishing rate. The blockade continued to choke the South's economy, and if Vicksburg, Mississippi, then under siege by an army led by Semmes's Mexican War colleague Ulysses Grant, capitulated, the supply and strategic advantages of the Mississippi River would be greatly diminished.

There was the toll on the ranks of officers believed to be indispensable to consider as well. Some losses were in battle, naturally—in a few weeks Semmes would read of the killing of Stonewall Jackson at Chancellorsville, accidentally shot by his own troops after a stirring victory. Some of the loss was from exhaustion. Semmes was beginning to fall into this category. In his midfifties, he noted on May 2, his wedding anniversary, he had not been home for over two years. He was homesick and tired and having to try harder to be optimistic about the South's future.

And yet with all this, the captain was about to set his ship on a course that would encircle the world and burnish his reputation and fame even brighter.

14

Life aboard the USS *Kearsarge* was tough, but not brutal. Captain Winslow ran a very tight ship and in this he was ably assisted by his executive officer, Lieutenant Commander Thornton, who was also a disciplinarian, but fair.

With the ship's twenty-four-hour-a-day routine there was little time for the men to get into mischief. Winslow usually ran a four-hour watch bill at sea which meant the crew, divided into sections according to their specialties, would have two four-hour work periods, two four-hour watch standing requirements, and one eight-hour sleep or rest period each day. In port, the routine usually changed somewhat with eight-hour watches, sleep, and work periods promulgated as needed by the XO and master at arms.

The ship was constantly trimmed up and cleaned. This was not only a matter of naval pride but a necessity for proper functioning of all the equipment. A poorly stowed line could trip up a sailor and break a limb. In a constantly pitching sea a loose solid shot could roll around like an errant bowling ball and knock men down like pins. The bright work (brass, and a lot of it) was polished frequently: If not, corrosion from salt air quickly set in. The deck was holystoned at least once a week.[61] The sails needed constant mending—even washing, given the gouts of black smoke belched forth by the *Kearsarge*'s coal-burning furnaces.

The gunners were constantly checking the ammunition, scrubbing the round shot to keep them, well, "round," and free of detritus that would whirl them away in the wrong direction when fired or, worse, foul the gun barrels. Powder, of course, needed to be kept dry, and the fuses too. Both needed constant monitoring. The big Dahlgren guns were cleaned and scrubbed regularly to keep them ready for action. The rails and pins that held the guns in place in the deck also needed frequent testing and lubrication.

In addition to his medical duties, Dr. Browne made sure the galley was clean and safe, that the cooks were preparing the ship's food with as much sanitary attention as could be mustered, and that the food itself was fit to eat. On one occasion, with the ship stopped in Cádiz, Spain, a group of unscrupulous merchants, who had not seen a ship stop for stores for some weeks, tried to foist on the *Kearsarge* their oldest supplies. The vigilant assistant paymaster, Joseph A. Smith, would have none of that. When he discovered insects in the flour and beans, as well as moldy sugar and meat, he immediately rejected it. The crew took care to return it to the merchants by tossing it overboard into the harbor, where the owners could come and get it if they wished. No one showed up to collect.

Regarding the victuals the crew did receive, the paymasters tried hard to follow the guidelines for the standard ration. For the U.S. Navy in 1861, as set by the Navy Department, the daily ration per sailor was as follows:

---

61 A "holystone" is a piece of soft sandstone that was used to scrub the wooden decks, thus clearing the wood of any dirt, grime, tar, etc. The practice continued in the U.S. Navy through World War II on any ships that still had wood in the decks.

Daily:

1 lb. of salt pork with ½ pint beans or peas; or
1 lb. salt beef with ½ lb. of flour and 2 lbs. of dried apples or other
dried fruit; or, — lb. preserved meat, ½ lb. rice, 2 oz. butter,
1 oz. of desiccated vegetables; or, — lb. preserved meat,
2 oz. butter, and 2 oz. desiccated potatoes
14 oz. biscuit (hard tack)
¼ oz. tea or 1 oz. coffee or cocoa
2 oz. sugar
1 gill (4 oz.) of spirits

Weekly:

½ pint pickles
½ pint molasses
½ pint vinegar

This menu would, of course, be altered to fit the available stores in any given port but as can be seen the navy finally understood by 1861 the value of including items like fruit, vegetables, pickles, and vinegar to balance the protein-heavy diet and stave off the dreaded scurvy that had plagued mariners for centuries.

In regard to the "spirits" ration, the navy had officially eliminated it in 1862 (how many songs were there, after all, about drunken sailors?) but beer, rum, wine, and whisky aboard ship was somewhat up to the captain's discretion. Winslow never drank very much, but he did see the value in handing out a tot or two to the crew after particularly stressful situations. He knew, as did all ship captains, that sailors will find their alcohol no matter what restrictions might be in place. In fact, on at least two occasions during Winslow's tenure, visiting coal barges came alongside with more than coal. Rum and whisky, hidden in the coal, were secretly sold to eager sailors willing to take the risk of being caught and tossed into irons. In every port, there were "bum boats" that would come alongside eager to sell all manner of souvenirs, food, and, of course, secret supplies of alcohol.

On holidays, Winslow encouraged the cooks to prepare special feasts for the crew, usually roast goose and pies. If a crewman snuck below decks or behind a mast to gulp down a purloined beer or shot of illicit rum Winslow would only turn his one unseeing eye in that direction. If they obeyed him, worked hard, and showed up for duty sober it was sufficient.

The greatest problem Winslow (and all other far-flung captains) had with alcohol was on liberty in the ports the *Kearsarge* entered. It was always a challenge for Winslow and Thornton to grant liberty—or not, and to whom. Sailors were like iron filings to the magnets of saloons and bordellos in any port of call. Bar fights were common and jailing by the local authorities was frequent. If the crew of a belligerent ship was also in port at the same time, the problems always got worse. If the men could not pound each other to bits on the high seas with their guns they were always more than eager to try and do the same with their fists while ashore.

Shore leave was also the time when desertions occurred, of course. It was most often the low-ranking malcontents and ill-adjusted landsmen who "took off," but not always so. The *Kearsarge* saw some experienced men simply walk away and disappear. Over time, the ship lost a quartermaster, three officer's stewards, one captain of the top, three coal heavers, and a slew of seamen.

The *Kearsarge* was always short at least a few hands, but never critically so. The men who deserted could always be replaced, it seemed, with eager recruits in almost any port. There were, however, two problems with foreign recruiting, one practical, the other political. The practical problem was that noncitizens with no true feelings for the Union cause could be pollutants to the esprit de corps of the crew. Men looking for a few quick bucks and transport to another country were also the readiest to desert. The political challenge was that the neutrality laws of most countries forbade "belligerents" from recruiting new men to supplement their crews. This situation became a particular irritant and a real challenge for Winslow one time while in Ireland in what became known as the "Queenstown Incident."

On November 3, 1863, the *Kearsarge* pulled into Queenstown Harbor on the Irish southeast coast. The *Kearsarge* needed coal, Winslow had business in Cork, and the warship needed a few recruits. The British Foreign Enlistment Act forbade the latter and the rules against belligerents in port required the *Kearsarge* to leave within twenty-four hours. With Winslow ashore on business Lieutenant Commander Thornton simply refused to leave until his captain returned—and there was no ship or force in Queenstown big enough to make Thornton do otherwise. That news quickly circulated in all the waterfront pubs and within hours the *Kearsarge* had sixteen eager and willing recruits aboard that the ship's petty officers took great pains to hide from the authorities and their executive officer (or perhaps he simply looked the other way).

With coal replenished and the captain back aboard on November 5, the *Kearsarge* sailed away after making a careful search for extra "visitors." The sixteen Irishmen remained hidden aboard and magically appeared amongst the crew the next day when the ship was far out to sea and headed for France. Winslow was far from happy when these men were discovered but he was not about to turn around and return them. He wanted to get to Brest with all due speed, believing that the raider CSS *Florida*, already in Brest Harbor, was about to sail. He also had been told in Cork that his opposite number, Captain Semmes on the *Alabama*, had illegally welcomed several recruits recently from Simon's Town (he had, indeed). Winslow decided to return the Queenstown men at his convenience—if at all.

Off the coast of Brest, the stowaways asked to speak to the captain. He acquiesced. The men pled their case, mostly that they were destitute and had no prospects other than with the ship. Winslow took pity on them, although he had half a mind to put them ashore in France. If he did that, though, these men might run straight to CSS *Florida* and try to enlist there, and he did not want to have that happen either. He decided to let the men stay aboard, at least for the moment.

On November 19, Winslow received a communiqué from William Dayton, the American ambassador to France. Dayton had heard about the Irishmen and in no uncertain terms told Winslow he must return them. Relations between the United States and England were just too fractious to take the risk. Reluctantly, Winslow was forced to agree.

On December 5, the *Kearsarge* left Brest in its wake and steamed back to Queenstown. Two days later, outside the harbor he had fifteen of the Irishmen put aboard a tug and taken ashore, with a letter to the local British commander that it had all been an honest mistake. Why only fifteen men and not sixteen? It turned out that one of the stowaways, Michael Ahern, a Queenstown native, had been a competent civilian clerk—and Winslow particularly needed a clerk for his paymaster. Ahern stayed aboard. Winslow and Thornton later insisted that there must have been some mistake because they clearly recalled putting sixteen men on the tug. The British must have miscounted. Ahern stayed put, and as future events will show, the deception was fortunate for Ahern as well as his new ship.

Meanwhile, the repatriated Irishmen, resplendent in their new Union Navy uniforms, and a month's pay in their pockets ($14), were all the rage in the local pubs and brothels—celebrated for their brief but good fortune.

When Winslow had taken command in April 1863, he faced a nearly impossible task. According to Captain John Morris Ellicott, Winslow's primary biographer, "The theatre of operations upon which Winslow now entered was a vast and perplexing one, but within it his judgment was supreme; in fact he scarcely got a single communication from the Navy Department until his long struggle was crowned with success. His cruising ground was thirteen hundred miles long. It was bounded on the east by the coasts of Europe and Africa and on the west by his discretion. He was to blockade, capture, or destroy vessels fitted out as Confederate cruisers. Of these he knew two, the *Florida* and the *Alabama*, to be on the high seas and that a third, the *Sumter*, had been laid up in Gibraltar.[62] Others were being fitted out in British and French ports, but of these he knew little yet: in fact, one, *Georgia*, was commissioned off Ushant at the very time he was assuming command."

For the first six months of his tenure, Winslow did not alter the tactics that had been employed by Pickering, who had received his orders from Welles, and who, not knowing any better, had told Pickering to chase Semmes wherever he needed to go. As Winslow dashed from one area to another, following rumors, supposed sightings, the littered wakes of destroyed vessels, phantoms, and false sightings (twice he mistakenly chased British mail steamers), he began to realize the tactics weren't working.

By early autumn of 1863 it finally dawned on him that all the reports of the sightings and prizes taken were secondary to the fact that the Confederate commerce raiders, at one time or another, would have to return to some port to coal, off-load their prisoners, buy supplies, and make repairs. Since the vast majority of Union oceangoing merchant traffic was between the eastern ports of America and Europe (except for many of the whaling ships), Winslow first decided to confine his activities to the northern half of his hunting grounds, which meant excluding shadow-chasing south of the equator.

Since he had complete discretion, his next task was to further narrow the field to the most logical ports and areas where the raiders might appear. Since so many supposed sightings and rumored refueling and arming stops had centered around the Azores, he made those islands the focus of his attention. It also dawned on Winslow, though, that the Azores were probably not a good choice for cruising. The islands were not central to

---

62   In this case the term *laid up* meant *put up for sale*.

the major lanes of ship traffic and communications between the Azores and other points in Europe were slow and unreliable.

Winslow pulled out a large chart of Western Europe and the British Isles and sat down in his cabin to study it, with his number two, Thornton. They knew for certain from various U.S. consuls and agents of the Union government that two Confederate rams were under construction in Nantes, two more rams were being built in Liverpool, the cruiser CSS *Rappahannock* (built under guise of becoming a Royal Navy ship) was getting ready for sea in the Thames River, CSS *Florida* was under repair in Brest, and CSS *Alabama* and CSS *Georgia* were at large but, logically, must return at some point to either where they were built or a major European repair facility. Winslow and Thornton reasoned that all potential home ports in the Confederate States were effectively blockaded by Union warships, the *Kearsarge* would need reliable coaling stations, or at least access to colliers that could come to her, and the *Kearsarge* would need repair facilities that were friendly and readily available, most likely in Spain or Holland.

Once all these points were plotted out, a solution became obvious: target the French ports, especially Brest, Calais, and possibly Cherbourg. By stationing himself astride the English Channel he had a chance to dash to any of those ports and Gibraltar and Ireland were within two days sailing. Coaling facilities were within striking distance or coal barges could come and meet him. Repair facilities in Spain and Holland were close enough to make them viable. A hostile England or a "hard neutral" France would have little impact on his cruising pattern.

It was not a perfect solution, but to Winslow the chance to make something positive happen rose from nearly zero to at least fifty-fifty that one raider or another would come under his guns. Of course, those odds also made it possible for his enemies to escape him. So began the delicate minuet between hunter and hunted that would last another nine frustrating months but ultimately end in a most desired confrontation.

15

What would have been the most notable display of Confederate Navy might was nearly put on display in the port of Bahia, Brazil, on the morning of May 13, 1863.

The *Alabama* crew thought they were anchored in Bahia alone, until the rising sun revealed another warship a half mile away. After some initial alarm on the *Alabama*, thinking a trap had been sprung, and a fight was in the offing, the mystery ship ran up the Confederate flag. Much to their relief, she turned out to be the CSS *Georgia*.

This raider was a recent addition to the South's small ocean-going fleet, and the second Confederate ship named after the Peach State. The first CSS *Georgia* was an ironclad built in Savannah in 1862. The Ladies' Gunboat Association had raised $115,000 for her construction. Commanded by First Lieutenant Washington Gwathmey,[63] the new warship was anchored in the Savannah River and employed as a floating battery to defend

---

63 Gwathmey (1817–1880) was born in England but became an officer in the U.S. Navy, then switched to the Confederate Navy in 1861. After the war he settled in Alabama.

the river channels below the city. Her cannons, if needed, were to check any Union advance from the sea as well as to guard Fort Jackson.

The second CSS *Georgia* had also been built in 1862 but started as the fast merchantman *Japan*. She was constructed with an iron hull, making her unsuited to *Alabama*-type extended cruises without dry-docking. Iron-hulled ships needed regular bottom maintenance in an era when antifouling under-body coatings were yet unknown. As eager as he was to expand the Confederate Navy, James Bulloch wanted nothing to do with iron-hulled ships, but Commander Matthew Fontaine Maury,[64] one of Bulloch's purchasing assistants, argued for the *Japan*. Vessels that could be purchased were few and far between and English shipbuilders were moving toward iron ships for greater hull integrity. Bulloch reluctantly went along and purchased her at Dumbarton, Scotland, in March 1863.

On April 1, the *Japan* departed Greenock, reputedly bound for the East Indies and carrying a crew of fifty who had shipped for a voyage to Singapore. She rendezvoused with the steamer *Alar* off Ushant, France, and took on guns, ordnance, and other stores. On April 9, the Confederate flag was hoisted and she was placed in commission as CSS *Georgia* with Commander William Lewis Maury[65] in command. Maury's orders read to prey on United States vessels wherever found. Though not quite as feared as the *Alabama*, the *Georgia* certainly made its mark on Union shipping.

The day after unexpectedly discovering each other, members of the crews of the *Alabama* and *Georgia* went on an excursion led by Semmes, who was senior captain over Maury. They boarded a train that took them up above the city of Bahia where they at-

---

64 Maury (1806–1872) was a world-renowned oceanographer and scientist. He was also a commander in the U.S. Navy until his home state of Virginia seceded. He transferred at the same rank to the Confederate Navy and, among other assignments, was sent to England to assist Bulloch in acquiring ships.

65 A cousin to Matthew Fontaine Maury, William (1813–1878) was also a commander in the U.S. Navy before "going South." He attained the rank of captain before the war ended.

tended a reception hosted by the British superintendent of the local railroad. There, the two captains learned that the CSS *Florida* had been in the area two days earlier. Conceivably, if Captain Maffitt had known of the nearness of the other Confederate warships (with his brother aboard the *Alabama* as a midshipman), the sudden Southern squadron could have managed a reunion.

Given the growing military strength of the North it is unlikely that these three formidable ships, had they been able to continue hunting Union prey, would have produced a different outcome to the war; however, victory for the North came at a much greater cost. And with three effective predators loose at one time, there were many more stories to tell. Unfortunately for the Confederacy, one by one, its "fleet" of sea tigers steadily diminished.

CSS *Georgia* certainly tried to copy the exploits of the *Alabama*. After spending two more weeks at Bahia, resupplying and enjoying more shore entertainments, she was off to hunt. She would capture a respectable total of nine prizes during the rest of 1863, but the *Georgia* never came close to that level of success the following year.

While the *Georgia* was undergoing repairs at Cherbourg in late January, it was decided to shift her armament to the CSS *Rappahannock*. However, the transfer was never conducted because *Rappahannock* could never get her cranky engines working properly and she ended up languishing pier side until the end of the war. Consequently, the *Georgia* was moved to an anchorage three miles below Bordeaux, where she remained until the beginning of May. The once-feared raider sailed to Liverpool and was sold a few weeks later to a merchant of that city. The steamer again put to sea on August 11, and four days later was captured by the frigate USS *Niagara* off Portugal. She sent to Boston where she was condemned and sold as a prize. As SS *Georgia*, she was placed in merchant service, home-ported in New Bedford on August 5, 1865. Her career ended on the coastal rocks of Maine in January 1875 as she foundered in a violent Nor'easter.

Of the very modest Confederate fleet, the ship with the most distinction—from the southern point of view—other than the *Alabama* was the CSS *Florida*.

After its near rendezvous with the *Alabama* and *Georgia* in May 1863, the ship, remaining under the command of Captain Maffitt, prowled the east coast of South America and the West Indies, with calls at neutral ports, all the while making captures and eluding the large array of Federal ships (including the USS *Kearsarge*) pursuing her.

In July, the *Florida* sailed from Bermuda for Brest, France, where she lay in the French naval dock from August 23 to February 1864. There, near collapse from various ailments, Maffitt relinquished command to Joseph Nicholson Barney,[66] whose own ill health prompted another handover, this time to Lieutenant Charles Manigault Morris.[67]

Returning to the West Indies (after embarrassing Captain Winslow and the *Kearsarge* with her narrow escape from France), the *Florida* reloaded her coal bunkers at Barbados. She then skirted the U.S. coast, sailed back across the Atlantic to Tenerife in the Canary Islands and then southwest to Bahia again, arriving on October 4, 1864. After being illegally captured and towed to sea three days later by the USS *Wachusett*, the *Florida* was sent to the U.S. as a prize, despite Brazil's protests at the violation of its sovereignty. Napoleon Collins of the *Wachusett* was

---

66 Barney (1818–1899) was a lieutenant in the U.S. Navy before switching sides in 1861. After commanding the *Florida* he was promoted to commander and became a CSA naval agent in Europe. After the war he took the Oath of Allegiance, settled in Virginia, and became a successful insurance agent.

67 Morris (1820–1895) was also a former U.S. Navy lieutenant before joining the CSA Navy in 1861 with the rank of first lieutenant. He was promoted to commander aboard CSS *Florida* but was stranded in Brazil when the *Wachusett* towed away his ship while he was ashore. He spent the rest of the war in South America as a Confederate Navy agent. After the war he moved to England with his family, only returning to the U.S. in 1880 where he spent the rest of his days living in Baltimore.

court-martialed and convicted of violating Brazilian territorial rights. This slap on the wrist was set aside by Gideon Welles, allowing Collins to enjoy fame and eventual promotion for his daring capture of the Confederate raider.[68]

The official end of the *Florida*'s career came at Newport News, Virginia, that November when she sank under dubious circumstances after a collision with the *Alliance*, a troop ferry. It was a loss to Brazil too as the *Florida* could not be delivered back to that country in satisfaction of a final court order returning her to Brazilian custody. The ship's success had been second only to the *Alabama*, with thirty-seven prizes taken, two of which, the *Tacony* and the *Clarence*, were christened into the Confederate Navy.

There were other raiders that tried to follow in the wakes of the bold Confederate Navy trio of *Alabama*, *Georgia*, and *Florida*. None met with anywhere near the success of the "big three."

CSS *Nashville* did not have a very long career. As reported earlier in this book, she was the first ship of war to fly the Confederate flag and the first raider to capture an American ship in the North Atlantic. As the privateer *Rattlesnake*, later in the war, she ran aground on the Ogeechee River, Georgia, and the guns of the monitor USS *Montauk* destroyed her.

An indication that Bulloch and his fellow agents in England continued to contribute to the South's maritime effort until late in the war was the brief but effective career of the CSS *Tallahassee*, named after what had become the Confederate capital of Florida.

Tallahassee was constructed on the River Thames by J&W Dudgeon to the design of one Captain T. E. Symonds of the Royal Navy. Ostensibly she was to be for the Chinese opium trade. Commissioned as the *Atlanta* she had made several blockade runs between Bermuda and Wilmington, North Carolina, before the Confederates bought her. Once recommissioned and prepared for sea in the summer of 1864, the *Tallahassee* was placed

---

68 Collins later retired as a rear admiral. Many of the artifacts from the CSS *Florida* can today be found at the Hampton Roads Naval Museum in Virginia.

under the command of John Taylor Wood,[69] who had quite a pedigree—Wood was a grandson of President Zachary Taylor and a nephew of Jefferson Davis.

The new Rebel raider conducted an impressive nineteen-day hunt off the Atlantic coast as far north as Halifax, Nova Scotia, destroying twenty-six vessels and capturing seven others that were bonded or released. But her success as an oceangoing warship was short-lived. Wood sailed the steamer into Halifax Harbor on August 18 to take on bunker coal and water. Neutrality laws limited her stay in Halifax to twenty-four hours. The *Tallahassee* was granted an extra twelve hours to fix a broken mast but was only allowed to load enough coal to take her to the nearest Confederate port.

Two Federal warships, USS *Nansemond* and USS *Huron*, were rumored to be waiting for the *Tallahassee* at the harbor entrance. But the wily Captain Wood hired legendary Halifax pilot John "Jock" Fleming, who guided the Confederate ship through the narrow and shallow Eastern Passage between Dartmouth and Lawlor Island, a route normally run only by small fishing boats.

The first Northern warship to actually arrive was the gunboat USS *Pontoosuc*, but this was several hours after the Confederate cruiser departed. However, unable to procure enough coal to continue long-range hunting, Wood was forced to return to Wilmington, arriving safely on August 26.

The *Tallahassee* was renamed CSS *Olustee* in honor of the Rebel victory at the Battle of Olustee in northern Florida in

69   Wood (1830–1904) graduated second in his 1852 class at the U.S. Naval Academy. When the Civil War commenced he was already a lieutenant in the navy but switched allegiance to the Confederacy and was commissioned a first lieutenant. He served on the CSS *Virginia* during her duel with the USS *Monitor*. His family connections also provided for him a promotion to commander and a simultaneous commission as a Confederate colonel of cavalry. Further promoted to captain while skipper of the *Tallahassee*, and as the Confederacy was ending, he accompanied his uncle on Davis's attempted escape from Union forces after Lee's surrender. Wood then fled to Cuba, and after the war relocated to Nova Scotia where he settled with his family for the remainder of his days.

February 1864. *Olustee* was placed under the command of Lieutenant W. H. Ward. She ran through the blockade off Wilmington again on October 29, 1864, but suffered some damage from Federal guns. She captured and destroyed six ships off the Cape of Delaware before having to return for coal. She warded off attempts by the USS *Sassacus* to capture her on November 6 and by four other Union warships on November 7, finally passing into the safety of Wilmington Harbor.

There *Olustee* went under yet another transformation and was renamed again, suitably, CSS *Chameleon*. She ran through the Union blockade on December 24 while the United States fleet was preoccupied with bombarding Fort Fisher. The *Chameleon* proceeded to Bermuda to obtain provisions for the Confederate Army then made two attempts to enter a Southern port. Finding it impossible, the *Chameleon* sailed to Liverpool. She arrived, ironically, on April 9, 1865, the day Lee surrendered to Grant at Appomattox. The *Chameleon* was seized and sold by the British authorities and was about to enter the merchant service when the victorious U.S. government instituted suit for her possession. She was handed over to the U.S. consul at Liverpool on April 26, 1866, and two months later sold at auction.

Even with the achievements of the other Rebel raiders, no ship inspired more headlines, especially in the outraged North, than the CSS *Alabama*. To add to its total of the previous year, during the first six months of 1863 the raider took twenty-seven ships (including the sinking of the *Hatteras*), destroyed twenty-one of them, and converted one, the *Conrad*, captured on June 20, into a Confederate vessel. July began auspiciously when the *Anna F. Schmidt* and the *Express* were boarded and burned on the 2nd and 6th.

Then it all changed: There would be only one prize in August, none in September and October, then three ships taken in November and the same in December—only seven captures for the balance of the year. The raider that had ruled the seas found itself cruising aimlessly with few sails sighted.

There were several reasons for the sharp decline in the *Alabama*'s fortunes. More merchant owners and captains were chartering neutral ships or at least had registered their cargoes with neutral countries, making them exempt from seizure. It became increasingly frustrating for Semmes to inspect the hold of a ship that the *Alabama* had run down, with cargo intended for the North but registered to another neutral nation. Without a legal foundation he could not burn these ships and risk international condemnation.

Another reason for slimmer pickings was that ship captains certainly knew by the second half of 1863 which waters were being prowled by the *Alabama*, and they devised alternate routes to their destinations. Even if these routes resulted in extra days or weeks at sea, that was better that being burned and the owner possibly bankrupted. One more reason was that Secretary Welles had more roaming warships, and even if they arrived too late after hearing of an *Alabama* sighting, those waters were at least temporarily closed to the Confederate raider.

Like the South itself, the *Alabama* was getting more worn around the edges. As the year went on, Semmes could follow the course of the war in captured newspapers. July had seemed an especially dismal month for the Confederacy with the surrender of Vicksburg and Lee's northern invasion stymied at Gettysburg. Losses of men and material that could not be replaced were mounting. The appointment of Grant as the overall commander appeared to have reinvigorated Union forces. The chance of Great Britain or France or any European country of significance aligning with the South became more remote.

As for the *Alabama*, she had been at sea nonstop for a year with only the most urgent of repairs and maintenance having been done. There had been some respite at the end of July when the *Alabama* put in at Saldanha Bay sixty miles north of Cape Town, South Africa, and some caulking and engine work could be completed. During a subsequent visit to Cape Town, the ship and its captain were treated as celebrities.

Still, the *Alabama* had lost some speed and was less agile. The same could be said of its skipper. "His face is careworn and sunburnt," wrote a reporter, adding that, "the features were striking—a broad brow with iron-grey locks straggling over it, grey eyes, now mild and dreamy, then flashing with fire as he warms in conversation, a prominent nose, thin compressed lips and well-developed chin." Unlike his reputation, "He has nothing of the pirate about him." Tellingly, "He was dressed in an old grey stained uniform with battered shoulder straps and faded gold trimmings."

As with his uniform, Semmes was frayed and tired. He was well into his third year of being away from home and hearth. He confided in his journal, "The fact is, I am past the age when men ought to be subjected to the hardships and discomforts of the sea." Even the sound of the wind in the rigging "gives me the blues." But there was no end in sight of the *Alabama*'s mission.

Or perhaps there was, sooner than expected and in the form of the USS *Vanderbilt*.

Word reached Semmes that the powerful Union vessel was in South African waters. If the *Alabama* could not avoid it or outrun it, the Confederate raider would be at a disadvantage in a battle with so powerful a ship. *Vanderbilt* may have begun as a pleasure vessel, but there was little about her like that any longer.

Originally a transatlantic passenger and mail steamer constructed by Jeremiah Simonson of Greenpoint, New York, in 1857, the following year the ship ran aground while on a voyage from Bremen, Germany, to Southampton, England. She was refloated and taken into Southampton in a severely leaky condition. The ship was offered to the Union Army by her owner, Cornelius Vanderbilt, the railroad and shipping magnate, in early 1862 and transferred to the navy that March.

The *Vanderbilt* began her military career in Hampton Roads, Virginia, intended for use as a ram against the Confederate ironclad CSS *Virginia*. Vanderbilt himself suggested filling the bow of the vessel with concrete and reinforcing it with iron plating. This was not done, however, and instead the ship was fitted with a heavy battery of fifteen guns at the New York Navy Yard that summer. She left New York in November to conduct a search for the *Alabama*. The cruise was fruitless, and the *Vanderbilt* returned to Hampton Roads in January 1863.

But she was not through with the elusive *Alabama*. After only ten days docked, the *Vanderbilt* received orders to conduct a much longer and more thorough search (and transport one Captain John Winslow to the Azores to meet his new command). Thus began a year-long cruise which took the vessel to the West Indies, eastern coast of South America, Cape of Good Hope, Saint Helena, Cape Verde, the Canary Islands, Spain, and Portugal. During the West Indies portion of her deployment, the *Vanderbilt* served as flagship of Commodore Charles Wilkes's Flying Squadron.

During its long voyage the *Vanderbilt* captured the blockade-running British steamer *Peterhoff* in late February 1863 off Saint Thomas, Virgin Islands. This incident touched off a dispute between the British and Americans as to the disposition of mail carried aboard the steamer. President Abraham Lincoln eventually ordered the mail returned to the British. The American warship's captures also included the British blockade runner *Gertrude*, taken off Eleuthera Island in the Bahamas in April, and the British bark *Saxon*, seized at Angra Peguena, Africa, in October. The *Saxon* was suspected of having rendezvoused with and taken cargo off the CSS *Tuscaloosa* earlier.

What of the *Alabama* and stalking her off the coast of South Africa? Fortunately for the Confederate cause at sea, a familiar pattern was repeated. The *Vanderbilt*'s captain and crew became increasingly frustrated as the Union ship arrived at a port to discover that her quarry had departed only a few hours or a few days earlier. Eventually, in January 1864, the *Vanderbilt* returned to New York City for repairs without ever having sighted the Confederate vessel. By then, the *Alabama* was long gone from the Atlantic Ocean.

To where? To a part of the world it had not visited before. With the *Vanderbilt* being only one of an increasing number of Union ships in the area and targets scarce, Semmes had the idea to explore a new theater of operations. He set sail for the South China Sea.

It took only two weeks to get there, thanks to benevolent weather and good winds. In late October 1863, the *Alabama* resumed stopping ships: They all turned out to be neutral and protected from seizure. It was closing in on three months without a capture, and possibly only out of aggravation and to mollify an impatient crew, Semmes determined to take on the USS *Wyoming*. While off the coast of Indonesia, Semmes had been told by the captain of an English vessel and then a Dutch one that the Union gunboat had been spotted nearby.[70]

It was uncharacteristic of the *Alabama* to seek a confrontation with a ship of war but the search which got underway alleviated some of the restlessness on board. As it turned out, the quest for the *Wyoming* was interrupted by, finally, a catch. Off Java Head, lookouts spotted a sail. It belonged to an American merchant ship, the *Amanda*. Its captain was both shocked and chagrined to encounter the by-now legendary Confederate captain and his ship so far from home. On the night of November 6, the *Amanda* burned brightly.

Four days later, cruising through the South China Sea, there was still no sign of the *Wyoming*, but the raider spotted and chased down the *Winged Racer*, which apparently could not race that fast after all. It was a clipper ship out of New York, and while its cargo was not valuable—though the coffee, sugar, and tobacco on board

---

70   This was the first of four ships in the U.S. Navy to be named the *Wyoming* and the only one named in honor of the Wyoming Valley in eastern Pennsylvania. This *Wyoming* had been launched in 1859 and had operated on the California coast during the war. It had combat experience, having been deployed to fight the forces of a Japanese warlord in the Battle of Shimonoseki Straits on July 16, 1863.

were welcomed—there was an impressive fire nonetheless. The next day brought another capture of another clipper out of New York named the *Contest*. That night she too became a bonfire.

This was more like it. But instead of three ships taken in five days being a promising harbinger of adventures to come, the remainder of November saw the *Alabama* in a nomadic and futile search for prizes. The *Wyoming* was nowhere to be found. (By then, it was in Singapore.) The restlessness of the crew returned, more pronounced than before. Semmes suspected at least some of the men would desert at the first port the *Alabama* put into, but he did need to find a place to do repairs. And desertions were preferable to a mutiny. Kell and the other officers were constantly on guard against one.

Like the emotions of the crew, the condition of the ship was deteriorating rapidly. Old leaks reopened and new leaks appeared. Rot was becoming rampant. The rigging needed to be redone with fresh, strong rope. The to-do list went on and on.

Pulo Condore offered a haven. This cluster of small islands sitting off the coast of Vietnam had recently been claimed by France, and the head of the small garrison invited Semmes to have the *Alabama* stay as long as she wanted to in order to undertake repairs. Another enticement was that the island where they anchored offered a welcome change in diet. A bullock was offered up, killed, and roasted. The fresh meat, Semmes noted, contributed to "a reasonable degree of contentment."[71]

The interlude for the Confederate officers and crew was a pleasant but brief one. The Pulo Condore cluster had no facilities for repairing ships. Crewmen supervised by Kell did what

---

71 France was at the beginning of an occupation that would last almost a century, to the Battle of Dien Bien Phu which resulted in the decisive defeat of its military forces in May 1954. The Treaty of Huế had been signed on April 14, 1863, between representatives of Vietnam and the French Empire. Based on the terms of the accord, three Vietnamese ports were opened (Tourane, Balat, and Quảng Yên). Moreover, freedom of missionary activity was permitted and Vietnam's foreign affairs were under French imperial protection. Saigon, seized by the French the previous year, was declared the capital of French Cochin China.

they could, which included creating a submersible compartment that allowed men to clean the Alabama's bottom from underneath. Then, after taking on fresh water and more meat, the ship continued its Asian sojourn.

The *Alabama* sailed south, and its next stop was Singapore, on December 21, where by then the *Wyoming* was only a memory. She was able to take on coal there, and while doing so, the captain sauntered around the city. Semmes enjoyed exotic sights he had never seen before but noticed that unlike in England and in previous British territory visits, he, his officers, and his ship were not treated like celebrities. The ongoing war in the United States, soon to enter its fourth year, had tested Great Britain's neutrality and its economy. In particular, because of ships like the *Alabama*—especially the *Alabama*—global merchant trade was down, and one of the impacts was that the tea trade upon which Singapore depended had suffered greatly. The last thing local officials wanted to do was celebrate the ship.

The chilly reception was not the sole reason for the *Alabama*'s abrupt departure. A mini–American Civil War was.

While refreshing themselves at a hotel bar, Arthur Sinclair and a few other Southern officers were approached by several Americans who were not Navy but served on U.S.-flagged merchant ships. Presumably, these vessels would not think of leaving Singapore until the *Alabama* did, which could explain what happened next. At first, the conversation over a new round of cocktails was cordial, but then one of the Americans proposed a toast that the Confederates deemed insulting. Less friendly words were exchanged followed by flying fists. The *Alabama* men may have inflicted more damage because they were the ones to successfully flee when the police arrived. After hearing about the brawl, Semmes immediately determined the ship had worn out the little welcome it had been shown and the *Alabama* weighed anchor.

After six weeks without a prize, there were to be end-of-year gifts for the Rebel raider. One came on Christmas Eve, right after the *Alabama* had left Singapore and entered the Strait of Malacca. The *Martaban* was bound for Singapore with rice from Burma. At first, after she was boarded, the American captain claimed his ship was British and had papers to prove it. But when Semmes examined them, he suspected a ruse. Placed under oath, the captain grudgingly admitted the *Martaban* was an American ship with the British documents being a cover story. It was torched before the end of the day.

After a quiet Christmas Day, the *Alabama* took two ships on December 26, the *Highlander* out of Boston and the *Sonora* out of Newburyport. After relieving both captured captains of their chronometers, Semmes had their ships burned.

In 1863, the Alabama had a tally of twenty-nine ships taken, with twenty-two of them destroyed. Every Union attempt to find and take her had been unsuccessful, with one of its warships, the USS *Hatteras*, sunk. The Northern press portrayed the larger-than-life and seemingly invincible Raphael Semmes as laughing at Gideon Welles and his incompetent, seagoing sloops of war.

But as the year came to an end, Semmes felt anything but invincible. He was very weary and farther away from his family than ever. He had heard little about the status of the Southern cause, but he suspected Confederate independence was not any closer than when 1863 had begun and could be in jeopardy altogether. His crew had been wrung dry by the thousands of miles of sailing, infrequent shore leave, and intervals of bad water, bad food, and bad weather. Without a complete overhaul, the ship could not take much more of the pounding of the high seas.

The *Alabama* was soon to leave the Strait of Malacca and enter the Indian Ocean. Perhaps this was the time, finally, to think about sailing for home.

16

The monotony of constant cruising back and forth was often broken by the drills that Winslow demanded, including firing of live ammunition. All the guns were exercised at one time or another, including the big, booming Dahlgrens. Actual targets of derelict boats were sometimes available.

The Parrot gun was easy to wrangle into various firing positions and the marines who manned this rifle took great pride in beating their navy opposites in timing drills and accuracy of fire. The 32-pounder, smoothbore, muzzle-loading cannons were each served by a crew of six or eight, depending on available manpower. There was at least a gunner, loader, sponger, rammer, and two or more men to handle the blocks and tackle that wrestled the guns back into place after firing and recoil.

The hefty Dahlgrens required enormous work to maneuver properly and swiftly. Each gun had a crew of at least ten sailors and an officer to oversee the sighting and firing. The captain and his exec also had to be mindful of the enormous weight of the guns. When pivoted to one side simultaneously, in a broadside firing position, the ship itself could be put nearly on its gunwales by the tonnage.

Captain Winslow also insisted on fire drills, boat drills (to get his cutters and lifeboats in and out of the water), boarding drills, and even abandon-ship drills. He may not have been the most judiciously discreet officer in the U.S. Navy, as Secretary Welles could attest, but he was a careful one. He also knew, even if the men grumbled about the drills, it took their minds off the boredom.

Sundays, either at sea or in port, were generally when the crew rested. Winslow had the men formed up on deck every Sunday morning to read to them from the Bible. The day was also a chance to shake out their bedding, wash their clothes and hang them in the rigging to dry, complete personal tasks, write letters home, smoke a pipe if they had tobacco, and grab some down time for the rigors of another week ahead. Winslow would usually look the other way if the men wanted to play cards, which he generally forbade, and if there was an extra tot available in the "grog tub" so be it.

There was no such thing in the Civil War U.S. Navy, as there is today, as formal "training." Each man was expected to have a certain level of basic competence equal to his rank—except for the clueless landsmen. To learn more and attain higher rank was up to each individual sailor. But in addition to on-the-job training, Sundays could be used for informal instruction, depending on the whims and dedication of the higher-up petty officers and junior officers.

From all accounts that could be discovered, the USS *Kearsarge* at that time was a more than competent ship with a generally well-adjusted and reasonably happy crew. *Happy*, of course, was a relative word in a life at sea that was tough, demanding, and far away from home port with almost zero chance of seeing family on any regular basis. The *Kearsarge* had not, in fact, touched home base for the two years since her commissioning and departure from Portsmouth.

Meanwhile, on November 24, 1863, with workmen still aboard banging away, the CSS *Rappahannock* slipped down the Thames estuary and put to sea. Just outside the harbor, a base crew of about fifty Confederates, including all her officers, was shuttled out to the ship by tug. They took over, unfurled the Stars and Bars, and put her in service to the Confederate Navy. As she pushed into the English Channel her bearings seized and she came to a dead stop. Embarrassingly, she had to be towed into Calais where emergency repairs began immediately. Captain Winslow was informed of all this by message.

As 1863 ended and 1864 commenced, the USS *Kearsarge* was on a storm-tossed sea still trying to cover her bases. Realistically, the threats—and targets—remained the same: CSS *Florida* under repairs in Brest, CSS *Rappahannock* undergoing repairs in Calais, CSS *Georgia* undergoing repairs in Cherbourg, and CSS *Alabama* out there somewhere.[72]

Captain Winslow was desperately hoping that the *Florida* would complete her long-stalled repairs and come out. Nothing would be more satisfying—or morale boosting—than capturing or destroying one of these four thorns in his side. Could Winslow have steamed into any one of these ports, charged up to any one of these stationary targets, and blasted it to splinters as she sat there helpless and immobile? Yes, he could have, and he was sometimes tempted to, but as he well knew, the political repercussions could have been devastating, especially with France, whose emperor, Napoleon III, seemed inclined to side with the Confederacy against the Union. There was also a sense of fair play and chivalry to consider.

The game of cat-and-mouse would continue. In mid-January 1864, Winslow received a report from Ambassador Dayton in Paris that the *Florida* was still experiencing problems getting her repairs completed. The *Kearsarge* was having her own problems too. Food and coal were running low, and the condensers were

---

72   She was, in fact, far south of the equator, as our previous chapters attest.

malfunctioning, decreasing fresh water needed for the boilers and the crew. Winslow decided to take a chance and dash for Cádiz where he could make repairs as well as take on supplies. The *Kearsarge* reached that city in Spain on January 23.

On January 26, while in port, Winslow received another communiqué from Dayton with some rather alarming news. The captain of the *Florida* had told the local papers in Brest that he was planning on "coming out" to fight the *Kearsarge* in early February. On top of this missive, Freeman Morse, the U.S. consul in London, sent Winslow a telegram indicating that his spies had told him that the *Florida* had even taken on two more steel Blakely cannons to add to its arsenal. Piling on more anxiety, the U.S. consul in Le Havre, France, also sent Winslow an urgent letter indicating that his spies were telling him that the *Georgia* and *Rappahannock* were on their way to Brest to join up with the *Florida* and that the three belligerents were planning to tackle the *Kearsarge* together.

Winslow had learned during the past nine months that a great deal of the information from land-based sources could often be unreliable. Still, he could not ignore the threat. Given what he knew about each of these three ships he was very confident that he could take on any single one of them and be victorious. He might even be able to take on two of them at a time, but three? That might be a bridge too far. Even given the *Rappahannock*'s limited speed and armament, all the Rebel cruisers would have to do would be to encircle him and the three ships in unison could blast him to bits. He decided to consult with his senior officers.

None of the officers had any qualms about taking on their opponents—even three at a time, although they collectively voiced an opinion that they thought it impossible that all three ships could be coordinated at once. The wild card, of course, was the *Alabama*. Still the risks seemed to justify the potential reward and the entire crew was anxious to get something done and end the cruise.

Lieutenant Commander Thornton broached the idea that he had employed during his battle with the forts in New Orleans while running the USS *Hartford* up the Mississippi River. He suggested taking all the excess chain aboard and draping it over the sides of the *Kearsarge*, especially along the hull where the boilers were housed. Winslow readily agreed to the idea and even went one step further: He directed the ship's carpenter to cover the chains with slats of thin wooden lathe and then paint them black to match the hull. The chains were soon bolted down on each side of the ship and covered with the boards. Even from close in, the deception was nearly impossible to detect. Going forward, the *Kearsarge* would essentially have a suit of armor protecting her most important internal parts.

On February 14, 1864, her repairs complete and restocked with coal and food supplies, the *Kearsarge* left Cádiz. Four days later, she arrived off the French coast at Brest. Imagine Winslow's chagrin when he took his telescope, stared into the harbor, and found that the pier where the CSS *Florida* had been berthed was empty. The Confederate cruiser was gone. Sailing into the harbor and tying up where his enemy had been, Winslow soon learned he had missed nabbing the *Florida* by two days. She had slipped out of the harbor on February 16 under the cover of darkness, all lights extinguished, apparently believing that the *Kearsarge* was still lurking in the vicinity.

Making matters even more depressing, Winslow learned that the CSS *Georgia* was no longer in Cherbourg. The French had ordered the vessel to leave, but that was only a small consolation. Three of four of Winslow's targets were once again in the wind. On February 19, he wrote a letter to Secretary Welles reporting these dismal facts. It must have been galling to him to do so.

Later in the day, he wrote a letter to his wife and in it we can almost hear some of the weariness he must have been feeling:

"I shall go up the Channel as far as Calais, and after hovering about to catch either of them should they remain, proceed as information may direct. It is very cold and our men suffer very much so far north. You have no idea what a flurry my numerous and constant correspondence keeps me in and I have so much to attend to besides."

As the winter storms in the Channel abated and the temperatures rose, life began to improve a bit for the crew of the *Kearsarge*. The schedule—and the boredom—did not change much, however. The pattern became one of a constant round of trips between the English, French, and Dutch ports, waiting for the enemy to show up, taking on fuel and supplies, and watching for the *Rappahannock* to come out and fight.[73] At the end of April, Winslow picked up a stack of newspapers in Dover. From among the broadsheets he learned that the *Florida* was in Havana,[74] the *Georgia* was on her way to Liverpool,[75] and the *Alabama* was rumored to be sailing from the area of South Africa up to the English Channel, possibly for repairs.

With his good eye squarely on the *Rappahannock*, and the *Georgia* and *Florida* at least temporarily out of reach, the news about the *Alabama*, if true, was particularly electrifying. Winslow redoubled his efforts to keep his ship in fighting form, fully supplied, and the crew drilled, ready—and sober.

If Winslow was lucky—and hadn't he earned some luck by now?—the *Alabama* would make itself available. In the late winter of 1864, no one would argue that this ship was the crown

---

73 Unbeknownst to Winslow, of course, was that the *Rappahannock* might as well have been nailed to her pier in Calais. She would never leave before the end of the war. French authorities kept her impounded and the many deficiencies in her design and engine suite left her constantly needing repairs. She was ultimately turned over to the U.S. Navy after the end of the war.

74 This was not quite true: she was in the West Indies, but certainly far enough away at that time not to be of concern to Winslow.

75 Again, what Winslow could not know was that the Confederate Navy had deemed the *Georgia* "unfit for further service." She was on her way to Liverpool to be sold to a private merchant.

jewel of the Confederacy's navy. It was both a feared and coveted adversary. To capture or sink the *Alabama* would make any Union captain's career. Winslow knew he did not have the charisma, reputation, and record of success that Raphael Semmes had. But being in Washington and presenting the Rebel captain's surrendered sword to Secretary Welles—maybe even President Lincoln himself!—now that would be reputation enough for any seagoing commander.

ACT IV:
THE BATTLE

I'd sooner have fought that fight than any ever fought upon the ocean!

Admiral David Glasgow Farragut

17

Sailing through the Indian Ocean, the *Alabama* did not encounter severe weather. This was more fortunate than typical. Raphael Semmes had to wonder that if his ship were to be struck by a tempest similar to the hurricane the *Alabama* survived in October 1862, would there be the same outcome this time? Leaks were constantly being plugged and it could not be known after all the almost unrelenting wear and tear what would break or collapse under the pressures of wind and wave.

What the *Alabama* did encounter was another ship—on January 14, 1864, and it was the *Emma Jane* out of Bath, Maine. Her cargo hold was empty, so there was not as much damage to the Union as Semmes would have liked when the merchantman burned. Worse, the capture of the *Emma Jane* was an aberration because the Indian Ocean proved not to be fertile hunting grounds. Home was still on the captain's mind but there was no sense retracing the miles he had just come. The *Alabama* sailed on, to Africa.

The good news for the crew the second week of February was finally putting into a port, one that was part of the Comoro

Islands between Mozambique and Madagascar. The bad news was the population was Muslim and there was not a drop of liquor to be found. For what was most likely the only time in the *Alabama*'s history, the disgruntled and sober sailors returned from shore leave early.

The ship set sail again and made its way south uninterrupted, rounded the Cape of Good Hope, then put into Cape Town. Semmes was still a popular figure there but otherwise the stay, only three days to take on supplies, was painful for the captain, on several scores. First, the speedy bark *Conrad*, which the *Alabama* had captured the previous June and turned into the CSS *Tuscaloosa* by Semmes's decree, was sitting in Cape Town, impounded by the British, as illegally seized and repurposed. Semmes even wrote a legal brief while at anchor arguing for her release. The argument was not settled, to Semmes's chagrin, until after he sailed.[76]

Secondly, his hosts in Cape Town organized a wild game hunt for Semmes and several of his officers. If the hunt bagged any grand prizes the results were not recorded. Tragically, though, one of Semmes's officers, Third Assistant Engineer Simeon Cummings, was accidentally killed when his hunting rifle, for unknown reasons, exploded in his hands.

If that wasn't enough bad news, thirdly, for the first time in the year Semmes had access to newspapers and additional information passed on by British officials. His suspicions were correct, and worse: The South's fortunes were declining.

Lee's unsuccessful invasion of the North that was stopped at Gettysburg the previous July had indeed been a turning point, but so had the other event that week, the fall of Vicksburg, allowing the Union's victorious commander, Ulysses Grant, to be appointed by Lincoln to direct all of the North's military efforts.

---

76 The Confederate crew, originally from the *Alabama*, got tired of waiting and left the ship. The British agreed with Semmes's brief and released the ship to her owners, but the owners refused to claim her. So she sat, until turned over to the Union Navy as a prize of war.

All this was not totally unknown to Semmes, but noticeable was the absence in news accounts from America of reports of Confederate victories. True, as tradition seemingly dictated, armies stuck to winter quarters until the ground thawed, but it seemed whatever momentum the South once had was gone. Thousands more men had been lost as well as large swaths of territory to Union invaders and there was stability in Union leadership—the combination could well mean doom to the Confederacy. And those who still believed in the cause and fought on, like Semmes and his loyal officers, were three years older and more tired than ever.

On March 29, Semmes recorded in his journal, "The Yankee Government and people, and with them a great portion of the English press and people, seem to have jumped suddenly to the conclusion that we are beaten, and that the war must soon end by our submission! Verily, the delusion of these men in the matter of the war is unaccountable. No power on earth can subjugate the Southern States."

There was no solace on the sea because there were no more prizes sailing into view—nothing the rest of March and the first three weeks of April. The *Alabama* had become something like the Flying Dutchman, a wandering and ghostly ship with no place to call home. She sailed northwest through the Atlantic. Semmes considered trying to find a British or French harbor in South America that would permit the *Alabama* to put in for repairs.

Spirits lifted near the coast of Brazil on April 22 when "Sail ho!" was shouted out from overhead. With the racehorse having more gray whiskers and injuries, it took several hours for the *Alabama* to run down the *Rockingham*, which was carrying guano from Peru to Portsmouth. Before burning and sinking her, Semmes had his crew use the *Rockingham* for practice with their 32-pounders. Lieutenant Kell did not think the exercise went well—not only was sufficient accuracy not achieved, but as many as a third of the shells that struck the *Rockingham* had not exploded. Unfortunately, no one on the *Alabama* followed up to examine the condition of the ship's shells and gunpowder.

There was one more capture before the end of April. While still near Brazil, the *Alabama* chased and caught the *Tycoon*. The only cargo worth transferring were cartons of clothing, which allowed those crew members who were interested to replace the shirts and pants that by now were little more than rags on their bodies. Leaving the ship engulfed in flames behind, the *Alabama* headed north. It crossed the equator on May 2, the fourth time the ship had done so since its launching. The Atlantic Ocean was free of prey, a frustrating testament to the fear the Confederate raider had instilled in the international merchant community.

Ten days later, it was an embarrassing moment for Semmes to discover the true state of the *Alabama*'s armory. Kell must have finally pressed his target practice disappointment with the captain and his reasons for doing so. Not only had some of the ship's powder been dampened by leaks and probably rendered unusable but many of the fuses in the shells were bad. Even if all powder and fuses could be replaced, Semmes had to wonder if the *Alabama* would become a toothless tiger considering that she was still leaking.

Three weeks later the captain and crew suffered another embarrassment. A British ship was spotted approaching from behind. It was not necessarily one of the fastest ships in Queen Victoria's fleet but with ease it caught up to and outdistanced the *Alabama*. His once-fast raider was, Semmes wrote, "like the wearied foxhound, limping back after a long chase, foot-sore and longing for quiet and repose." And like his ship the captain "was well-nigh worn down" and the three years of war he had been at sea were "a load of a dozen years upon my shoulders."

He could have made the decision to turn west and head for America. The thought of finally being back with Anne and the younger children still at home had to be powerfully alluring.

He could also learn about the fates of his sons Samuel Spencer and Oliver.[77] And it could not escape the captain's thinking that by breaking the blockade then coasting into a Southern harbor there would have been a cause of celebration for all.

But here was the rub: by late spring 1864, Semmes could not be sure what harbors were still in Confederate hands. As he had noted in his journal, "The last batch of newspapers captured were full of disasters. Might it not be that, after all our trials and sacrifice, the cause for which we were struggling would be lost?"

The *Alabama* could wander down the East Coast looking for a friendly port and even into the Gulf of Mexico without ending its journey. And what if she could break through the Union blockade into Charleston or Savannah? Even a repaired and refreshed *Alabama* might not be able to break back out and the Confederacy would lose one of its more potent weapons.

Another consideration for the captain: Would his ship survive one more crossing of the Atlantic Ocean? Even in May a destructive storm could attack, and the *Alabama* was already a seriously wounded animal. As tempting as setting a course for the Carolinas was, Semmes decided the more expedient and prudent course was north to France. He knew British sympathy and any possible support for the South had waned. He would roll the dice with the French. With luck, they did not consider the Confederate cause lost.

Inside the English Channel, Semmes steered his ship east. He determined that Cherbourg would be the best port for refitting and repairing of the *Alabama*. She arrived there at noon on Saturday, June 11. Semmes had prisoners from the *Rockingham* and *Tycoon* escorted off the ship and he prepared to meet with French officials.

This was "a great relief," Semmes recorded in his journal.

---

77 Both were serving in the Confederate Army and were, thus far, unscathed. His youngest son, Raphael Jr., was about to enter the Confederate Navy as a fifteen-year-old midshipman.

"And thus, thanks to an all-wise Providence, we have brought the cruise of the *Alabama* to a successful termination."

However, upon her arrival in Cherbourg, Raphael Semmes could not truly have suspected it would be the *Alabama*'s final port of call. The war was not over, and in fact the South's fight for independence would rage on for another ten months. If his weary and leaky ship could be sufficiently repaired and resupplied, the captain knew he would have to return to the hunt and inflict more damage to Union commerce.

No one, even the most ardent supporter of the South, would have blamed Semmes if he decided in Cherbourg that the war had ended for his weary ship and crew. The *Alabama* had sailed and steamed a total of 75,000 miles, run down and boarded almost three hundred vessels, and taken sixty-four, with all but twelve set aflame. It had cost the Union cause well over $6 million in lost cargo. And the one Union warship that had challenged the *Alabama* to a straight-up fight had been sunk, "the only defeat of a Federal warship in single combat during the war," according to John M. Taylor. "Semmes's record would not be approached by any other sea raider until the era of the submarine."

The *Alabama* had represented the best of the Confederate Navy on the ocean. But despite James Bulloch's yeoman efforts, there simply had not been enough ships, nor enough ports to welcome and maintain them. In nearly two years at sea, the *Alabama* had not put into a Confederate port. Officials and residents at several neutral ports had lauded the exploits of the legendary ship and its captain, but the *Alabama* had never been home. A homecoming would have to wait.

The first order of business was for Captain Semmes to ascertain what kind of reception and, he hoped, cooperation he would receive in Cherbourg. He sent a request to Admiral Augustin Dupouy, admiral of the port, asking that he have time for his hull and boilers to be repaired. Recently appointed to the position, Dupouy was not about to make that decision on his own. He kicked it to higher-ups in Paris.

Two days later, on June 13, when Semmes had still not received a reply, he went ashore to pay a call on the French admiral. Dupouy tried to explain that France was not as receptive to the possibility of Southern independence as it may have once been and was now more sensitive to Confederate ships visiting its ports, in its territories as well as the homeland. As a lawyer and by now a seasoned diplomat with foreign authorities, Semmes grasped the nuances: The tide had turned against the South and France was not going to get caught aiding the losing side.

He returned to the *Alabama* and pondered his next move. The captain's initial plan had been to dry-dock his ship for at least a month, maybe two, and give it a complete overhaul. Well before the summer's end the *Alabama* would be back in action, scourge of the sea once more. However, what if the response from Paris was that even the most basic repairs could not be done? And there was another dilemma—his crew. Attempting to keep them on board could become too volatile a situation. But giving them shore leave in Cherbourg could mean half of them would disappear. Many of them had been at sea for far too long, and more than a few had discerned the *Alabama*'s fortunes were declining. "Fortunes" indeed—the men had seen next to nothing of the promised prize money.

And Semmes had to take a calculating look at himself. In three months, he would be fifty-five years old. Most captains were retired by then or confined to shore duty, not at the helm of their country's most famous ship and one that had logged so many miles in all kinds of climates no less. And he was ill: He had picked up some kind of bug during the *Alabama*'s recent travels and could not get rid of the fever and chills. As much as he loved his cause and his ship, Semmes could have willingly turned both over to another captain to continue the *Alabama*'s journey. But Cherbourg was certainly not full of Confederate Navy officers waiting for assignments.

He may have assumed that there was more time to resolve at least some of the vexing issues while waiting to hear from Paris. But then word began to spread—a Union warship was approaching. A ship that crossed the Channel from Dover had docked in Cherbourg and brought news of a Yankee vessel named *Kearsarge* and that it could arrive as soon as the following day.

When Semmes heard of this, he summoned Lieutenant Kell to his cabin immediately. Whatever the *Alabama* did, it would have to be done without delay.

18

On the final day of May, the *Kearsarge* had cruised into Flushing, Holland, for some minor repairs to the engines. Winslow was also curious: On his way, he had sailed by Calais again, and it appeared that the peripatetic *Rappahannock* was off-loading its coal, not preparing for sea. *What could that be about?* he wondered. He was hoping to get ashore and get some news or perhaps a telegram.

There was no news awaiting him, but a telegram did arrive about a week later once Winslow's presence in Flushing was known. It was, again, from Ambassador Dayton in Paris. It was not information he had been expecting at all, but what he read made his heart leap. He said nothing but immediately turned to the officer of the deck.

"Sound the gun. Quickly."

Sounding a deck gun, probably the Parrot, with powder and no charge, was a signal for the crew to return to the ship. Many of the men were on liberty in Flushing. No doubt the boom would be heard all over the city.

"Now send for Mr. Cushman."

The chief engineer came scampering up the gangway from below and jogged across the deck to where Winslow stood.

"You called for me, sir?" Cushman saluted smartly but coughing.

"Yes, Mr. Cushman. Get up a full head of steam as quickly as you can."

Detecting what he thought was an uncharacteristically wry smile on Winslow's face, Cushman inquired, "Yessir. Right away. Have you had news?"

"Indeed. I'll tell you when we're away."

Shaking off their various leisure pursuits, the crew came running, in clumps and knots. With surprising alacrity, everyone was accounted for and the *Kearsarge* loosened her lines and pulled away from the quay. She chugged upriver, gathering way, and soon poked her bowsprit into open water.

Three miles from shore, with the crew still wondering where they were headed in such a hurry, Winslow had the duty boatswain muster the men on deck amidships. The captain came out of his cabin and strode to the gathered throng. He pulled out the telegram he had received.

"Men, this telegram is from Minister Dayton, in Paris. He has informed me that the *Alabama* is in port at Cherbourg. We are to go there and wait."

The entire crew erupted in spontaneous cheers. They knew exactly what this news meant: If the *Kearsarge* could get there in time, they could bottle up the most elusive and most dreaded of their targets—at long last. If they poured on the coal and could gather a speed of at least ten knots, they would be there in under two days. First, however, a quick dash to Dover, to pick up the mail, more coal, and fire off a message to Captain George Preble,[78] commander of the USS *St. Louis*, whom Winslow knew to be in Gibraltar. *St. Louis*, a sloop of war with twenty-four

---

78 Nephew of the famous Commodore Edward Preble and granduncle to Lieutenant Edward Preble of the USS *Kearsarge*.

guns, could be of help if she could join up with *Kearsarge* in time. As a pure sailing ship, the *St. Louis* was not going to be of much value in chasing a steamer, but she could sit on one of the two entrances to Cherbourg while the *Kearsarge* guarded the other.

On the way down to Cherbourg the crew was a beehive of activity. They were going to make all preparations possible for battle and they also wanted their ship to look polished and perfect in front of their archenemy. The *Kearsarge* arrived off the Cherbourg breakwater on the afternoon of June 14. She slid slowly through the eastern entrance and within a boat-length of her nemesis. At long last, the two rivals were nearly hull to hull. The crews of each ship lined up along their respective rails to take a long, hard, silent look at one another. There was no cheering or jeering from either crew.

The *Kearsarge* slowed to a stop but did not anchor. She simply launched a gig and sent two of her officers ashore to present the ship's papers to the port captain. Once these formalities were complete, the *Kearsarge* steamed slowly out of the harbor by the western entrance and took up a position on blockade.

Upon the occasion of these two great ship rivals finally meeting one another Captain John Ellicott wrote: "What were the feelings of the two commanders, Semmes and Winslow?— shipmates, messmates, and roommates in a previous war, in which each had won commendation for brave deeds. In that war they had fought side by side with all the ardor of youth; now, in the maturity of years and experience, they had come together again, grim if not bitter opponents in a far more stupendous conflict, duelists as equally equipped as such can ever be in naval warfare. Each was familiar with the other's characteristics. Semmes knew that he would be blockaded with ceaseless vigilance; Winslow felt sure that his opponent would ultimately fight his way out rather than be smothered in a hole."

What next? Winslow would not have long to wait. The very same day, June 14, Captain Semmes sent a note to the local Con-

PHIL KEITH WITH TOM CLAVIN

federate consul that read, in part, "I desire to say to the U.S. Consul that my intention is to fight the *Kearsarge* as soon as I can make the necessary arrangements. I hope these will not detain me more than until tomorrow evening, or after the morrow morning at the furthest. I beg she will not depart before I am ready to go out."

A copy of Semmes's note was promptly forwarded to Winslow on June 15. *So, there it is, then*, Winslow mused. The note even elicited a chuckle between Winslow and Thornton when they read the part about begging them to stay. They were not leaving—even if it meant that Semmes might send them to the bottom of the English Channel. Winslow did not bother to respond to Semmes. He did not feel he needed to do so as the terms seemed to be set.

Let's get on with it, he thought.

19

By the time the *Alabama*'s first officer entered the captain's cabin, Raphael Semmes had already made his decision. What the captain decided to do would be done, of course, but it would be of great help if Kell was in agreement.

Upon his arrival, the lieutenant was invited to sit. He could not help but observe and admire the dozens of captured chronometers, a collection fit for a museum. Semmes then informed him that he intended to fight the *Kearsarge*. Kell knew of the Confederate Navy Department's directive not to voluntarily engage with Union warships, but at that moment it mattered more that the captain—as he was apparently disposed to do—outline his reasons for going against policy.

The first obvious reason was that the *Alabama* was running out of time. Most likely, the *Kearsarge* was just one of several Yankee gunboats in European waters. Thanks to the telegraph, word had spread rapidly of the *Alabama*'s presence in Cherbourg. As of that day the only ship on the *Alabama*'s horizon was the *Kearsarge*, but in a few days that could change, and Semmes would be reliving the blockade of the *Sumter*.

Another reason: By now, with no definitive word from Paris, Semmes expected that he would wait in vain for permission to do the extensive repairs his ship required. The *Alabama* might have to find a more accommodating reception in Spain or perhaps Italy, and the sooner the better.

There was yet another reason: The *Alabama* was the undefeated champion of the high seas. Semmes knew there was a reputation and aura about her that intimidated the officers and crews of other vessels, even warships. Every Union captain was aware of the battering given to the *Hatteras*. Semmes knew his former shipmate John Winslow was unlikely to be intimidated, but the Rebel captain believed his ship, even in its deteriorated condition, could beat the *Kearsarge*.

On this last point, Kell expressed doubts. He reminded his skipper of the faulty fuses and damp gunpowder. In a sea battle at that point, the *Alabama* really did not know her true capabilities. For the first time since the *Hatteras* almost eighteen months ago, the *Alabama* would be confronting a ship that could more effectively fight back. *Kearsarge* had at least as many guns of equal caliber. Another factor had become increasingly clear: The Confederate ship had lost speed. Two years ago, it could have outmaneuvered any Union ship of similar size. What if the *Kearsarge* could sail rings around her?

Semmes dug in his heels. He was certain his ship had enough left to win a fair fight. And there was pride involved. While it might be prudent to try to flee today to prey upon more Union shipping tomorrow, the captain did not want to risk losing a reputation while trying to run from the enemy. After years of selfless service to the Confederacy, Semmes did not want his legacy to contain a hint of cowardice. Better to die in battle, if it came to that.

Kell could not disagree with that. And he had his pride too, not only as an officer but as the first lieutenant of a renowned warship. No one, including the captain, had spent more time on board the *Alabama* since it had begun its global journey in August 1862. Accepting the fate of being blockaded and sidelined until the end of the war was out of the question. It was essentially fight now or surrender. And his ship, Kell believed, could thrash any Yankee vessel.

So, when Semmes affirmed his decision to engage the *Kearsarge* and ordered the *Alabama* cleared for action, Kell did not hesitate. Kell knew his fellow officers would not do so either. Semmes also sent Kell off to search for any better fuses, shells, and powder that might be available for purchase.

The captain had correspondence to attend to. He had already composed and sent off letters to John Slidell,[79] the Confederate States of America's chief representative in France, and Samuel Barron,[80] the flag officer commanding Confederate Navy forces in Europe, such as they were. Semmes had informed them of the *Alabama*'s arrival in Cherbourg and detailed the repairs his ship would need. And as a poignant conclusion to the letter to Barron, Semmes had written, "As for myself, my health has suffered so much from a constant and harassing service of three years, almost continually at sea, that I shall have to ask for relief."

However, all of that became moot once the *Kearsarge* appeared. Semmes wrote another letter to Barron informing him of his new plan of action and, of course, that this was not the time to be relieved of duty. He wrote out a requisition for coal, knowing that keeping his wheezing boilers supplied would be necessary in a battle. He alerted Dupouy that the *Alabama* would not be remaining in Cherbourg for repairs. The port admiral promptly replied that this was just as well because the govern-

---

79 Slidell (1793–1871) was a native New Yorker who moved to Louisiana and became an active promoter of states' rights and secession. He had been a senator from Louisiana before the Civil War.

80 Barron (1809–1888) was a U.S. Navy officer until Virginia seceded from the Union in 1861. He was offered a commission in the Confederate Navy as a commander and was sent to Europe (England, at first) to supervise Confederate shipbuilding activities. He became the senior Confederate Navy officer in Europe in 1863. After the war he returned to Virginia and became a farmer.

ment had decided not to allow a "belligerent ship" to take advantage of France's neutrality.

And then there was the most important message to write. At his desk in his cabin, Semmes once more put pen to paper. "Sir," he began, and after a businesslike preliminary, he continued with the note that became the challenge to the *Kearsarge*. The gauntlet had been thrown down, and Semmes finished with: "I have the honor to be, very respectfully, your obedient servant, R. Semmes, Captain."

He had the challenge note delivered to the American consul in Cherbourg, as we have related, and the note was forwarded to Winslow on the *Kearsarge*. Semmes had no doubt of this and was not perturbed when there was no response. He would not have responded either.

It was time, without delay, to complete the necessary arrangements for battle. Semmes believed he would win the contest with the *Kearsarge*, but to be on the safe side he made a wrenching decision and had his collection of chronometers removed from his cabin. All through the journeys of the *Sumter* and then the *Alabama*, these had been his prizes and symbols of his success as a captain. To part with them was very difficult but he did not hesitate to have the chronometers transferred to the *Hornet*, a merchant ship under the command of a Captain Hewitt. He promised to transport them to Liverpool for safekeeping should the battle go against the *Alabama*.[81]

There were financial matters to finalize: Remaining in Semmes's possession were four sacks of gold sovereigns, worth about $25,000, and a sealed package containing the ransom bonds of the vessels the *Alabama* had captured then released.

---

81 Hewitt did sail the chronometers safely to Liverpool. Semmes never saw them again and they were eventually sold off at auction. The proceeds were to be paid out to the surviving *Alabama* crew; however, the crew had scattered. Semmes never saw any money from the sale. It's likely that most if not all the proceeds went into Captain Hewitt's pockets which, after all, might be fair since he took the risk of protecting the clocks and spiriting them away: the spoils of war.

The captain still hoped that the bonds would be redeemed for cash which the Confederacy could undoubtedly use. The coin sacks and bond package were delivered to Mssr. A. Bonfils, the Confederate States' agent stationed in Cherbourg. Accompanying them was the paymaster's last payroll.

Semmes was relieved when his request for fuel was approved, and on the 15th the coaling process began. Kell kept the crew busy preparing for battle—cleaning the guns, stacking the ammunition within easy reach, making sure pistols and rifles were ready, and sharpening cutlasses. Antonio Bartelli, who served as Semmes's steward, expressed his confidence by polishing glasses that would be used to toast victory. But a disturbing note was that Kell's search for replacement powder, shot, and fuses proved to be fruitless, meaning the *Alabama* would have to go into the fight with what she had on board.

Before retiring on the night of the 15th, Semmes wrote in his diary, "My crew seems to be in the right spirit, a quiet spirit of determination pervading both officers and men. The combat will no doubt be contested and obstinate; but the two ships are so equally matched, I do not feel at liberty to decline it. God defend the right and have mercy upon the souls of those who fall, as many of us must!"

During the daytime hours, crowds gathered in an area of the docks where the *Alabama* could best be observed at its mooring. Word had spread throughout Cherbourg and its surroundings that there was to be a mano a mano duel on the sea between the Union and Confederate warships. As mundane as the onboard preparations and the coaling operation were, there was still a sense of spectacle about them. Here in the form of a ship was one of the gladiators about to go out into the watery arena. It could return the champion, or it could not return at all. The *Alabama* was already world-famous, and, many believed, it was about to begin its greatest adventure of all.

A few such musings may have crossed the captain's mind, but

Semmes could not indulge in them. There was too much to do. This included not taking on volunteers who had offered to serve on the *Alabama*—who knew what their true loyalties were— and refusing visitors. People wanted to tour the *Alabama* like it was a theater readying a new production. One would-be visitor was Evan Jones, the skipper of a yacht named the *Deerhound*. It too had been built by the Laird company and was owned by an Englishman, John Lancaster, who with his family was to end their European vacation in Cherbourg and sail home. Jones was turned away, but he and Semmes would meet soon.

On Saturday, June 18, with most preparations complete, Semmes took a risk: He granted his crew liberty. He believed it was the right thing to do for the long-suffering sailors and officers, but he had to fear that a few—or more—would not return to the *Alabama*. How appealing was it to serve both on a ship and for a cause in decline, and on top of that, to go into a battle where a cannonball could turn a man into bloody rags? Then again, the crew would be lionized on shore; and, indeed, after the crew members left the ship and strode across the docks, they were cheered by the growing crowd drawn to catch glimpses of the two combatants, the *Alabama* moored in the harbor and the *Kearsarge* anchored just outside. Some of the crowd were quick enough to follow sailors to the nearest pubs and buy drinks. How could men leave such a reception behind and defect or disappear?[82]

Semmes and his officers remained on board. For Lieutenant Kell, a virtually empty ship was the best opportunity for

---

82 Back in Virginia, this date also saw the end of the four-day Second Battle of Petersburg, which extended Southern resistance. The battle consisted of repeated assaults by Union forces against substantially smaller forces commanded by General P. G. T. Beauregard. Beauregard's strong defensive positions and poorly coordinated actions by the Union generals made up for the disparity in the sizes of the armies. By the 18th, the arrival of significant reinforcements from Robert E. Lee's army made further assaults impractical. The failure of the Union to defeat the Confederates in these actions resulted in the start of the ten-month Siege of Petersburg.

a thorough inspection. The crew had prepared well for battle. There was nothing further to be done, and this he reported to his captain.

Sometime that day, John Lancaster and his wife and four children had arrived in Cherbourg and boarded the *Deerhound*. The family voted not to set off for England right away but to remain to witness the battle that everyone in the city was talking about. Lancaster had no enmity for the Union, but he would be rooting for the *Alabama*, seeing as how it was something of a sister ship to his own. He and his family could not have imagined how important that relationship would be the next day.

That evening on the *Alabama*, Semmes invited his officers to a meeting. In the cramped cabin he looked Kell, Sinclair, Wilson, and the others in the eye and saluted each man. There was silence as no doubt the men did not feel confident about keeping emotions in check while speaking. Finally, the captain addressed them: "Gentlemen, tomorrow we fight the *Kearsarge*. Only the good God knows what the outcome will be. Thus far, He has shielded us. I believe He still watches over us. I have taken this responsibility alone. It was the only way out with honor. If I have done wrong, if I fail, the fault will be mine. The *Alabama*'s record speaks for itself. You can be proud of it. It is my intention, with God's help, and yours, to sink or capture the *Kearsarge*."

The officers muttered and nodded their agreement. The captain informed them that he would have a chest brought to shore containing some of his valuables and that they might want to make use of it too. The lawyer in Semmes could not help advising them it would be prudent to write up and also put into the chest their last will and testament. Finally, with one more look at the men who had served him so well, especially his first officer, the captain ended the gathering.

The next day was Sunday. It would be impossible to attend services. But to the devout Catholic captain, an impending battle was not an adequate excuse to avoid worship altogether. Semmes left his ship—by this time of night, the crowd had dispersed—and after a stroll of a few minutes came upon a small church. He walked quietly down the aisle and entered a pew near to the altar. For close to an hour he prayed, then he returned to the *Alabama*.

A surprise greeted him there—his entire crew had returned. Semmes couldn't be sure if every single sailor was back, but clearly his ship was near if not at its full complement. And they were sober, or startlingly close to it. They had done their captain a great honor by following not his order but his request. Once again that night, Semmes saluted. The watch was set, and the rest of the crew and officers retired. Bring on the *Kearsarge*.

20

Though Captain Semmes claimed his officers and crew were ready for action, the *Alabama* remained at the dock on Sunday morning. She was observed taking on more coal—so much coal, in fact, that she was lying exceptionally low in the water. Winslow, no fool, knew exactly what Semmes was doing: He was packing the ship with as much coal as possible to reduce her profile against Winslow's guns and to better protect her engines. The coal was stored amidships on the *Alabama*, against both sides of the hull and surrounding the boilers. The extra weight might make her a bit slower, but she was better protected at the waterline, which is where Winslow was sure to aim his powerful Dahlgrens.

Was this tactic also a counter to the *Kearsarge*'s chain mail "armor"? Concerning this, there has been considerable controversy. After the battle, Semmes cried "foul" at the news that Winslow had girded his ship's midsection in chains. Semmes felt it had been "ungentlemanly." There is ample evidence, however, that Semmes knew exactly what Winslow had done.

Ellicott reports the following: "The port admiral [of Cherbourg] manifested a fellow feeling and interest…by informing Semmes, a day or two before the fight, that an officer detailed to visit the *Kearsarge* in the offing had reported the fact of the chain armor arranged on the ship… Semmes knew all about it and could have adopted the same scheme. It was not his election to do so."

Semmes had plenty of chain aboard the *Alabama* too. He could have done the same as Winslow. Semmes never indicated, in any subsequent writings, why he did not. Perhaps the best explanation is that he felt the extra coal would do as well. Another explanation was put forward in subsequent years by his supporters, who contended Semmes viewed the chain as an artificial and ungallant ploy.

The *Kearsarge* had received an unexpected guest the day before: William Dayton Jr., son of the ambassador and himself second secretary of the American legation in Paris. Young Dayton was carrying a note from his father for Captain Winslow. He had taken a train from Paris and hired a boat in Cherbourg to take him out to the *Kearsarge*—but only after promising the French port commander that he would return, and not join the *Kearsarge*'s crew. Young Dayton also brought with him a large basket of fresh figs—a gift for Captain Winslow.

Ambassador Dayton's note expressed the hope that Winslow would not engage the *Alabama* inside the three-mile territorial offshore zone. Dayton felt it best that Winslow conduct the fight even farther out, perhaps six or seven miles offshore. He need not have worried. That was already part of Winslow's thinking.

Dayton left the *Kearsarge* with Winslow's assurances. He did not immediately return to Paris, however: He, too, wanted to stick around and see the battle, at least from shore. The crowd there had grown even larger.

After Dayton departed, Winslow had called a meeting of his officers. He polled all of them concerning their feelings about the coming contest. Every single one voiced the opinion that once the *Alabama* engaged them, they would not surrender. They would fight to the last man and "if need be, go down with the colors flying."

As Saturday had progressed, more people began streaming into the town of Cherbourg. Every hotel room was booked. Homeowners took in strangers for a fee. Even some haystacks in barns were rented out. The headlands surrounding the harbor offered a view far out to sea—if the weather would cooperate.

Meanwhile, the *Kearsarge* steamed slowly back and forth guarding the harbor's dual entrances. She was easily within view of the many cliffside onlookers.

Sunday had dawned bright and cloudless. All who would watch from the shore would be afforded an unobstructed and perfect view. The temperature would be mild, with a slight westerly breeze. An exact count was not taken but eyewitness reports from the observers who wrote accounts of that day indicate that there were thousands of excited onlookers. For these French citizens, the civil war in America of over three years' duration was about to be played out in front of them. With luck, the victor in this contest would presage the winner of the war.

The crowd started to stake out the best viewing spots along the bluffs right after dawn. Blankets were spread, umbrellas popped, picnic baskets opened, and champagne began flowing. Vendors appeared out of nowhere hawking all sorts of pastries, hot coffee or tea, sandwiches, and ices. The crowd could easily spot the long sleek black Union ship that prowled offshore. Her sails were neatly stowed. A thin, grayish plume of smoke trailed steadily from her single stack.

As the first beams of sunlight touched the steeples of Cherbourg, the *Kearsarge* had chugged slowly through a light chop three miles out, making large, lazy circles. Small whitecaps dotted an otherwise wine-dark sea. A cool air mass pressed down from on high creating an offshore breeze of about ten knots. The yards creaked as the *Kearsarge* heeled to port ever so slightly on her northerly track, then did the same as she reversed her helm and made turns back south. Occasional cinders sparkled from her stack as the day expanded. Below, the crew not on watch rocked in their hammocks. Some sailors slept soundly, but many others were already awake, gripped by anticipation.

Captain Winslow, who had been awake for hours, paced the quarterdeck. Morning dew glistened on his oilskin coat and fog droplets formed on the bill of his cap. As usual, his latent fevers, from his torpid days on the Mississippi, plagued him. His blinded eye was throbbing again. His blood raced and his heart pounded. He was not a well man, but that day he knew he would be able to push all of that aside.

Semmes, his old comrade, had indicated he needed only to lay on some coal and then he would come out. That was five days ago. Winslow's patience was wearing thin. He was trying to quell an urge to steam into the anchorage, glide up to the *Alabama*, and blast her to pieces right there at the dock. Winslow knew that in doing so, he would cause an international incident, but he was beginning not to care.

At 6:00 a.m., the crew of the *Kearsarge* was rousted out by Ham Fat's drum roll. On that day, no man had to be told twice. Each sailor donned their Sunday best uniforms and then quietly began to go about their duties.

It was typical aboard *Kearsarge* that twelve to fifteen men gathered in a "mess group," and this was done promptly at 7:00 a.m. Each gang designated one of their own to draw the rations for a meal and act as cook—a duty that was frequently switched around, some lasting much longer than others, depending on their culinary skills. Ham Fat prepared the captain's food, which Winslow sometimes shared with his officers. The rest of the wardroom had their own mess. The senior petty officers ate with one group of sailors or another. The marines had their own mess too.

That morning Ham Fat doled out hot biscuits, sliced ham,

fresh figs, and the very rare treat of hard-boiled eggs to Winslow and Thornton. Some figs found their way to the various crew messes, as did the balance of the preserved ham. Mostly, the fare was fresh-baked biscuits and a porridge made from dried oats and desiccated apples. There was plenty of food to go around since the captain did not want his crew fighting on an empty stomach. Plus, no one knew when the next meal would show up—if at all. The experienced hands ate with gusto. Many of the new men did not eat at all, or hardly. The nervous anticipation of real combat curbed some appetites.

On the *Alabama* that morning, Captain Raphael Semmes could survey the deck of his ship with great satisfaction. As expected, his first officer had done well in preparing the *Alabama* for a fight. The crew had cleaned her up, including scrubbing the brass work, and Lieutenant Kell, preparing for any eventuality, had ordered sand strewn around the guns on the deck to make footing less slippery and, if or when it came to that, to absorb blood. The crew wore their Sunday outfits with the exception of the gun crews who, expecting fast and furious action, had not donned shirts. It was told to Semmes soon after he appeared on deck that down below the surgeons and their assistants had their instruments cleaned and ready for use.

It was also reported to Semmes by Kell that there had been a visitor to the *Alabama* that morning. A French naval officer had been rowed over from the *Couronne* to say that he had been instructed to report that his ship would sail along with the Confederate cruiser until it was outside the three-mile limit to make sure international law was observed. He and Kell had saluted each other, then the officer returned to the *Couronne*.

There were other preparations that Semmes thought could give his ship an advantage. One was he had had the port guns moved to the starboard battery, his plan being to fire first with this enhanced starboard firepower, damage the *Kearsarge* as much as possible, and draw near to board her. Because of concerns about the effectiveness of the fuses and gunpowder, Semmes wanted to avoid a prolonged duel that would require numerous broadsides. Also, when coaling, he had overfilled (as Winslow had observed), even to having coal piled around the boilers. This would indeed offer more protection to these essential machines and mean the *Alabama* rode lower in the water and thus was a smaller target.

There was, of course, still a chance Winslow might not engage. But what reason could Captain Winslow have to make *Kearsarge* veer away when the Confederate warship left the Cherbourg harbor? The *Alabama* was the top prize Winslow had sought since he took command. Anything less than outright victory could ruin his career as well as be a fresh embarrassment to the North.

At 8:30 on the *Kearsarge*, with the morning meal complete and the dishes washed and stowed, the crew worked on their final pre-battle tasks: cutlasses were sharpened, pistols made ready, and the marines cleaned their rifles. A first round was carefully loaded in every chamber. No one knew if a boarding party would be called or if there might be a need to repel boarders, but the crew would be prepared for either scenario. Gunners sorted out their shots and shells and the powder monkeys carefully placed buckets of water near all the guns in case they were needed to douse any fires. Every cannon was loaded with a shell and primed.

Then, the waiting began. Would there even be a battle that day? Despite the bravado of Captain Semmes, no one really knew if he was bluffing. Perhaps this whole exercise would turn into nothing more than another standoff, like those the crew had experienced with the *Sumter*, *Florida*, and *Rappahannock*. Men with pipes were told they could not smoke them. There was too much powder and loose ammunition on deck.

The temperature began rising, and the heat beat down on the men and the freshly holystoned deck. There was little chatter.

The predominant sound was the sea swishing down the sides of the *Kearsarge* as she prowled back and forth.

There was no reason for further delay. Finally, Semmes gave the order. Moments later the *Alabama* was under light steam power and gliding through the harbor. He could see not just the *Kearsarge* beyond the entrance to Cherbourg but the *Couronne* too, ready to escort the Rebel raider beyond the three-mile limit. Also, on the move through the harbor was the *Deerhound*. Captain Jones would keep a safe distance while providing the Lancaster family with a good view of the action.

As the *Alabama* departed Cherbourg, its officers and crew could see the tops of buildings and nearby hills lined with those people who hoped to witness a unique event.

Whatever was to happen, the captain of the Southern ship aimed to be the best-dressed participant. Just before the trip away from the French city had begun, Semmes had gone below. He returned wearing his best and hardly ever worn Confederate States of America uniform, the gold epaulettes and brass buttons shining in the strong June sunlight. The captain had even allowed his steward, Bartelli, to wax his mustache. As the *Alabama* moved through the harbor in an almost stately way, those with sharp eyes on shore noted the proud captain's outfit and posture.

When it passed the berth of the French warship *Napoleon*, the *Alabama* was treated to three cheers. The French frigate's band followed this up by the closest it could get to playing "Dixie." As Arthur Sinclair recorded, "We were surprised and gratified. It was much appreciated by us, and no doubt stirred our brave lads to the centre."

At the same time, Captain Winslow slowly paced the quarter-deck of the *Kearsarge*. His head was down, hands clasped behind his back, his brow deeply furrowed. *What do we do if he does not come out today? Where is the damn* St. Louis? *What will Welles do with me if I let another raider elude my grasp?*

Lieutenant Commander Thornton quietly approached his

captain, trying not to overly disturb his private thoughts. As he drew close, he cleared his throat and whispered to his leader, "It's time, sir."

"Very good, Mr. Thornton."

Per Sunday tradition, all the crew not performing critical tasks would fall in on the main deck in their very best uniforms to hear the Bible read by the captain, maybe a homily, and hopefully a few words on the situation they were facing. Winslow took his customary position between the two long rows of his officers and sailors who were lined up port and starboard, stiffly at attention. Nearly all his crew were there. Two engineers were below deck, maintaining *Kearsarge*'s head of steam and a gang of coal shovelers were feeding the furnaces. The normal deck watch was posted and alert.

Winslow cleared his throat and began, "At ease, men. Today I want to read to you a few passages from…"

"Cap'n!" a bosun positioned high above the main deck cried out from his mizzen mast perch, "She's a-comin! She's comin' out!"

It was as if a bolt of Saint Elmo's fire had been shot through the crew. Every man stiffened, waiting for the command to "Take stations!"

Winslow slapped his Bible shut and handed it to Thornton. "My glass!" he barked.

The captain's yeoman ran to the fo'c'sle, grabbed his chief's spyglass, and dashed back to his commander's side.

Winslow strode to the port rail and lifted the powerful brass and optical instrument to his one good eye and peered at a large vessel, belching gray smoke, steaming out of the mouth of the harbor. He could not resist declaring, "And so there you are, you bastard. At last!"

The crew, overhearing, broke into wild cheers, waved their hats, and jumped up and down in place. They were on a hair trigger, some on tiptoes even, waiting for the captain's next command.

He lowered his glass, turned to his exec, and said, simply, "Battle stations, Mr. Thornton."

All Thornton had to do was turn to the crew and yell, "Go!"

Every sailor knew his place, and the mass of men dissolved into a wild scramble for their assigned posts. Some dashed to the engine room, others headed for the guns. Loaders began sweating in the ammunition lockers hauling out more shot and shell. The surgeon and his staff prepared a medical station in the wardroom, laying out battle dressings and bone saws. Hospital stewards began spreading sand around the guns to soak up the blood that was bound to be shed. The gunners' mates grabbed rammers, lanyards, spongers, and firelocks. Stokers shoved more coal into the fires and the engineers hefted rags and oilcans. Landsmen, seamen, and powder monkeys distributed powder bags, round shot, and shells. The marines positioned their rifles, grappling hooks, pistols, and even cutlasses while also taking over the forward Parrot gun.

As every man settled in, the hard-charging shape of the *Alabama* grew larger. She had a bone in her teeth, and she was headed straight for the *Kearsarge*.

"Helmsman!" Winslow shouted. "Point her out to sea!"

Winslow would not fight this battle in French territorial waters. He would take a position six miles out, then turn and face the enemy. He was a cautious man, a careful man. Thirty-seven years in the navy, many of them at sea, had taught him that preparation and practice beat daring and impetuosity. He would make sure his men were fully ready, then reverse course and head straight for his old friend and former shipmate, with every intention of blowing him and his cursed ship to kingdom come.

21

It was quite the procession: Trailing the Confederate warship was the French Navy ironclad *Couronne*, trailing farther behind her were two French pilot boats, and bringing up the rear was the yacht *Deerhound*.

On the headlands and walls of the breakwaters the spectators—most of them partial to the daring *Alabama*—cheered when Winslow turned the *Kearsarge* out to sea. Many of them thought the Union warship was already fleeing. Such, of course, was not the case. Winslow was only trying to get more sea room in which to fight.

At 10:45,[83] the Union warship neared a point nearly six miles out from the coast. Winslow ducked into his cabin for a few minutes. When he reemerged, Thornton noted with some amusement that the captain had exchanged his Sunday-best dress hat for his old, weather-beaten, salt-encrusted sea cap. He held his

---

83 All times are approximate, but certainly within sixty minutes of being the true local time on June 19. Participants' accounts vary slightly as to the exact times of the day's major events due to the lack of accuracy of the chronometers of the day. Winslow's "10:45" might be Semmes's "10:42," or William Dayton Jr.'s "10:57," etc.

speaking trumpet[84] in his right hand and he had strapped on his standard-issue navy pistol. It was clear the captain was ready to engage in a fight.

Winslow climbed atop a sea chest on the quarterdeck, well aft and close to the starboard bulwarks. This would be where he remained throughout the action. The position was an ideal one for the commanding officer. With half his body above the rail, he had a perfect view of his adversary, and was himself in plain view of the helmsman and the men at the batteries. Within easy range of his voice were the quartermaster at the wheel, the officer at the engine bell, and the officers directing the fire of the guns.

Winslow's first order, shouted across the deck, was, "Helmsman! Shift your wheel!"

"Aye, aye, captain," came the reply from Quartermaster William Poole. The large double wheel positioned amidships spun rapidly, putting the *Kearsarge* nearly on her beam ends. When she had completed that 180-degree turn, she came up and was pointed straight at the *Alabama*.

"Steady up! Put us on her stern!" It was clear the captain wanted to slip behind the *Alabama*, cross her stern and rake her with the *Kearsarge*'s starboard guns. The big Dahlgrens had already been pivoted to starboard for that very purpose.

"Engineering! Pour it on!"

Third Assistant Engineer Henry McConnell, stationed at the engine companionway, rang up the bell for full power and full speed ahead. Below, Chief Engineer Cushman answered as directed and bellowed to his coal heavers to stoke both furnaces to the max. Second Assistant Engineer William Badlam opened both boilers wide. The *Kearsarge* shuddered, then leaped forward. Cinders flew skyward and deep gray smoke belched from the stack. Fortunately, the west wind pushed the choking smoke to port, away from the guns and the captain.

---

84 A short megaphone which could amplify and better direct the captain's voice over the sounds of battle.

With both ships on a collision course, the closing speed was almost twenty-five knots, a frantic speed for those times.

By then, the *Alabama* was a full seven miles outside Cherbourg—both the *Couronne* and *Deerhound* had dropped behind. Semmes saw the *Kearsarge* come about. Obviously, Winslow had determined this was far enough. And no sense taking a chance the Rebel ship would catch a sudden wind and with full sails take off for another neutral European port.

This seemed an appropriate time for the crew to hear from their captain, and Semmes did not disappoint. After mustering all of the ship's company on the deck, he addressed them: "You have, at length, another opportunity of meeting the enemy—the first that has been presented to you since you sunk the *Hatteras*! In the meantime, you have been all over the world, and it is not too much to say that you have destroyed, and driven for protection under neutral flags, one-half of the enemy's commerce, which at the beginning of the war, covered every sea. This is an achievement of which you may well be proud; and a grateful country will not be unmindful of it. The name of your ship has become a household word wherever civilization extends. Shall that name be tarnished by defeat? The thing is impossible!"

Captain Semmes waited for the cheers to end before continuing: "Remember that you are in the English Channel, the theater of so much of the naval glory of our race, and that the eyes of all Europe are at this moment upon you. The flag that floats over you is that of a young republic, which bids defiance to her enemies, whenever and wherever found. Show the world that you know how to uphold it."

The men dashed back to their stations as the *Kearsarge* closed in. This was it. As Sinclair reflected, "It is the hour of prayer in old England; and many a petition is now going up to the God of battle and of mercy for these brave fellows, many of them about to embrace their watery winding-sheets."

At the distance of a mile the *Alabama* showed the Yankees her starboard side and let loose with a crashing volley. The breeze swept smoke across the deck. The battle had commenced. It was nearing 11:00 a.m.

Through their telescopes, Semmes and Kell could not detect any direct hits. The shells appeared to have overshot the enemy. The first mate realized the gunners had overcompensated for the ship's list to that side because of the extra cannon. While they attempted to make the necessary adjustments the *Kearsarge* drew closer. At a thousand yards, she opened fire.

With the *Alabama* bringing her starboard broadside to bear, Winslow's plan to cut across his opponent's stern and rake her went into the wind. With both ships then favoring the starboard guns, Winslow was forced to fall off slightly to port and then begin a continuous starboard turn to keep his power side against the foe.

The *Alabama*'s Blakely gun had the distance on any gun aboard the *Kearsarge*. Winslow knew this, of course, and as Semmes let fly, Winslow decided he would have to wear his ship ever closer to avoid being pounded by the Blakely before his Dahlgrens got in range.

Both sides began a delicate minuet, tracing circles around one another. *Alabama* tried to keep the circle wide, using her superior range while *Kearsarge* attempted to tighten the circle with each turn, closing the range. Winslow's guns could do more damage than Semmes's could, but only if they got in closer to do it.

Alabama's first salvo had indeed gone high but had clipped the Union ship's foremast backstay, which snapped like a parted bow string. The 32-pounders let fly seconds later, but the shots were not yet in range and fell short of the *Kearsarge*.

The Union marines fired their Parrot rifle, and a single shot flew toward the *Alabama*. It fell short, too, to the cheers of the Confederate crew, but now the *Kearsarge* had the range: nine hundred yards. The Dahlgrens could be fired.

When *Alabama*'s 32-pounders fired their second volley, Winslow noticed something curious: there seemed to be four puffs of smoke emanating from the *Alabama*'s gun deck, not three from the guns Winslow believed were there. Focusing on the gun ports Winslow saw the snouts of four guns and not three. *Damn! Semmes has shifted one of his guns from port to starboard*, Winslow realized. That would give him a one-gun advantage from any starboard volley.

"Mr. Thornton!" Winslow trumpeted above the din.

The executive officer came running. "Yes, sir?"

"*Alabama* has shifted one of her guns to starboard. Get to the gun deck quickly. Let us do the same—perhaps even two!"

Thornton raced below to the gun deck and ordered Gunner Franklin Graham to shift one of the port-side 32-pounders to a vacant gun port on the starboard side. Thornton tried to shift two guns, in fact, but quickly realized that a fourth gun would interfere with the recoil and reloading of the third gun. Three 32-pounders would have to do. Winslow shouted, "All guns! Open fire!"

The first salvo from the pivot guns fell short and great geysers of water shot up near the *Alabama*. But a high-flying shell, probably from a 32-pounder, sheared off the *Alabama*'s spanker gaff which brought it clattering to the deck still holding the Confederate colors. It was the turn of the *Kearsarge* crew to cheer. Semmes, however, had a backup: a larger flag was ready at the truck of the mizzen mast and the captain ordered it unfurled and run to the top.

Winslow and Thornton both noticed that the *Alabama*'s gunners were firing rapidly—and wildly. Most of their shots were high and way off target.

"Mr. Thornton," the captain ordered, "tell the Dahlgren crews to fire low. Aim for the waterline. I want to punch holes in her hull. Have the other guns rake her decks. Tell them all to take aim, for God's sake. No wild firing!"

From that moment forward, Lieutenant Commander Thornton spent the rest of the action going from one gun crew to another, constantly reminding the men to take their time, aim their guns: "One good shot, boys, aimed well is worth 50 flying high and wide," he kept reminding them.

The *Kearsarge* gunners were using only shells: Winslow wanted the explosive power of a striking shell to create havoc and inflict maximum damage on the *Alabama*. He would switch to solid shot if he could get in close and pound away against his opponent's hull. (Shells had been around a long time, since the fifteenth century, but only recently had they become the modern, rifled projectile favored for long distance use and explosive power after they struck the target. The traditional round shot were typically used in close combat to punch holes in a ship's hull or batter the ship with brute force.)

During the battle, Ham Fat's station was in the captain's galley awaiting orders from his commander. He was not a cowardly soul, but glad to be in one of the safest parts of the ship. With each mighty blast he stuffed another biscuit in his mouth and chewed away.

Below deck, aft, Dr. Browne, with his repertoire of bone saws, sharp scalpels, tourniquets, and bandages, paced nervously while waiting for the inevitable. His steward spread buckets of sand all around Browne's makeshift operating platform, which normally served as the senior officer's dining table. Browne knew the screams of the wounded and the wailing of the dying would come soon enough.

22

As the *Alabama* and *Kearsarge* circled one another, each ship tried to savage the other's stern section. Taking out one of the pivot guns, smashing the rudder, or killing a captain could wound a ship mortally, and Semmes and Winslow were both in exposed positions to better direct their ship's actions.

One of the *Alabama*'s Blakely's fired a 100-pound shell that smashed into the *Kearsarge*'s sternpost. The projectile imbedded itself in the stout timbers surrounding the rudder but inexplicably failed to detonate. Had it gone off, it would have likely destroyed the *Kearsarge*'s ability to maneuver—and that could have been a fatal blow. As it was, the damage done by the shell casing itself bound up the rudder, making it difficult to turn. From that moment forward it would require three sailors on the wheel instead of the usual single helmsman.

By 11:15, the *Alabama* was firing at a rate of about two-to-one compared to the *Kearsarge* guns. The Confederate gunners were working so fast and firing so quickly that many of their shots were errant—and sometimes the necessary steps in loading and firing the guns were either forgotten or ignored. For example, the *Kearsarge* crew was treated to a bizarre sight when they witnessed a round belching out of one of the *Alabama*'s guns preceded by a sponger that had been left in the barrel. The enemy gunners' haste was also evident in that two ramrods were inadvertently fired off, resembling what one sailor later described as "black meteors" as they soared through the air.

Not all the shots were wild, of course. The *Alabama*'s rear pivot gun fired a shell that blasted into and through the bulwarks near the aft pivot gun on the *Kearsarge*. Contact with the side of the ship caused the shell to spin end over end and as soon as it cleared the solid oak it exploded near the big gun.

Ordinary Seaman James McBeth, who had joined the crew in Cádiz in January, lay against the base of the gun with a compound fracture of the left shin. Quarter Gunner John Dempsey, an original *Kearsarge* crewman, struggled to his feet staring wide-eyed at what was left of his right arm. Shrapnel had ripped it to shreds from his tattooed bicep down. Most seriously injured was ship's clown and entertainer, the Ordinary Seaman William Gowin. He lay sprawled on the deck covered in blood, mostly his own. Both his left femur and left tibia were poking through his trousers—horrible double-compound fractures.

McBeth and Dempsey staggered away to find Dr. Browne. Gowin refused all help, telling his mates to stick to their guns. He painfully crawled away on his own to find the doctor.

One deck below, Acting Master David Sumner had command of the 32-pounders. His men were working furiously amidst the blinding smoke and throat-burning cordite residue. The crews on each gun had done good work, especially the Number 1 gun where Seaman Joaquin Pease, stripped to the waist and sweating liberally, was conducting a Herculean effort readying and loading his gun with superior efficiency. All the men were functioning well under trying conditions, but Pease caught Sumner's eye.

Finally, one of the *Alabama*'s better-aimed Blakely shells slammed into the side of the *Kearsarge* amidships, right where the boilers were housed. A great cheer went up from the *Alabama* as Semmes, Kell, and everyone who could see the impact believed they had landed a killing blow. Imagine their amazement when the shell, which did not explode, bounced off and fell harmlessly into the sea.

The round did, however, tear off several batter boards hiding the chains protecting the *Kearsarge*'s vital innards. It was then that the crew of the *Alabama* knew they were not up against an ordinary wooden-hulled ship: They were fighting what amounted to an ironclad.

Another Blakely shell struck in the same area moments later. It, too, did not explode, but did burrow itself into the hull after its energy was partially absorbed by the chains.

By this time, the ships were within five hundred yards of one another, but Winslow wanted to be even closer. He motioned for the helm to take a slightly tighter turn toward his enemy. Earlier in the battle Winslow had given thought to trying to ram the *Alabama*, if he could get in close. He was confident that his prow could stove in the side of his foe and still maintain the structural integrity of the *Kearsarge*. He also wondered about boarding the *Alabama*. He abandoned both thoughts, however, after witnessing the punishment his guns and his crews were dealing out. He was convinced the *Alabama* would soon be nothing more than mangled spars and wreckage.

That was certainly not the view of Captain Semmes. However, he was watching his own plan of charging then boarding the *Kearsarge* fade. Already, it was clear the Union ship was faster in the water and more accurate firing its broadsides than the *Alabama*. The Confederate ship would be turned into splinters before getting within boarding distance. He would have to depend on the aim and resiliency of the *Alabama* gunners and that extra firepower on the starboard side.

The *Kearsarge* was content to do the same. The adversaries continued circling each other, exchanging broadsides. As the minutes passed, the turns contracted until there was only four hundred yards between the two ships. *Alabama* kept blasting away frantically but the *Kearsarge*, though firing more slowly, was firing with more telling effect.

According to the *Alabama*'s executive officer, John Kell, "The 11-inch shells of the *Kearsarge* did fearful work, and her guns were served beautifully, being aimed with precision, and deliberate in fire. She came into action magnificently."

Semmes became puzzled by how little harm was being done to the *Kearsarge*. It did appear, as Kell had ruefully predicted, that some of the Alabama's shells did not explode because of the ineffective fuses and apparently tainted gunpowder. The shells were failing in greater numbers than he had thought possible.

Both captains were making fearful demands on their ships' steam boilers. Observers noted that the smoke billowing out of the *Kearsarge*'s funnel was black, leading a few at first to think the Union ship was on fire. Those more knowledgeable surmised correctly that the smoke spewing from the *Kearsarge* was darker and thus more visible because of the origin of the coal it burned—from Newcastle, whereas in Cherbourg the *Alabama* had taken on coal clawed out of mines in Wales, which burned with a much lighter, grayish hue.

As the ships fought each other, destruction and casualties mounted higher on the *Alabama*. And it became clear the Southern ship was not giving as good as she got. It was not just the dubious quality of the ammunition, but the ability of *Alabama*'s gunners compared to their adversaries.

One of the sailors on the Confederate cruiser was Henry Higgins, who had quite the pedigree as the son of Commander Thomas Higgins of the Royal Navy. In May 1860, at age twenty-three, the younger Higgins joined Her Majesty's Indian Navy in Bombay as an able-bodied seaman. He served for more than three years in the sloop of war *Elphinstone* before being discharged at Bombay in late 1863. It was in Singapore that Higgins signed aboard the *Alabama*. Once at sea, he soon soured on his choice and when the *Alabama* made a stopover at the island of Johanna off the southeast African coast, he and three other crew members deserted. Semmes offered local natives a reward and the men were soon captured and brought back to the ship. The four were demoted to landsmen, forfeited a month's pay, and clapped in irons for two weeks.

As part of his account given a month after the battle, Higgins reported, "We had not a single competent gunner on board, excepting the captain of the forward pivot. He was an old English man-of-war man, trained in the British navy. The captains of the other guns were not competent gunners, though brave men."

At the same time as the *Alabama*'s guns were causing minimal damage, the Dahlgrens on the *Kearsarge* fired true. As those shells struck, shards of wood sliced through the air, shredding the clothes and piercing the flesh of crew members. At times the Union shells hit more directly, as when one struck the *Alabama*'s aft pivot gun and several sailors manning it were killed immediately. Abruptly, the air around the gun was filled with gore, the bloody remnants and rags of what had moments before been men. One of the young officers, Michael Mars, keeping his head if not his breakfast, grabbed a shovel and tossed the gobs of quivering red remains overboard.

"The shell man belonging to our gun crew was cut right in two by one of the *Kearsarge* shots while he was bringing a shell to our gun," recalled Higgins. "His name was James Hart. He was blown all to pieces, and nothing was found of him which could be recognized except the collar of his shirt. Several men were wounded and carried below."

Undeterred by the carnage, the *Alabama* kept firing two shells for every one of the *Kearsarge*. But attrition would soon take its toll. Singly and then in twos, wounded men, some moaning in agony, were brought below to see if Dr. Galt or Assistant Surgeon Llewellyn could do anything for them. But given the conditions below and the state of battlefield medicine in 1864, most of the wounded would die or be permanently maimed.

Semmes now stood on the stern, atop a horse block (a raised step for securing sail sheets). While this made him even more exposed to enemy fire as well as flying shrapnel and splinters, it also provided a better view of the contest. That included the damage being done to his men and his ship. Suddenly, he too was hit—a piece of hot shrapnel struck his right hand. Straight away a quartermaster was at the captain's side, binding the wound and putting his arm in a sling. Given the destruction all around him, Semmes was almost embarrassed by the trivial injury.

It was easy to ignore his own pain given the horrid condition of his ship and crew. As the Confederate captain's eyes swept over the scene before him, it was obvious that the *Kearsarge* was closing in for a finish. The battle was nearing its climax.

23

Below deck on the *Kearsarge*, Chief Engineer Cushman and his gang were doing man-killing work. The roar of their own guns was making them deaf, plus each powerful broadside shoved the ship sideways a few feet. The noise and the vectors rattled the gauges, sloshed the water in the boilers, shook the pipes, and knocked men off their feet. The heat and the coal dust were nearly unbearable. Several pipes sprung leaks that spewed scalding water on the men. It was like being inside a giant, heated tea kettle.

An *Alabama* shell tore off the roof of the engine room, which was covered by a glass skylight. Shards of glass and deadly splinters flew everywhere, but no one was seriously injured. The shell unintentionally alleviated much of the heat and choking dust by opening the engine compartment to the elements, but it did not do any good for the nerves of the men stationed below.

Another shell struck the stack with a loud metallic clang. Cushman thought he had lost his smoke pipe, but when he ran topside to take a better look, he saw that the missile had only punched a three-foot circular hole in his vent.

Farther aft, Dr. Browne was fighting valiantly to save Gowin's life. There was no saving the mangled leg. Both bones were shattered, and pieces had punctured every muscle and the femoral artery. Gowin's life was flowing out of him and onto the sanded deck around Browne's feet. As Gowin shouted fevered encouragement to his shipmates, through his screams of pain, Browne removed the useless leg eight inches from the hip. Browne felt Gowin might survive—if he had not lost too much blood already.

Browne turned next to Dempsey. Here, too, saving the shredded arm was not an option. Browne grabbed his bone saw and cut through the mess near the top of Dempsey's bicep. As soon as he was bandaged, Dempsey requested permission to go back to his gun. Browne said no but he was distracted setting McBeth's fractured ankle and did not see Dempsey slip away to rejoin his mates. When he turned around and saw Dempsey was gone all Browne could think was, *What good is a one-armed gunner?*

Other than cuts, burns, scratches, sprains, splinters, and a few cracked ribs, the injuries to these three men would be the only major casualties of the day aboard the *Kearsarge*. Browne marveled at the relatively small butcher's bill and said a silent prayer of thanks.

On the *Alabama*, Drs. Llewellyn and Galt were also saying prayers—in this case, for the dying. As the battle raged above, more men were being brought below. For most, there was little the surgeons could do. Shrapnel and splinters had made an unholy scarlet mess of bodies. The groans of suffering almost drowned out the noise of the explosions.

In a way, the Confederate raider was groaning too. Shortly after 11:30 a.m., a shell from one of the *Kearsarge*'s Dahlgren cannons struck and broke the *Alabama*'s rudder. This had an immediate impact on steering. Then the ship took a hit at the waterline, where the shell penetrated the engine room and then exploded. Semmes felt the entire ship shudder—the *Alabama* had sustained a mortal wound. He idly noted an *Alabama* shell striking the *Kearsarge* at just below the waterline yet there was no similar damage. By now in the battle, such impotence on the part of the *Alabama*'s ammunition had become all too routine.

Still, the firing from the *Alabama* continued to be frequent though often wild. Two solid shots from *Alabama*'s 32-pounders, fired at about this time, could have done serious damage, except for some incredible providence. One round shot flew directly in the Number 2 starboard gun port of the *Kearsarge* as that crew was reloading—which meant that the gun and the crew were pulled back from the opening. Somehow, the shot missed every sailor and as if it had "eyes" exited through the Number 2 gun port on the port side, splashing harmlessly into the sea. Several Union sailors later reported feeling the "whoosh" and hot air brush them as the round flew by. Seconds later yet another shot came flying through the very same gun port, an amazing and statistically improbable occurrence. This time, though, the shot landed with a thump into a large pile of hammocks the crew had stored to make room for working the guns. The hammocks immediately caught fire.

Second Assistant Engineer Sidney Smith had charge of a fire-fighting crew and one of the two firefighting pumps. The hoses were already primed and ready for use. Within seconds, Smith and his men were on the hammock fire and quickly extinguished it. The gun crews kept up their firing all through the incident, never pausing.

The marines on the foredeck, led by Acting Masters Mate Charles Danforth, had the honor of firing the first shot, for range, at the beginning of the battle. They had been at it hotly ever since. One of their shells entered a port by the *Alabama*'s forward pivot gun. It bounced off that gun's slide rack and exploded. One man's leg was crushed by the flying shell itself, and another sailor was nearly cut in two by shrapnel from the explosion. He expired seconds after spilling guts and gore all around the gun.

The marines' later fire was much less effective, and unlike the other gun crews on the *Kearsarge*, the marines seemed to be exercising much less fire discipline—they were hurried, firing too rapidly, and somewhat wildly. The pivot gun finally overheated and the next shell could not be rammed down the full extent of the tube. If the gun were fired—or if the shell cooked off in the heat—it was entirely possible the barrel would explode. Working frantically, fearing the gun would erupt any second, two of the marine gunners managed to manhandle the shell from the tube.

Aboard the ironclad *Couronne*, several French officers made the astute observation that the gun smoke from the *Kearsarge* was powdery white while the smoke from the *Alabama*'s guns was dark gray or black. Dark smoke could only mean that the gunpowder was not burning completely. It had either deteriorated in storage or was damp, or both. It would also mean that each shot from the *Alabama* was not carrying a complete "punch" equal to its explosive potential.

At the forward pivot gun on the *Kearsarge*, Captain of the Top John Bickford was acting as Number 1 loader. It was his responsibility to get the 100-pound shells into the muzzle of the enormous Dahlgren. It took at least two brawny sailors (like Bickford) to get the shell to the lip of the muzzle, but before that step occurred, the loader had to physically tear off the lead cap to expose the shell's all-important fuse. If the fuse was not exposed, the firing cartridge would not light it when the lanyard was pulled. The fuses were cut or set for various times, such as five or ten seconds (or more if a delayed reaction was desired). Without a lit fuse, the shell became nothing more than a solid shot.

Bickford was careful to remove each lead cap, and he was setting the fuses for five seconds, which at the current range between the *Kearsarge* and the *Alabama* would be the time needed for the shell to be fired, travel the distance, slam into the *Alabama* and explode.

When the guns finally ceased firing, Bickford checked his pockets. He had been mindful to preserve every lead cap that he had pulled. The acting master Wheeler, in charge of the forward pivot, had counted thirty-five rounds fired—a rate of about one shell every two minutes. Bickford pulled all the caps from his pockets. He counted out thirty-five.

At noon, it began to be clear to sharp observers that the battle would not continue much longer. After seven circles around one another the distance between the two great vessels was shrinking. From his perch on the quarterdeck Winslow could see the *Alabama* beginning to slow down and settle in the water. Obviously, great damage had been done.

He pondered his next move. Should he try and ram her, to finish her off? Or should he try and send a boarding party to capture the ship and thereby win a great prize? Nothing would give Winslow more pleasure than accepting Semmes's sword in defeat then towing his battered and vanquished foe back into port.

"Mr. Thornton!" Winslow shouted. "Bring grape to the guns. Maybe we can sweep her decks clean and take her." Grapeshot were shell canisters full of small, round metal balls. When fired (always at close range) they acted like giant shotguns. They were a devastating antipersonnel weapon.

Under Thornton's command, the powder monkeys scurried below and retrieved shells full of grapeshot. They disbursed them to the main and gun decks and laid them near the guns.

All throughout the action, Thornton had made it his particular duty to see to the guns. He circulated among the pieces constantly, encouraging the gunners to take careful aim, make the shots count, and pay no attention to how many rounds were fired—just make them score. He was continually reminding the pivot guns to "aim low." He wanted his big beasts to punch holes in the *Alabama*, below the waterline, and once the gun crews steadied up and got into the rhythm of the action, that is exactly what they did. Thornton also kept the powder, shot, and shells coming, making sure the powder monkeys were distributing the ammunition before a gun ran out. Practice and the many tedious gun drills were finally paying huge dividends.

A shell from the *Kearsarge* "came into our coal bunkers and penetrated the boilers, putting out the fires and burying several of the firemen under the coal," according to Higgins. "Some were killed, and others dug out alive. The vessel was filled with smoke and steam." This combined with the shot that had hit the Rebel ship's rudder meant that "all our power of movement then was over."

The Federal gunners were suffering mightily, however successful they were being. The smoke stung their eyes until, red and watered, they could hardly see. Each roar of a gun assaulted the ears until they were temporarily deaf. It was nearly impossible to breathe as particles of gunpowder, smoke, dust, and fumes from the ship's stack choked their lungs nearly shut. Snaking lines wrenched arms and legs; deadly splinters flew with each shot the enemy landed; shrapnel was always flying about, and the noise and the pounding literally rattled their brains inside their skulls. Ship's boys hurriedly ran from gun to gun with buckets of water, but there was never enough to clear parched throats and remove the sting from the eyes. They kept at it, though, never slacking, and eagerly cheering through their hoarseness whenever a round struck their foe.

"We are making a desperate but forlorn resistance, which is soon culminated by the death blow," Lieutenant Sinclair reported. "Our ship trembles from stem to stern from it."

Indeed, the *Alabama* had suffered more than one fatal blow. There was a jagged opening in the ship's hull and water was pouring into it. The location was particularly ominous because some of that water washed directly into the engine room. It extinguished the fires under the boilers. Another consequence was the pumps ceased working. The *Alabama* had now lost steering and steam power and could not remove the water it was taking in.

Still, the men on the Confederate warship fought on, even as the toll mounted in the most gruesome ways. "Our men were then very fatigued and many disabled and wounded," Higgins would soon testify. "We still fired as well as possible from the port side, though we knew the day was lost. When the headsails were loosed the loader of our port gun, John Roberts, a young Welshman, while engaged in the work, had the lower part of his body cut open, which caused his entrails to protrude. With his entrails hanging out, he walked toward his gun and fell dead on deck." Higgins also observed that "a midshipman stationed in the after division was knocked overboard, his leg, which was shot off, remaining on board."

Semmes, where he stood at the stern, could feel the *Alabama* was lower in the water. He ordered that fore and aft sails be set. The only chance to save his ship was to make a run for it—not farther out to sea but back to Cherbourg, or even just to the three-mile limit with, presumably, the French ship *Couronne* prohibiting further combat within sovereign waters. That boundary was barely four miles away. However, given the *Alabama*'s severely wounded condition, the chances of outrunning the *Kearsarge* were quite low.

And then they fell lower.

24

Within a minute after the *Alabama*'s sails were set, the *Kearsarge* broke off its circling and took up a position between the damaged Confederate cruiser and Cherbourg. Semmes knew the French port was no longer an option. And by now, steaming or at least sailing for another neutral port anywhere in Europe was not possible either.

Lieutenant Kell went below to see for himself how badly the ship was wounded. Water was everywhere, and the level was rising. He saw that the steadfast Dr. Llewellyn continued at his table, trying to stop the flow of blood from a sailor writhing in agony. Suddenly, the table and the sailor were gone—a shell had come through the hull and carried both the wounded sailor and the operating table through the other side of the ship. After a stunned moment to take this in, Llewellyn, by then standing knee deep in water, turned to the next blood-drenched sailor.

Dazed and emerging from below, Kell reported to the captain that water was pouring into the ship and there was no hope of restarting the boilers or the pumps. In the first mate's estimation, the *Alabama* could stay afloat only another ten minutes.

As though to punctuate that pronouncement, the shells from a fresh *Kearsarge* broadside raked the Rebel ship's deck, causing even more carnage.

On the Union ship, a few minutes after noon, Winslow bellowed, "Cease fire!" He lowered the speaking trumpet. Thornton went from gun crew to gun crew. The *Kearsarge* fell silent.

From his perspective on the quarterdeck Winslow had instantly seen Semmes pull out of his circling pattern and point the bow of the *Alabama* toward the shore. Winslow had his helm come about and parallel the *Alabama*'s course. Given that the *Kearsarge* was still at full propulsion potential and the *Alabama* was wallowing and barely making headway, it did not take long for the *Kearsarge* to pull ahead and begin crossing the *Alabama*'s path to block her.

As the two ships grew closer, it was obvious to Winslow that his opponent was finished. Her decks were strewn with wreckage. Many of her spars had been shot away and numerous untethered lines fluttered in the breeze. Coming up the *Alabama*'s port side several gaping holes were clearly visible at her waterline—the work of Winslow's powerful, battering Dahlgrens. Only two 32-pounders pointed to port. The big pivot guns were still shifted to starboard, apparently unmovable. The *Alabama*'s gunwales, near the stern, were already awash, the waves licking over the main deck.

With the guns then silent, despite the ringing in all their ears, the primary sounds Winslow heard were the creaking of the masts, the hissing of the boilers, and the staccato beat of the big cylinders driving the engines. That was not all, however: Winslow heard moans and screams coursing over the whitecaps from the crippled ship he was sliding by.

The men at the *Kearsarge*'s guns took in clean breaths with huge gulps. They were fagged, to be sure, but the air was clearing and the smoke dissipating, which made it much easier to breathe. Buckets of water with tin cups were passed around. It had barely been an hour since the battle commenced, yet to some it seemed like they had been at the work all day.

One of the aft gunners suddenly shouted, "Look, she's struck her colors!"

The Confederate ensign was, indeed, being hauled down and a white flag took its place. But just as the men aboard the *Kearsarge* were about to cheer, the *Alabama*'s two port-side guns fired again.

Shocked, Winslow shouted, "They're playing us a trick! Give it to her, boys!"

The Dahlgrens and the 32-pounders opened again, punching another two holes in the hull and raking the main deck. At the same time there was confusion aboard the *Alabama* about who was still firing and why. From the after-action reports, especially from Winslow, it seems that at least a couple of the *Alabama* gun crews were so angered with the surrender order that they decided to keep on firing. Their ardor was short-lived as the *Kearsarge*'s Dahlgrens did their fearful work.

"We may dismiss the matter as an undoubted accident," Sinclair concluded about the last exchange of gunfire. Perhaps.

By this time, the *Alabama* had come to a standstill. Her stack no longer produced any smoke. Her engines had stopped working. Her stern was nearly awash, and Winslow could already see men jumping into the sea, abandoning ship. He told his helmsman to circle the ship and ease closer in.

On the stricken ship, Semmes told Kell to have the wounded brought up from below and put into the lifeboats. As this was being done with haste, it was discovered that only two of those boats were still intact. Semmes ordered Master's Mate George Fullam to command one, and once it was filled with wounded crewmen, to immediately set off in the direction of the *Kearsarge*.

The Confederate captain now faced doing what he had never thought possible. He could have paused to ponder the action, but he knew any hesitation would cost lives. He shouted for a white flag to be raised. Two Rebel sailors were seen to jump up on the spanker boom, aft, and unfurl a large white sheet.

Another surrender? Winslow wondered suspiciously, yet he ordered a cease-fire once more and there was silence. All guns had stopped shooting but the memory of them was like thunder in Semmes's ears.

A whaleboat came around the *Alabama*'s stern, pulled by six oarsmen, and headed to the *Kearsarge*. The gray-clad Fullam stood in the stern, tiller in his left hand, and a sword in his right. Several wounded *Alabama* sailors were carefully laid in the space remaining. When the gig pulled alongside the *Kearsarge*, Fullam shouted up to Captain Winslow, "My captain has surrendered, sir. And I hereby surrender to you." Fullam then pitched his sword into the sea. "Captain Semmes requests that you help us rescue our men, sir."

"Very well. Come aboard."

Fullam was helped to the *Kearsarge*'s deck and then the Confederate wounded were brought aboard.

Winslow had only two gigs remaining that had escaped damage and remained seaworthy. He ordered them launched immediately to help in the rescue.

Fullam gazed up and down the *Kearsarge*'s deck. There was no blood on the boards and no signs of carnage, which puzzled him. He asked Captain Winslow, "Sir, where are your dead and wounded?"

"We have three wounded only, and they are below deck already being treated."

Fullam was thunderstruck. "Only three wounded? My God, it's a slaughterhouse over there!"

"I am heartily sorry for your losses, sir," Winslow told him, then pointed to the Stars and Stripes fluttering at the masthead. "You see that flag above? That is the one you should have signed to sail for."

Fullam had no ready answer. Instead, he asked, "May I have

your permission, sir, to return to my ship? I wish to help further in the rescue. I give you my word, sir, that when we're done, I will return to you as your prisoner."

"On that basis, and your word, you may return," Winslow replied.

"Thank you, sir." With that, Fullam was back over the side and into his whaleboat. He never did return, however, as promised, which left a stain on his honor and a black mark against him in Winslow's memories.

Fullam had yet to return when Kell's voice rang out: "Abandon ship! Abandon ship!" Crewmen dived or tumbled over the side facing the *Kearsarge* and the second lifeboat with more wounded in it was lowered to the water. When his ship appeared empty of living men, Semmes took off his coat and boots. Then he and his first mate jumped overboard.

Sinclair was one of the last to leave. "The decks present a woeful appearance," he observed, "torn up in innumerable holes, and air-bubbles rising and bursting, producing a sound as though the boat was in agony. Just before she settled, it was a desolate sight for the three or four men left on her deck."

With its captain safely away and its mission at an end, the *Alabama* could die. Its stern sank under the waves and its bow rose. The damaged mainmast broke apart. The ship stood vertical and began to slip down deeper into the water. Then the *Alabama* was gone, Sinclair reported, "making a whirlpool of considerable size and strength."

25

Even in the waters of the Atlantic Ocean, Raphael Semmes was still in command. He and his first lieutenant called out to the men thrashing about to stay close to each other. The water was surprisingly cold for the third week in June and hypothermia would set in quickly. Semmes hoped the men would help each other stay afloat, though the grim reality was some would cling so desperately they would drag each other under.

He tried to locate David White and Antonio Bartelli, last seen too afraid to leave the ship. Despite all their time at sea, neither man could swim. The captain had to assume they had gone down with her (they had). Suddenly, the dead body of someone he recognized floated by—David Llewellyn, the assistant surgeon. The poor man must have stayed with whatever wounded remained and had tried too late to leave the *Alabama*. Semmes then saw that, thankfully, Michael Mars was still alive. The young man was gamely treading water with one hand while with the other he held the captain's journal and other papers aloft.

Lieutenant Kell was grabbed by Eugene Anderson Maffitt, whose father commanded the CSS *Florida*. The young midshipman, even though he could not swim, was offering his life preserver. It would mean exchanging one life for another, and Kell would not do it. Instead, he looked about for rescue boats from the *Kearsarge*. He spotted two being rowed toward the flailing *Alabama* crew members. Why just two? They would not be enough.

But then another ship neared. It was the *Deerhound*. At the request of the Lancaster family to gain a better view of the battle as it reached its peak, Captain Jones had drawn the *Deerhound* as close as he could without actually being part of the battle. With the sinking of the *Alabama*, Captain Jones had drawn closer still. As soon as he was within hailing distance of the *Kearsarge*, Captain Winslow trumpeted down to him, "For God's sake, do what you can to save them!"

The yacht began to roam the water, and when the crew spied two men, they lowered a boat and hauled them in. One of them was Semmes. He had already been in a somewhat fragile state of health the previous couple of weeks, and the stress of combat and especially being in the cold Atlantic water did not make him any more resilient. His energy was rapidly dissipating, and it felt like his arms were heavy logs, more likely to drag him under than help to keep his head above the waves.

Suddenly, from above him came a shout; it was from William Roberts, the chief steward of the *Deerhound*. A hand clasped the captain's and Semmes was yanked up and into one of the yacht's rescue boats. He lay gasping in the bottom of it like a fresh-caught fish. He was soon joined by Kell.

The first lieutenant of the *Alabama* would recall that he was "pulled into a boat in which was Captain Semmes, stretched out in the stern sheets, as pallid as death."

Fortunately for the men thrashing in the water, two French pilot boats also arrived. They began hauling in *Alabama* crewmen. One of them would be Mars, but his rescue was a bit complicated. He had initially been fetched by one of the two

Kearsarge boats, but when a pilot boat drew near, Mars jumped back into the water and swam for it. If he could help it, Semmes's journal and other papers would not fall into Yankee hands.

Roberts directed his boat to make its way back to the *Deerhound*. He had placed a sail over the Confederate captain and his first mate huddled in the bottom. This attempt to avoid detection worked as the boat returned to the yacht without being stopped. Roberts had reasoned that the top priority for rescuers from the *Kearsarge* would be Semmes and being a Southern sympathizer, he did not want him taken prisoner.

Once on the *Deerhound*, Semmes was taken to Jones's cabin. There it was discovered the Confederate captain's splinter wound had reopened and his right hand was bleeding badly. He was treated and both he and Kell were given strong hot coffee made even stronger by stiff shots of rum. Semmes asked Lancaster about survivors of the *Alabama*. The yacht owner replied that it now appeared every man who was alive in the water had been taken aboard by the ad hoc rescue flotilla.

Greatly relieved, Semmes had a request: Because he had no desire to become a prisoner of war and thus conclude his efforts on behalf of the South, would Lancaster be kind enough to bring him to England? The owner instructed Jones to do so as soon as he had ascertained that there were no more men left in the water. In fact, the *Deerhound* would haul aboard a total of forty-two men, including most of Semmes's officers.

Semmes said to Jones, "I am now under English colors and the sooner you put me, with my officers and men, on English soil the better."

That was good enough for the English captain and Lancaster. Barely noticed in all the confusion, the yacht began to casually extricate itself from the recue site, drifting away from the *Kearsarge*. When a lane was wide enough, the *Deerhound* poured on steam to speed away from the *Kearsarge* and toward the English coast.

Semmes would record in his memoir, titled *Service Afloat*, that as he looked back to where his ship had sunk he mused, "A noble Roman once stabbed his daughter rather than she be polluted by the foul embrace of a tyrant. It was with a similar feeling that Kell and I saw the *Alabama* go down. We had buried her as we had christened her, and she was safe from the polluting touch of the hated Yankee!"

Semmes gratefully watched the *Kearsarge* recede into the distance. He desperately did not want to fall into Federal hands. He, along with many of his officers and crewmen, did not know whether they would be treated as prisoners of war or as pirates. If they were deemed to be pirates, they could all be hanged on the spot, legally. In addition, Semmes certainly did not want to suffer the embarrassment of having to surrender to his old shipmate Winslow.

Semmes may well have recognized how fortunate he was that it was John Lancaster and his yacht that snatched him and his men from the sea. Under the then-existing rules of war, it would have been proper and certainly expected that any *Alabama* crewmen taken aboard the *Deerhound* should have been relinquished to the *Kearsarge* or, at worst, landed back in Cherbourg with instructions to turn them over to Captain Winslow. It is not clear, however, that Lancaster knew about these niceties. Captain Jones probably did, but he not only was following the owner's instructions but his own inclinations.

Lancaster's actions reflected the fact that English sympathies, though they did not include favoring slavery, had for a long time generally favored the Confederacy because its success would result in another trade partner and weaken the United States as a rival. Nearly all the Rebel commerce raiders had, after all, been built in England. Could Lancaster, as a good English citizen, do less than to try and help those he believed to be friends of his own government?

Henry Higgins of the *Alabama* was one of the men rescued

by Union sailors and was relieved to find that they did not view him as a pirate. "We were all treated with every possible kindness on board the *Kearsarge*," he later reported. "Our grog was given us as soon as we got on board, and we were treated much better than any prisoners had ever been treated on the *Alabama*. On board the *Kearsarge* the crew was very much dispirited because they had not taken either Semmes or the *Alabama*. Captain Winslow came forward among us and gave us dry clothing and gave orders to treat us with every possible kindness."

But courtesy went only so far. As the *Deerhound* pulled farther away, several of the *Kearsarge* officers shouted for Winslow's attention. The Union commander could not believe what he was witnessing. Thornton wanted his captain to put a shell into the *Deerhound* or at least across her bow to get her attention. To Winslow's credit, he declined to do so. He had personally seen that there were women and children aboard the *Deerhound*. Blowing up an English yacht and killing innocent civilians would absolutely take the sheen off his tremendous victory. And indeed, that was what it was.

As the summer of 1864 began, the Confederate Navy was not officially finished. A handful of ships continued to ply the waters hoping to pounce on Union prey and there would still be attempts to penetrate the relentless and ever-thicker blanket of blockaders. But the *Alabama* had been the crown jewel of the South's oceangoing campaign. Now it was gone. Its sinking was a decisive nail pounded into the coffin of the Confederate States of America.

But while it lived, the CSS *Alabama* and its relentless adversary, the USS *Kearsarge*, had made history.

EPILOGUE

With a gaggle of prisoners and wounded men from the *Alabama*, the *Kearsarge* sailed back into Cherbourg Harbor about three o'clock the same Sunday afternoon. The ship had battle damage, to be sure, but her battered hull was still whole, her engines were working well, her spars and masts were intact; and, most important of all, she was afloat and her colors flew proudly in the gentle breeze. A sizeable crowd lined the banks of the harbor, spilling down to the piers, and they were waving their hats and cheering loudly—the very same citizens who had huzzaed the *Alabama* as she sailed from the same spot only six hours earlier.

Snugged to the pier, the process of off-loading the wounded began. The local mariner's hospital was ready to receive them. Lieutenant Commander Thornton supervised the sorting out of the wounded and the prisoners. There were, at first count, about seventy *Alabama* men on board the *Kearsarge* had plucked from the sea or taken from the lifeboats. What was to be done with them, other than the wounded? There was certainly not enough room on the *Kearsarge* to berth them all.

As Thornton was figuring all this out, Winslow retired to his cabin. He was emotionally and physically drained yet bursting with pride for what he and his magnificent crew had accomplished. He sat down at his desk and began to write.

Winslow's first communiqué concerning the battle off Cherbourg went via Ambassador Dayton in Paris. The captain penned the following:

USS *Kearsarge*
Cherbourg, France, June 19, 1864 Afternoon
Hon. Gideon Welles,
Secretary of the Navy, Washington, D.C.

SIR: I have the honor to inform the Department that the day subsequent to the arrival of the *Kearsarge* off this port, on the 14th instant, I received a note from Captain Semmes, begging that the *Kearsarge* would not depart, as he intended to fight her and would not delay her but a day or two.

According to this notice, the *Alabama* left the port of Cherbourg this morning about 9:30 o'clock.

At 10:20 a.m. we discovered her steering toward us. Fearing the question of jurisdiction might arise, we steamed to sea until a distance of 6 or 7 miles was attained from the Cherbourg breakwater, when we rounded to and commenced steaming for the *Alabama*. As we approached her within about 1,200 yards she opened fire, we receiving two or three broadsides before a shot was returned. The action continued, the respective steamers making a circle round and round at a distance of about 900 yards from each other. At the expiration of an hour the *Alabama* struck, going down in about twenty minutes afterwards, and carrying many persons with her.

It affords me great gratification to announce to the Department that every officer and man did his duty, exhibiting a degree of coolness and fortitude which gave promise at the outset of certain victory.

I have the honor to be, most respectfully, your obedient servant.

JNO. A. Winslow
Captain

The glorious news was off to Paris, as was young William Dayton Jr. In the meantime, what to do with the prisoners? Winslow had to make a command decision before supplies and goodwill ran out. Thinking clearly of the welfare of his own men and wanting to avoid the possibility of having to sequester seventy former enemy combatants amongst his own crew, Winslow decided to parole all the enlisted prisoners, keeping only the four *Alabama* officers that he had taken: Third Lieutenant Joseph Wilson; John Pundt, third assistant engineer; Chief Engineer Miles Freeman; and Boatswain Benjamin McCaskey.[85]

The electrifying news of Winslow's victory still took sixteen days to reach Washington. Welles was gobsmacked; first, because the sinking of the *Alabama* had finally taken that menacing piece off the chess board; second, because it was whiny, sickly, obstreperous, seemingly useless John Winslow who had done it.

Welles was delighted by the outcome, no doubt, but he wanted more—and expected more, in terms of Winslow's reports. He would get more reports, many of them, over the following days. His first duty, however, was to convey the good news to President Lincoln, who was said to be so delighted he did a little jig.

As soon as Welles returned from the White House, he fired off the following telegraph to Winslow:

85   Wilson was exchanged in late 1864, but Pundt, Freeman, and McCaskey were imprisoned at Fort Warren in Boston Harbor until the end of the war.

NAVY DEPARTMENT, July 6, 1864
Captain JOHN A. WINSLOW
Commanding USS *Kearsarge*, Cherbourg, France

SIR: Your very brief dispatches of the 19th and 20th ultimo, informing the Department that the piratical craft *Alabama*, or *290*, had been sunk on the 19th June, near meridian, by the *Kearsarge*, under your command, were this day received. I congratulate you on your good fortune in meeting the *Alabama*, which so long had avoided the fastest ships and some of the most vigilant and intelligent officers of the service, and for the ability displayed in the contest you have the thanks of the Department.

You will please express to the officers and crew of the *Kearsarge* the satisfaction of the Government at this victory over a vessel superior in tonnage, superior in the number of guns, and superior in the number of her crew. The battle was so brief, the victory so decisive, and the comparative results so striking that the country will be reminded of the brilliant actions of our infant Navy, which have been repeated and illustrated in this engagement.

The *Alabama* represented the best maritime effort of the most skilled English workshops. Her battery was composed of the well-tried 32-pounders of 57 hundredweight, of the 68-pounder of the British navy, and of the only successful rifled 100-pounder yet produced in England. The crew were generally recruited in Great Britain, and many of them received superior training on board Her Majesty's gunnery ship the *Excellent*.

The *Kearsarge* is one of the first gunboats built at American navy yards at the commencement of the rebellion. The principal guns composing her battery had never been previously tried in an exclusively naval engagement, yet in one hour you succeeded in sinking your antagonist, thus fitly ending her predatory career, and killed many of her crew, without injury to the *Kearsarge* or the loss of a single life on your vessel.

Our countrymen have reason to be satisfied in that this, as in every naval action of this unhappy war, neither the ships, the guns, nor the crews have deteriorated, but that they maintain the ability and continue the renown which have ever adorned our naval annals.

The President has signified his intention to recommend that you receive a vote of thanks, in order that you may be advanced to the grade of commodore. Lieutenant-Commander James S. Thornton, the executive officer of the *Kearsarge*, will be recommended to the Senate for advancement ten numbers in grade, and you will report to the Department the names of any others of the officers or crew whose good conduct on the occasion entitles them to special mention.

Very respectfully, etc.,
GIDEON WELLES
Secretary of the Navy

Letter writing style and language usage has certainly changed a great deal since 1864, but it is hard not to notice some of the undertones of Welles's reply to Winslow's welcome news. Instead of being jubilant that the nemesis has been eliminated, it is almost as if Welles cannot believe that Winslow and the *Kearsarge* pulled it off. Why, for example, does Welles compliment Winslow's "good fortune" instead of his "diligence and hard work"? Why does Welles have to point out that some of the "most vigilant and intelligent officers of the service" could not do what he'd somehow managed to do? Welles also spends a whole paragraph decrying the inferiority of the *Kearsarge* versus the *Alabama*. At least, at the very end, he speaks of rewards for Winslow and Thornton and asks for the names of any others in the crew who might merit awards.

In the first sentence of Welles's letter there is also the ominous two-word phrase "brief dispatches." This seems to presage Welles's desire for much more information; and, indeed, Winslow is pestered over the next few days with a flurry of letters requesting more details. Winslow, to his credit, answers each inquiry with more and more specifics, and often attaches reports from his officers to back him up. It never seems to be enough to satisfy Welles, however.

The most egregious sin that Winslow commits, in Welles's eyes, is paroling his many Confederate prisoners. Welles wanted them returned and would have certainly imprisoned them if not put them on trial for piracy. Semmes's men were no fools, however, and as even Winslow would have predicted, their paroles meant nothing to them. Not a single *Alabama* prisoner who was released ever returned to custody.

Raphael Semmes was no longer captain of a ship but there were still CSS *Alabama* matters to resolve. One was paying off the crew members who had survived, and once that was done, to arrange to have money sent to the families of those who had perished.[86] He also needed to field queries about the battle. Despite having lost his ship—or perhaps for having done so—Semmes was an even bigger celebrity in England.

"Notwithstanding that it had been a notably one-sided engagement, an aura of romance clung to the *Alabama*'s last battle," biographer John M. Taylor offers up for excuse. "For Southern sympathizers, and there were many in Europe, the clash off Cherbourg was the Civil War in microcosm: the gallant but outgunned South, ignoring its deficiencies in materiel, fearlessly taking on a superior force."

(The battle was certainly not as lopsided as Taylor explains. With the exception of bad gunpowder and fuses aboard the

---

86 He still had four sacks of gold coins at his disposal.

Alabama, both ships, as Captain Ellicott has noted, were very evenly matched in nearly every regard.)

Outwardly, Semmes presented the somber demeanor of a warrior who had done his best against steep odds. His actual suffering he expressed only in his journal: "No one who is not a seaman can realize the blow which falls upon the heart of a commander, upon the sinking of his ship. It is not merely the loss of a battle—it is the overwhelming of his household, as it were, in a great catastrophe."

Of some comfort was the respect shown to Semmes by members of the Royal Navy. A group of officers led a successful effort to raise money—a total equivalent to $800 was collected—to replace the Confederate captain's sword that had gone down with the Alabama. The gold scabbard featured the national emblems of Great Britain and the Confederate States of America and letters forming "Peace and friendship." And Semmes was lauded for his achievements at a dinner given by John Laird, the member of Parliament whose sons had constructed *290,* which became the *Alabama.*

Also comforting was the friendship of the Reverend Francis Tremlett, one of the more prominent Southern sympathizers in England. Semmes and Kell accepted the clergyman's invitation to stay indefinitely at his home in Belsize Park. Kell remained only a short time, leaving the second week in July on a journey that the lieutenant hoped would return him to Confederate service. For Semmes, however, the respite could not last long enough. Reverend Tremlett was not only a courteous host but he was glad to act as a travel guide, leading Semmes and several others on a tour of Europe that included Germany, Switzerland, and France.[87]

And most comforting of all, the group of travelers included the reverend's sister, Louisa Tremlett. Yet to turn thirty, the unmarried Louisa had met the Southern captain before, in May

---

87 To elude cloying Southern sympathizers as well as Union spies on the Continent, Semmes traveled under the name "Raymond Smith."

1862 during a brief stay Semmes had made in London while awaiting orders to the *Alabama*. There may have been nothing more than flirting at that time, but during their next months together the relationship went beyond idle affection. Louisa, of course, knew that Semmes was married and that he was twenty-five years older than she was, yet she apparently did not make much of an effort to block any of the captain's interest. For his part, it had been over three years since he had seen Anne Spencer Semmes, and in the summer of 1864 the captain of a sunken ship was at possibly his lowest period—other than maybe the discovery of his wife's earlier infidelity and pregnancy. When Louisa presented him with a ring, he wore it on the same finger as his wedding band.

It is not known if Semmes and Louisa engaged in physical intimacy during the two-month European sojourn, but they were together daily. Her brother had to be aware of feelings between his sister and his friend but seems to have kept his eyes on the other attractions of the Continent. Finally, though, the apparently blissful excursion had to end. Louisa and Semmes and the others returned to Belsize Park in September.

Restored emotionally as well as physically, Semmes prepared to return to America. There were temptations in addition to Louisa that enticed him to remain in Europe and away from the fray, but the Confederate captain could not abandon the Southern cause, especially when it needed loyalists the most. As Semmes would quickly learn, Atlanta had been taken by William Tecumseh Sherman, the CSS *Florida* had been captured in Brazil, and Phil Sheridan's campaign in the Shenandoah Valley was rampaging toward a highly successful conclusion.

After leaving his journal, the *Alabama*'s flag, and his new sword with the Reverend Tremlett and Louisa (to be shipped to him later), Semmes boarded a ship bound for Cuba. This would be the first leg in the journey that would finally bring him home.

★ ★ ★

While in port at Cherbourg (the French government gave the *Kearsarge* a dispensation from its normal rules for length of stay) there was an unwanted duty to perform on June 27 when William Gowin unexpectedly died. Dr. Browne was puzzled by his expiration. Although he had suffered a serious wound and the loss of his leg (along with a large quantity of blood), Gowin seemed to be on the mend. His normally ebullient spirits had sagged, however, and he also seemed to have had a recurrence of a bout of malaria that had plagued him previously. The crew was saddened to lose their fun-loving jester and talented musician. A plot was located for Gowin in a cemetery overlooking the harbor. The men even took up a contribution among themselves to purchase a fine gravestone for their former shipmate. Gowin was the only Union fatality of the newly famous fight.

Over the next few weeks, the crew of the *Kearsarge* repaired whatever battle damage was within their capabilities. Thankfully, there was not a great deal of work to do—except for the rudder. The 100-pound shell that the *Alabama* had deposited in the sternpost was still there, and the crew had no desire to remove it, fearing that it might finally explode. It was a job, frankly, for the shipfitters in a major repair facility. The crew was able to carefully place wedges between the posts in the stern to make the steering less difficult.

Following a cruise of over two and a half years, the crew was spent. After their tremendous victory over the *Alabama*, they were ready to go home—so was their ship. The *Kearsarge* needed some major repairs and modifications. Winslow anxiously awaited orders to secure the ship's return as it plied back and forth between English and French ports, somewhat at a loss as to what to do next. There were consolations, though: everywhere the *Kearsarge* went she and her crew were greeted as heroes. Local newspapers relived the battle in large headlines. The officers and crew were feted at numerous celebrations, parades, and banquets in their honor. When granted shore leave the sailors did not have to worry about spending their own meager wages in the local bars. The brothels? Well, that was another matter, but it was rumored that liberal discounts could be had.

Winslow finally had time to write extensively to his long-suffering wife, although the Boston papers had already gotten wind of the *Kearsarge*'s smashing victory. In a letter to Catherine he wrote:

Off Hastings, July 7, 1864… I have written a letter to the Department, which must carry the *Kearsarge* home, for we have such shot in our stern post and otherwise, as will make it dangerous to keep at sea in gales of wind. Well, I suppose you have read enough about our fight, what a terrible sensation it had made in Europe, and as for poor me, I have been inundated with letters, etc. I took the opportunity I had and went to Paris to see about my eye. There I became a lion—dinners, speeches, writing, painting, permission to dedicate to me—Had to have a reception from 11 A.M. to 3 P.M. one day, general hand shaking, etc.: parties and nonsense afterward. I wished I was in the *Kearsarge*, where I got as soon as I could. I can't write a word, but someone gets hold of it, garbles and publishes it.

Well, of my eye—Oculist says, irrevocably gone!—might have saved it had I had an operation performed when first attacked—must be careful of the other.

Everyone very kind to me in Paris. Strange things have come to pass—I am, they say, a hero. It would have been gratifying to me when I was young; but now my hope is peace and rest. God grant it may arrive at an early day!

On August 11, 1864, at Dover, Winslow finally got the orders he had been hoping to receive, but they were not exactly what he would have wished. Welles directed Winslow and the

Kearsarge to proceed immediately to Martinique. There, Welles hoped the *Kearsarge* might catch up with the CSS *Florida* and do to her what the *Kearsarge* had done to the *Alabama*. If so, wonderful; but if no contact, then Winslow was cleared to return home.

That very same day, the *Kearsarge* was relieved on station by the USS *Iroquois*, Commander C. R. P. Rodgers as her captain.[88] Winslow immediately set sail for Cherbourg to pick up his wounded men, Dempsey and McBeth. From Cherbourg, the *Kearsarge* steamed to Fayal to pick up coal and supplies for her transatlantic journey to Martinique.

By the time the *Kearsarge* got to Martinique and searched around for the *Florida*, the USS *Wachusett* had already found her in Brazil, entered port, rammed the *Florida*, captured her, took her in tow, and fled Brazil before the Brazilian Navy could catch up. Naturally, this invasion of Brazilian territory caused a gigantic kerfuffle, but that is another tale. The *Wachusett* caught up with the *Kearsarge* in Martinique. Overflowing with crew and *Florida* prisoners, Winslow agreed to take seventeen POWs from the *Wachusett* and head for home while the slower *Wachusett*, *Florida* still in tow, steamed for Union waters.

A tired, threadbare *Kearsarge* and her crew sailed into Boston Harbor on the afternoon of November 7, 1864. A raucous crowd was on hand to greet her. More importantly to a haggard, sickly, exhausted Captain Winslow, he was finally home, in the arms of his family in Roxbury, by midnight.

Welles, true to his word, had President Lincoln sign a proclamation allowing the House of Representatives to pass a "Thanks of Congress" bill on December 20, 1864, designating Winslow a commodore. Likewise, Thornton was advanced "ten numbers in grade" which were sufficient to promote him to full commander.

---

88 Rodgers (1819–1892) was related on both sides to the most famous of the Perries and Rodgers who had been so prominent in U.S. Navy history. He was during his career a noted seafarer and ship's captain but also president of the U.S. Naval Institute (twice) and superintendent of the U.S. Naval Academy. He rose to the rank of rear admiral before retiring and both of his sons also became admirals.

There were honors for some of the men too. An astonishing seventeen Medals of Honor were awarded. They went to the following crewmen, with their ranks at the time of the action:

MICHAEL AHERN, PAYMASTER'S STEWARD, Queenstown, Ireland: for gallantry under enemy fire.

JOHN F. BICKFORD, CAPTAIN OF THE TOP, Tremont, Maine: First loader of the pivot gun who exhibited marked coolness and good conduct.

WILLIAM S. BOND, BOATSWAIN'S MATE, Boston, Massachusetts: Carrying out his duties courageously, Bond exhibited marked coolness and good conduct.

JAMES HALEY, CAPTAIN OF THE FORECASTLE, Ringaskiddy, Ireland: Acting as captain of a gun during the bitter engagement, Haley exhibited marked coolness and good conduct.

MARK G. HAM, CARPENTER'S MATE, Portsmouth, New Hampshire: Distinguished himself in the face of the bitter enemy fire.

GEORGE H. HARRISON, SEAMAN, Middleton, Massachusetts: Acting as sponger and loader of the 11-inch pivot gun during the bitter engagement, Harrison exhibited marked coolness and good conduct.

JOHN JAYES, COXSWAIN, Newfoundland, Canada: Acting as second captain of the No. 2 gun during this bitter engagement, Hayes exhibited marked coolness and good conduct.

JAMES H. LEE, SEAMAN, Long Island, New York: Acting as sponger of the No. 1 gun during this bitter engagement, Lee exhibited marked coolness and good conduct.

CHARLES MOORE, ORDINARY SEAMAN, Reading, Pennsylvania: Acting as sponger and loader on the 11-inch pivot gun of the second division during the bitter engagement, Moore exhibited marked coolness and good conduct.

JOAQUIN PEASE, SEAMAN, Fogo Island, Azores: Acting as loader on the No. 2 gun during this bitter engagement, Pease exhibited marked coolness and good conduct.

THOMAS PERRY, BOATSWAIN'S MATE, New York, New York: Acting as captain of the No. 2 gun during this bitter engagement, Perry exhibited marked coolness and good conduct.

WILLIAM B. POOLE, QUARTERMASTER, Cape Elizabeth, Maine: Stationed at the helm, Poole steered the ship during the engagement in a cool and most creditable manner...gallantry under fire.

CHARLES A. READ (JOHAN A. LINDEROTH), COXSWAIN, Sweden: Acting as the first sponger of the pivot gun during this bitter engagement, Read exhibited marked coolness and good conduct...

GEORGE E. READ, SEAMAN, Newport, Rhode Island: Acting as the first loader of the No. 2 gun during this bitter engagement, Read exhibited marked coolness and good conduct and was highly recommended for his gallantry.

JAMES SAUNDERS, QUARTERMASTER, Boston, Massachusetts: Carrying out his duties courageously throughout the bitter engagement...and it is testified to by Commodore Winslow that he is deserving of all commendation, both for gallantry and for encouragement of others in his division.

WILLIAM SMITH, QUARTERMASTER, Providence, Rhode Island: Acting as captain of the 11-inch pivot gun of the second division, Smith carried out his duties courageously and deserved special notice for the deliberate and cool manner in which he acted throughout the bitter engagement. It is stated by Rebel officers that this gun was more destructive and did more damage than any other gun of *Kearsarge*.

ROBERT H. STRAHAN, CAPTAIN OF THE TOP, New Jersey: Acting as captain of the No. 1 gun, Strahan carried out his duties in the face of heavy enemy fire and exhibited marked coolness and good conduct throughout the engagement.

Some notes on these awards seem warranted: Prior to the Civil War, neither the army nor the navy (which included the marines) had any officially authorized medals or decorations for exceptional service or valor. This lack of recognition had been intended since the first days of the Republic. As a democracy, where "all men are created equal," the armed forces of the new United States had forsworn these "gewgaws" and badges which, to the Founding Fathers, seemed to represent the military systems of the Old World, Great Britain in particular. The idea of strutting peacocks in gaudy uniforms festooned with epaulettes, golden cords, medals, and ostentatious badges was anathema to the views of the War Department and the secretary of the navy. Uniforms were, at first, plain and simple: brass buttons and frock coats for the navy, and blue tunics with simple shoulder straps or chevrons designating rank for the army.

Rather than medals, recognition for superior performance or valor in combat was attained through being "mentioned in dispatches" or brevet promotion, or both. A heroic charge up a foreign hill while under enemy fire might earn a brave army first lieutenant a brevet promotion to captain. Capturing an enemy ship at sea after a spirited engagement might merit an ambitious navy lieutenant a promotion to commander. Getting a letter from the government as in a "Thanks of Congress" was visual recognition and something to frame and hang on your wall. Likewise, a victorious general or senior captain who mentions you favorably in his glowing reports (as with Lieutenant Commander Thornton) might move you up on the promotion list.

There was one small exception: The Purple Heart. During the Revolutionary War, General George Washington usually recognized the meritorious deeds of his soldiers with a promotion to the next higher rank, whether the individual was an enlisted man or an officer. After a number of these brevet promotions, the Continental Congress, always crying about spending more money, curtailed the practice because it increased the payroll (when and if the soldiers were paid at all!). To compensate, Washington initiated a "Purple Heart" award, for valor or exceptionally meritorious service. In the beginning the award was, indeed, a small, purple cloth heart with the word *Valor* stitched upon it. The badge was meant to be worn over the left breast of the soldier's tunic.

Washington started these awards in 1782, very near the end of the Revolution; so, only three original Purple Hearts were ever awarded, but they remained the only "medals" officially designated, until 1861. Interestingly, the Purple Heart was revived and recodified, in Washington's honor, 150 years after our first president inaugurated them. In 1932, Congress reintroduced legislation adding the (new) Purple Heart to the Pyramid of Honor. It is made of metal these days and not cloth, but it is still (mostly) purple, and heart shaped, with Washington's profile on its face, in honor of the originator. To be awarded a Purple Heart, the recipient must have been wounded or killed in action, against "an enemy foreign or domestic." In precedence, it ranks directly above the Bronze Star, and just under the Silver Star.

Thoughts had changed, in 1861, concerning awards and medals. The Union began raising enormous amounts of volunteers, for both the army and the navy—larger numbers than ever before in American history. President Lincoln and the Congress wanted to offer up a special form of recognition; so, a Medal of Honor was proposed and ratified in early 1862. It took an Act of Congress to make the award official and many mistakenly began calling the decoration the "Congressional Medal of Honor." That is not the correct designation: It has always been, and is today, simply the "Medal of Honor." In the beginning it was the only such award, but today it is the highest award for valor that the United States can bestow on any member of the armed services.

There was another interesting distinction for the MOH (the official abbreviation) in the beginning: It could only be awarded to enlisted soldiers—not officers—and it was for the army only. The navy MOH came along as separate legislation in 1862 but it, too, was only for enlisted sailors and enlisted marines, not officers. The army began allowing the MOH to be awarded to officers in 1863, but the navy did not include its officers in awards of the MOH until 1915.

Had navy officers been eligible for the MOH in 1864, one might think that Captain Winslow and Lieutenant Commander Thornton might have been considered. Alas, they could not be. They would soon be promoted to the next higher rank, however, as was customary.

The MOH to Seaman Pease was extraordinary. It was quite rare that Black people of the day would be singled out for high recognition or advancement much beyond where Pease already was. It seems to say a great deal that Winslow would advance Pease's name for consideration for an MOH, but we do know the captain was an ardent abolitionist. Since record keeping was not always exact, we do not know if Pease was the first Black person in the navy to be awarded an MOH, but if he wasn't the very first, he was very close to being so designated.

Pease finished his navy enlistment in January 1865 and disappeared. There are no records after 1865 that note his activities, even his death. Some have speculated that he went back to sea to serve on a whaler or a commercial ship, but no ship logs with his name have yet been found. Some believe he might have returned to his native Fogo Island, but there is no record of his return or even his demise in any Cape Verde Islands records. Pease's MOH has been carefully preserved and is today in the care and custody of the Navy History and Heritage Command waiting to be claimed by a descendant—if any exist.

Paymaster Steward Ahearn's MOH is also somewhat exceptional: as the reader may recall, Ahearn was one of the "Queenstown Men" who snuck aboard the *Kearsarge* in Ireland in December 1863. He was the only one of the sixteen stowaways that Winslow elected to keep, in the face of all the controversy surrounding the enlistments. Ahearn was retained because he actually had decent experience in keeping books and accounts, which the *Kearsarge* paymaster desperately needed. Ahearn was not awarded his MOH for his ability with pen and ink, however; he was actually assigned to one of the Dahlgren guns when the ship was engaged in combat, and apparently he was very good at those duties as well.

One more MOH note, about John F. Bickford. He was a seafaring man down to the soles of his boots. First, he had been raised in a family that made its living on the water and the seagoing life came easily and naturally to him. In today's U.S. Navy he would be called a "plank holder"—that is, a sailor who was a member of the initial crew of a commissioned vessel. In Bickford's case, of course, he was part of the original crew of the *Kearsarge*. He enlisted as an ordinary seaman, but quickly started moving up the ladder—to seaman, captain of the top, to acting master's mate, and ultimately an acting master, which put him in the ranks of the junior officers.

When the *Kearsarge* crew was paid off and sent on its way in November 1864, Bickford requested and was granted leave to go home to Maine for three months. It was at home, in fact, that he received his Medal of Honor, via the U.S. Mail. To be granted his leave, Bickford had agreed to enlist for another two years. In January he reported to the USS *Lenapee*, a double-ended, side-wheel steamer of eight guns that the navy would use primarily for shore bombardment and as a tug.

But by April 1865, Bickford was not a well man. During service on the *Lenapee* he had contracted a severe case of malaria in the swampy terrain along the Cape Fear River. Bickford was hospitalized for nearly two months. In June he requested a discharge from the navy to return home to recuperate. An honorable medical discharge was granted. After recovering his health in Maine, Bickford moved to Gloucester, Massachusetts, in 1867 to find suitable employment. He was hired as a supervisor at the Stockbridge Fish Company in Gloucester and had the good luck to marry the boss's daughter two years later. The couple had five children, two of whom died in infancy.

Over the years his former shipmates held annual reunions on or close to June 19, recalling their great triumph of 1864. The last meeting was in 1925 at Bickford's home, with only Bickford and fellow Gloucester resident William Giles present. Bickford outlived his wife, Elsie, by fourteen years, dying from heart disease at age eighty-four on April 27, 1927. Only two other *Kearsarge* survivors outlived him: Giles and William Alsdorf in far-off New Mexico. Bickford was buried at Mount Pleasant Cemetery in Gloucester.

The months of November and December 1864 were chockablock with parades, parties, and banquets honoring the officers and men of the USS *Kearsarge*. President Lincoln had been reelected by a substantial margin the day after the *Kearsarge* returned from her cruise, and that also occasioned many celebrations. The merchants of Boston took up a collection on behalf of the crew and they raised $21,000 to divide among the men ($347,760 in today's dollars, or about $2,400 per man). Captain Winslow was given $25,000 by the New York Chamber of Commerce ($414,000 in today's dollars) which effectively alleviated the family's worries about money for the rest of their days.

In late October 1864, three and a half years after he had left, Raphael Semmes was back on the North American continent. After disembarking in Havana, he boarded another ship, this one taking him to Matamoros, just south of the border with Texas. From there, he traveled by horse and stagecoach to Brownsville, relieved to be on Southern soil again. He would have preferred to be on a Southern ship, but Semmes knew by now the Confederate Navy was little more than a ghost.

The remainder of his journey was bittersweet. On one hand, there were incessant reports of how badly the South was faring. There appeared to be little hope for the rebellion other than the endurance of General Lee's troops and the fortifications around Petersburg. Possibly, there was still a chance that if the siege went on long enough the Union tolerance for seemingly senseless death would cease. However, Lincoln's easy reelection that November, buoyed by the mail-in ballots of hundreds of thousands of Union troops, had only positive indications for victory by the North.

On the other hand, Semmes was welcomed as a returning hero. As he made his way through Texas, Louisiana, and finally into

Alabama the captain of the courageous *Alabama* was cheered and feted. Whatever money remained in his pockets stayed there because hotels and restaurants refused payment. No doubt the biggest bonus Semmes received was the company of one of his sons. Oliver Semmes was a major in the Confederate Army in command of a battalion of Rebel artillery in Louisiana. The captain and the major traveled together, sneaking across the Mississippi River to avoid roaming Union patrols, and reaching Mobile ten days before Christmas. There Semmes was reunited with his wife.[89]

The household included Anne's daughter Anna, no longer banished to Philadelphia, and their daughters Katherine and Electra. Once again, Semmes was faced with the prospect of sitting out the rest of the war, and in a city still held by Confederate forces. (Mobile Bay, however, was under the control of Admiral David Farragut's ships.) But he believed that would be irresponsible. Semmes sent a message to Secretary Mallory's office that he had returned, and almost immediately came a reply ordering him to Richmond. He left Mobile the first week of January 1865.

His journey smacked of a farewell tour. As he worked his way east and north, Semmes was again hailed as a hero of the War for Southern Independence and the speeches he was called upon to give offered a brighter picture of the Confederacy's situation than what he was observing out train and stagecoach windows. The war would last another three months but privately he wondered if it would end before he got to Richmond.

It did not, and when he presented himself to Mallory, Semmes was promoted to rear admiral. There were other honors—he dined with President Davis, was received by General Lee at his field headquarters, and was given accolades when visiting the chambers of the Virginia legislature and Confederate Congress. While it was most satisfying to be awarded such highly visible

---

89　Samuel Spencer Semmes was still in the field with the First Louisiana Infantry and the youngest son, Raphael Jr., had joined the Confederate Navy as a midshipman and was serving in Virginia with the James River Squadron.

recognition for his achievements and sacrifices, Semmes wanted to serve for however long the war lasted. Mallory appointed him commander of the James River Squadron.

This was a rather dreary position, with the only silver lining being Raphael Jr. being appointed to his staff. Semmes's "squadron" consisted of five rotting ships and three ironclads badly in need of repairs. Its sole role was to guard one of the gateways to Richmond. There was no hope of going on offense. The only real action the squadron engaged in was going after deserters, of which there was a growing multitude.

After two months of this the James River Squadron was scuttled. Lee abandoning Petersburg and then Richmond were the latest and most destructive blows to what lingered as the Confederate States of America. However, the war was still not over for Semmes. His next stop was Danville, Virginia, where he exchanged his commission as rear admiral for appointment as a brigadier general, and Raphael Jr. became an aide. The new assignment was to organize the men left from the squadron into an artillery unit that would be under the command of General Joe Johnston.

A few days later, Lee surrendered to Grant at Appomattox, yet Semmes continued to serve the Confederacy. With a force of 250 men, he moved on with Johnston's army to Greensboro, North Carolina. Finally, on April 26, Johnston surrendered to Sherman, the last major Confederate Army to do so. It took four weeks for father and son Semmes to travel by horse and sometimes on foot the eight hundred miles to Montgomery, Alabama, burdened by dashed hopes, the disappointment of total defeat, and the incessant images of destruction wrought by the Union forces. In Montgomery, they stepped onto a steamboat which took them to Mobile. During the last week of May, Semmes Sr. arrived home to stay—he hoped.

Tall, broad shouldered, with a full, dark beard, James Thornton looked every inch the resolute navy man that he was. He had nerves of steel and ice in his veins during combat, as exhibited aboard the USS *Hartford* at the Battle of New Orleans (1862) and stalking the decks of the USS *Kearsarge* during the Battle of Cherbourg. His reward for helping defeat the CSS *Alabama* was almost immediate promotion to commander; and, after the *Kearsarge* was decommissioned in November 1864, Thornton was given command of the gunboat USS *Iosco*. After the Civil War Thornton had duty at the Portsmouth Navy Yard. He returned to the recommissioned USS *Kearsarge* in 1868, this time as her commanding officer, and spent two years aboard her cruising with the Pacific Squadron. In 1870 it was back to Portsmouth where, in 1872, he was promoted to captain. In August of 1873 he was sent to command the steam sloop USS *Monongahela* assigned to the South Atlantic Squadron.

After successfully dodging bombs, torpedoes, bullets, and shells during Civil War combat Captain Thornton was ironically done in by an accident. On January 14, 1875, while in his captain's cabin aboard the *Monongahela*, a freak wave slammed into the side of the ship. The sloop lurched violently sideways and Thornton was knocked off his feet and thrown awkwardly against his own desk. His spine was nearly severed. From that time forward, he could not walk and only moved the rest of his body with great pain and difficulty. He was invalided out of the navy the next month and returned to his hometown of Germantown, Pennsylvania.

He continued to deteriorate and the doctors could do nothing for his internal injuries. He died three months later, May 14, at just forty-nine years old, a sad and unfortunate end to a proud and brave sailor.

The USS *Kearsarge* had a thirty-two-year career, all told, but during her decades of service she was in and out of commission five different times. Repaired and refurbished once more in 1873, she cruised to Japan, China, the Philippines, and Russia. After transiting the Suez Canal in the autumn of 1878, she visited several Mediterranean ports before returning to her "birthplace" in Portsmouth, New Hampshire, and being taken out of service once more.

Not done yet, the *Kearsarge* was reactivated in May 1879 to cruise four more years to Newfoundland, the Caribbean, West Africa, and Panama. She was present at the opening of the Brooklyn Bridge in May 1883. After three more years in European waters, and visiting the site of her famous victory, she was back in Portsmouth for another inactive period until November of 1888. Her last active duty period was among West Indies, Venezuela, and Central American ports.

She was heading to Nicaragua on February 2, 1894, when she ran up on Roncador Cay (now part of Colombia) during a storm. Fortunately, every member of her crew was rescued, but the ship herself could not be pried off the reef. Considering the provenance of the vessel, a valiant effort was made to refloat or at least salvage her, but the reef had done too much damage. Subsequent storms and wave action ripped her apart, but not before a number of important artifacts were saved. By the middle of 1894 both the *Kearsarge* and the *Alabama* were denizens of the deep.

The *Kearsarge* name would not disappear from the navy's roster for long, however. In 1896, a new pre-dreadnaught battleship, BB-5, would be launched by the Newport News Shipbuilding Co., and named USS *Kearsarge*—this time not memorializing the mountain in New Hampshire but the famous Civil War ship. BB-5 would be the only U.S. Navy battleship not named for a state. In an interesting nod to history, a new captain took over command of the battleship *Kearsarge* in 1905. His name was Herbert Winslow. Captain (later Rear Admiral) Winslow was a son of John Ancrum Winslow. The battleship *Kearsarge* was in commission until 1920, and even after that continued to serve the navy as *Crane Ship No. 1* until sold for scrap in 1955.

As noted previously, the U.S. Navy honored the *Kearsarge* name again with an *Essex* class aircraft carrier, CV-33, which served in Korea and Vietnam until she was laid up in 1974. Today, there is yet another USS *Kearsarge*, LHD-3, launched in 1992. She is still serving thirty years later as an amphibious assault ship that can carry up to 1700 U.S. Marines and their motorized equipment and helicopters, and put them on any beachhead on the planet. When the current *Kearsarge* is decommissioned, there will no doubt be another—the name has earned a hallowed place in American Navy history.

Once the fanfare faded, newly promoted Commodore Winslow was able to spend the balance of the Civil War ashore, in Boston, near his family. He was appointed president of the navy board supervising the construction of ironclads.

Late in 1865 diplomatic relations with France began to sour over Mexico with the installation of the Austrian puppet Maximillian as Mexican emperor. Secretary of State William H. Steward feared a war. It was decided to beef up naval forces in the Gulf of Mexico with an additional squadron of ships. Steward wanted a "fighter" in command of the new squadron and personally tapped Winslow for the job.

Winslow's first stop on his way to his new command was New Orleans on January 2, 1866. As soon as he arrived, however, he was turned right around and ordered to Washington, D.C. By this time, his old nemesis, Raphael Semmes, was under arrest for violating his "parole" by fleeing to England after the sinking of the *Alabama*. Winslow was needed as the key witness in any trial of Semmes. The commodore had mixed feelings about confronting his old shipmate once again, especially under these unpleasant circumstances—but the necessity never came into being after all. The attorney general of the United States, Henry Stanbery, determined that Grant's general terms for the surrender and release of Confederate officers applied in this case and Semmes was released. Winslow turned around again and headed to the Gulf. He arrived and took command of the Second Gulf Squadron on May 4 in what turned out to be one of the shortest command tours in navy history.

Maximillian surrendered on May 15, tensions with Mexico and France immediately cooled, and Winslow was ordered to stand down on May 21. He was "parked" in New Orleans to assist with occupation and Reconstruction activities for Louisiana. His wife was able to join him in the Crescent City in November. The tour ended the following May 1867, after which Winslow requested and was granted extended leave to take his family to Europe and hopefully enjoy several fetes in his honor. Sadly, his daughter Fanny, only twenty-three years old, died, and the trip was cancelled. The next year was spent surveying many of the old ironclads he knew so well from his service on the Mississippi River: These boats were no longer needed and Winslow was in charge of getting them sold. That task completed, in June 1869 he was given command of the Portsmouth Naval Shipyard.

More honors came Winslow's way in March 1870 when he was promoted to rear admiral and ordered to command the Pacific Fleet, headquartered in San Francisco. Reporting in July, he was able to bring his wife with him and together they occupied the admiral's quarters aboard the Fleet's new flagship, USS *California*, a large wooden steam frigate. In peacetime, a fleet admiral did not have much to do but enjoy the ride: a modern equivalent would be the captain's cabin aboard a luxury cruise ship. Admiral and Mrs. Winslow had their own servants, chef, and aides and spent the next two years cruising the Inside Passage in Alaska, the Hawaiian Islands (including a reception with the king of Hawaii), and several ports up and down the western coasts of North and South America.

It would have been a well-deserved and fitting conclusion to Winslow's career if it hadn't been for his poor health. His diseased right eye (which should probably have been surgically removed) gave him constant pain and neuralgia. He was still subject to the recurrence of sudden fevers. In January 1872, while cruising off the coast of the beautiful French Polynesian island of Rimatara, Winslow seemed to suffer a mini-stroke. He recovered quickly but Catherine and his aides knew that this was not a good sign. The ship made two more stops in South America but then headed for Panama. There, Winslow's health took another dip and a medical board recommended he resign his command, which he did, and he and Catherine then boarded a mail steamer bound for San Francisco.

The California climate seemed to revive his health and after another year he was much improved. The family took a cross-country train to Washington, D.C., where Winslow reported to the Navy Department in April 1873. On May 9, while still in Washington awaiting orders, he was felled by a severe stroke. He recovered sufficiently to be able to travel to his home in Rox-bury, but his remaining months were filled with undeserved pain and suffering. At last, on September 29, 1873, the valiant, tough old sea dog slipped his cable one last time, age sixty-three.

At Catherine's request, the funeral was small and private. Winslow's casket was draped in the old battle flag of the *Kearsarge*, the one that flew at the masthead on June 19, 1864. The admiral was interred in Forest Hill Cemetery, Jamaica Plain, Boston. Fittingly, the stone that marks his grave is a boulder from Mt. Kearsarge in New Hampshire.[90]

Three U.S. Navy ships have honored John Winslow. The first was USS *Winslow*, TB-5, a torpedo boat that saw considerable action in May 1898 engaging Spanish warships in Cárdenas Harbor, Cuba. The only U.S. Navy officer killed in the Spanish-American War, Ensign Worth Bagley, was part of her crew. TB-5's ultimate fate was to be scuttled, in 1923, to form part of a breakwater near Teddy Roosevelt's home at Sagamore Hill, Oyster Bay, Long Island. She rests there today, housing the fishes.

The second USS *Winslow* was DD-53, a four-piper destroyer launched in 1915. She saw service in World War I and was one of the famous destroyers sent to protect England from the U-boat menace. She was decommissioned in 1922 and sold for scrap in 1936. The third USS *Winslow* was also a destroyer, DD-359, put in service in 1937. She served mostly on Atlantic convoy duty

---

90   Catherine passed away in Boston in 1890 at age seventy-seven. She was buried next to her husband.

through World War II and was headed to the Pacific in 1945 when the war ended. She was decommissioned in 1950 and sold for scrap in 1959.

When the Civil War ended, Arthur Sinclair Jr., formerly of the *Alabama*, returned to Baltimore. He did not live very well, becoming impoverished. His hopes of a financial revival through the publication of his memoir, the unimaginatively titled *Two Years on the Alabama*, were dashed because the Southern supporters he wanted to attract shunned the book and its critical comments about Raphael Semmes. Sinclair's life was as long as it was unhappy—he died in 1925 in his eighty-eighth year.

John McIntosh Kell did find his way back into Confederate service, once again under Raphael Semmes. After being promoted to commander, Kell was captain of the ironclad CSS *Richmond* in the James River Squadron until it was disbanded. After the war, Kell returned to Georgia and became a farmer, and in later years he served as adjutant general of his home state. He also wrote a memoir, *Recollections of a Naval Life Including the Cruises of Confederate Steamers "Sumter" and "Alabama,"* which was published in 1900. That same year the loyal first lieutenant passed away. He was buried in Oak Hill Cemetery in Griffin, Georgia.

Briefly, in his first days back in Mobile, Raphael Semmes considered accepting a commission in the navy of Brazil. That country was in the process of luring five thousand men and women still loyal to the Confederate States of America and providing them with land for themselves and their slaves to use as farms and ranches. But he was too worn out for such a remote adventure. Perhaps he would become a businessman in New Orleans, but no immediate ventures were adequately appealing.

His ongoing ruminations were interrupted in mid-December 1865 when he was arrested at his home by a detachment of U.S. Marines. Semmes was charged—the order was signed by Gideon Welles—with escaping after he had surrendered the *Alabama* off

Cherbourg. He was hauled north and imprisoned at the Washington Navy Yard. Anne Semmes soon followed and made personal appeals to President Andrew Johnson. As noted above, after four months of bureaucratic wrangling, Semmes was released, on April 7, 1866, with all charges dropped. Welles was furious but there was nothing he could do about it by then.

Semmes returned to Alabama and what was most likely his first love: writing. His *Memoirs of Service Afloat, During the War Between the States*, all 833 pages of it, was published in 1868. With that out of his system, the former Confederate admiral moved from one occupation to another. He was a professor of philosophy and literature at what is now Louisiana State University, served as a county judge, and then toiled as a newspaper editor in Memphis. Almost inevitably, though, Semmes returned to Mobile and resumed his legal career.

In the court of public opinion, he defended both his actions at sea and the political actions of the Southern states. These activities and his several occupations barely kept Anne and him afloat financially. They were very much helped when the citizens of Mobile presented the Semmes family with what became known as the Raphael Semmes House, and it remained his residence until his death.

In early 1877, when he was sixty-seven, Semmes began to suffer from intestinal attacks. They persisted for months. However, it was consuming bad shrimp in August that finally proved his undoing. He was diagnosed with ptomaine poisoning and what remained of his health deteriorated rapidly. In his final hours Semmes imagined himself once again on the deck of the CSS *Alabama*, issuing commands and conferring with his officers. He died on August 30, 1877.[91]

Among the honors accorded Semmes was to become a member

---

91 Anne Spencer Semmes would pass away in March 1892 at the age of seventy-two, in Memphis. She would be buried next to her husband in the Old Catholic Cemetery in Mobile.

of the Alabama Hall of Fame. One of the streets on the Louisiana State University campus carried his full name. It no longer does but Semmes Avenue in Richmond, Virginia, still exists (as of this writing). A suburban area of western Mobile County is named for him as well as The Admiral Hotel in downtown Mobile. There was a life-sized statue of Raphael Semmes in Mobile, but it was taken down early in the morning on July 5, 2020, by city officials.

Two U.S. Navy ships have been named in Semmes's honor: The first USS *Semmes* was DD-189, a *Clemson* class destroyer launched in 1918 that served through World War II and, incidentally, was also a U.S. Coast Guard ship from 1932–34. The second USS *Semmes* was DDG-18, a guided missile destroyer commissioned in 1962. She served the fleet until 1991 when she was sold to the Greek navy.

There was just the one CSS *Alabama*, but the name has been used by three more navy ships so christened to honor the state. The first was USS *Alabama*, BB-8, a pre-dreadnaught battleship launched in 1900 and scrapped in 1924; the second was USS *Alabama*, BB-60, another battleship commissioned in 1942 and still afloat today as a museum ship docked in Mobile; and the third is USS *Alabama*, SSBN-731, an *Ohio* class nuclear submarine launched in 1985 and still in service—also famous as the platform for the movie *Crimson Tide*.

★ ★ ★ ★ ★

AFTERWORD

The CSS *Alabama* has been the focus of a transcontinental salvage effort for close to four decades. The wreck lies in French territorial waters seven miles from Cherbourg. In November 1984, 120 years after it was sunk, the ship was discovered by the French Navy minesweeper FNS *Circe*. Subsequently, French divers went to work led by French Navy Commander Max Guerot, who confirmed the *Alabama*'s identity. With further research, Guerot's fascination grew. When he retired from the French Navy, he joined several others in forming, in 1988, the CSS *Alabama* Association to support additional investigation of Semmes's long-lost ship.

Based in Mobile, the association continues to raise funds for dives at the site, the recovery of artifacts, and more historical research. Unlike the wreck at the center of the book *Ship of Gold in the Deep-Blue Sea*, the *Alabama* is not hiding a fortune in gold coins. However, it is the wreck of a Confederate ship of war, one of only eight true warships that made up the Confederate States Navy. The artifacts recovered so far are of great significance to historians and archaeologists as well as Civil War buffs everywhere.

Although the wreck is in French territorial waters, the U.S. government, as the successor to the former Confederate States of America, is the rightful owner. In October 1989, the U.S. and France signed an agreement recognizing the wreck of the *Alabama* as an important heritage resource of both nations and establishing a joint French American Scientific Committee for archaeological exploration. This agreement established a precedent for international cooperation in archaeological research and in the protection of a unique historic shipwreck. In 1995, the CSS *Alabama* Association and the Naval History and Heritage Command signed an agreement accrediting the association as operator of the archaeological investigation of the remains of the ship.

The *Alabama* was fitted with eight pieces of ordnance after she arrived at the Azores, six of them being 32-pounder smoothbores. Seven cannon were identified at the wreck site—two were cast from a British Royal Navy–pattern and three were of a later pattern produced by Fawcett, Preston, and Company in Liverpool. One of the Blakely-pattern 32-pounders was found lying across the starboard side of the hull, forward of the boilers. A second Blakely 32-pounder was identified outside the hull structure, immediately forward of the propeller and its lifting frame; the forward 32-pounder was recovered in 2000. Both of the British Royal Navy–pattern 32-pounders were identified: One lies inside the starboard hull, forward of the boilers, adjacent to the forward Downton pump. The second was identified as lying on the iron deck structure, immediately aft of the smoke pipe; it was recovered in 2001. The sole remaining 32-pounder has not been positively identified, but it could be underneath hull debris forward of the starboard Trotman anchor.

The ship's heavy ordnance consisted of one Blakely Patent 7-inch 100-pounder shell rifle mounted on a pivot carriage forward and one 68-pounder smoothbore similarly mounted aft. The Blakely was found beside its pivot carriage, atop the forward starboard boiler, and was the first cannon recovered from the *Alabama*. The smoothbore was located aft, at the stern, immediately outside the starboard hull structure. Both heavy cannon were recovered in 1994. In 2002, a diving expedition raised the ship's bell along with more than three hundred other artifacts, including structural samples, tableware, ornate commodes, and numerous other items that reveal much about life aboard the Confederate warship.

One of the most surprising finds was a human jawbone. It was found in the silt underneath one of the recovered 32-pounder cannons. That and the very cold water around the wreck site probably account for the bone surviving intact in the ocean for more than a century and a half. DNA analysis of the jawbone found that it was, not surprisingly, male, from an individual in relatively good health, of European heritage, between twenty-five and forty years old and, because of the wearing of some of the teeth, a pipe smoker. We'll probably never know who this individual was, but his remains were laid to rest in the Magnolia Cemetery in Mobile in 2007.

Many of the four hundred artifacts recovered from the *Alabama* wreck are now housed in the Underwater Archaeology Branch, Naval History and Heritage Command conservation lab in Washington, D.C.

ACKNOWLEDGMENTS

"What is it like to write a book with another author? How do you divide the work?" These are two questions we often get when discussing this project as well as the bestseller we did together, *All Blood Runs Red*, the biography of Eugene Bullard, the first-ever African-American fighter pilot (Hanover Square Press, 2019). I guess it really depends on your co-author. Tom and I have been friends for many years, and thank goodness, we're still friends even after going through these two manuscripts together. Tom is an "old pro" at collaborations, having done them also with Bob Drury, including such smash hit titles as *The Heart of Everything That Is* and, more recently, *Blood and Treasure*.

With this book, Tom and I decided to simply take "North" and "South," with Tom writing all the materials on Raphael Semmes and *Alabama* and me taking on John Winslow and the *Kearsarge*. After we each completed our assignments, Tom put on his editor's hat and stitched it all together, then I took one last swipe at the manuscript to smooth out any last wrinkles. There were a billion emails between us as the process moved along, and several pleasant lunches and excuses for drinks along the way too. Alas, not as many as maybe we would have liked as the COVID-19 virus tamped everything down including most of our favorite watering holes.

Research, too, had to be handled differently with the virus touching everyone and everywhere. Thank the gods for the internet and the increasing resources available via that medium.

Hopefully by the time this book is in print the cloud will have lifted, and, with widespread vaccines, we can get back to one of the great pleasures of authorship, which, in my view anyway, is interacting with the reading public.

There are some people I'd like to thank for getting me through the challenges. Certainly, first, to Tom, who made this a smooth and pleasurable experience. The whole book concept was his idea to begin with, so I also thank him for including me in the process.

Our agent, Nat Sobel, at Sobel Weber Associates, deserves many thanks, as usual, for navigating us successfully through the contract and publication process. Our editor at Hanover Square Press, Peter Joseph, is a delight to work with and provided us with invaluable guidance as the book progressed.

My angel, my life partner, Laura Lyons, always by my side, seeing me through the vicissitudes of the creative process and the pandemic—I could not have done it without her.

—*Phil Keith*

I second my co-author's sentiments and want to add my thanks to librarians, curators, and similar folks who were helpful to us during our research. And as always, my gratitude to friends and family members, especially Leslie Reingold, Kathryn and James VunKannon, and Brendan Clavin.

My friend Phil Keith passed away on March 10, 2021. This book reflects the ex-Navy man's spirit and the writer's enthusiasm for a darn good story.

—*Tom Clavin*

SELECTED BIBLIOGRAPHY

BOOKS:

Bowcock, Andrew. *CSS Alabama: Anatomy of a Confederate Raider*. London: Chatham Publishing, 2002.

Bradlee, Francis B. C. and James Magee. *The Kearsarge-Alabama Battle, the Story as Told to the Writer by James Magee of Marblehead, Seaman on the Kearsarge*. Middletown, DE: Big Byte Books, 2019.

Ditzel, Paul. *The Ruthless Exploits of Admiral John Winslow: Naval Hero of the Civil War*. New Albany, IN: FBH Publishers, 1991.

Editors of Time-Life Books. *The Civil War: The Blockade*. Alexandria, VA: Time-Life Books, 1983.

Ellicott, John Morris. *The Life of John Winslow*. New York and London: G.P. Putnam's Sons, 1905.

Ferapontov, Maxim. *USS Kearsarge vs. CSS Alabama, Personal Accounts and Official Reports, a View of the Fight From a Yankee Standpoint*. Ferapontov Anthology, 2017.

Fox, Stephen. *Wolf of the Deep: Raphael Semmes and the Notorious Confederate Raider CSS Alabama.* New York: Knopf, 2007.

Gindlesperger, James. *Fire on the Water: USS Kearsarge and CSS Alabama.* Shippensburg, PA: Burd Street Press, 2005.

Hearn, Chester G. *Gray Raiders of the Sea.* Camden, ME: International Marine Press, 1992.

Kell, John McIntosh. *Recollections of a Naval Life.* County Mayo, Ireland: The Neale Company, 1900.

Lardas, Mark. *CSS Alabama vs. USS Kearsarge.* Long Island City, NY: Osprey Publishing, 2011.

Luraghi, Raimondo. *A History of the Confederate Navy.* Annapolis, MD: U.S. Naval Institute Press, 1996.

Madaus, H. Michael. *Rebel Flags Afloat: A Survey of the Surviving Flags of the Confederate States Navy, Revenue Service, and Merchant Marine.* Winchester, MA: Flag Research Center, 1986.

Marvel, William. *The Alabama & the Kearsarge: The Sailor's War.* Chapel Hill: University of North Carolina Press, 1996.

McPherson, James. *War on the Waters: The Union & Confederate Navies, 1861–1865.* Chapel Hill: University of North Carolina Press, 2012.

Musicant, Ivan. *Divided Waters: The Naval History of the Civil War.* New York: Castle Books/HarperCollins, 2000.

Official Records of the Union and Confederate Navies in the War of the Rebellion (30 volumes, 1894–1922). Government Printing Office, Washington, D.C.

Prickitt, Jeff. *The Leadership of John A. Winslow and Raphael Semmes.* Ft. Leavenworth, KS: U.S. Army Command and General Staff College, 2018.

Secretary of the Navy. *Sinking of the Alabama—Destruction of the Alabama by the Kearsarge.* Annual report in the library of the Naval Historical Center, Washington, D.C., 1864.

Semmes, Raphael. *The Cruise of the Alabama and the Sumter (Volumes I & II)*. New York: Carleton, 1864.

Ibid. *Memoirs of Service Afloat, During the War Between the States*. Fredericksburg, VA: Blue & Grey Press, 1987.

Ibid. *Service Afloat and Ashore During the Mexican War*. Cincinnati: Wm. H. Moore & Co., 1851.

Sinclair, Arthur. *Two Years on the Alabama*. Boston: Lee and Shepard, 1896.

Spencer, William F. *Raphael Semmes: The Philosophical Mariner*. Mobile: University of Alabama Press, 1997.

Still, William N. Jr., John M. Taylor, and Norman C. Delaney. *Raiders and Blockaders: The American Civil War Afloat*. Lincoln, NE: Potomac Books, 1998.

Symonds, Craig L. *Lincoln and His Admirals*. New York: Oxford University Press, 2008.

Taylor, John M. *Confederate Raider: Raphael Semmes of the Alabama*. McLean, VA: Brassey's, 1994.

Troyer, Byron L. *Yesterday's Indiana*. Miami: E. A. Seemann Publishing, Inc., 1975.

Welles, Gideon. *The Diary of Gideon Welles, Vols. I & II*. Bellevue, WA: Big Byte Books, 2011.

MAGAZINES:

Browne, John M. "The Duel Between the Alabama and the Kearsarge." *Century Magazine*, Vol. 31, April, 1886: 923–934.

Bedlam, William H. "Kearsarge and Alabama." *Rhode Island Soldiers and Sailors Historical Society*. Providence, RI, 1894.

Sinclair, Arthur. "When the Kearsarge Fought the Alabama." *Hearst's Magazine*, Vol. 25, January-June, 1914; International Magazine Co., New York, NY.

OFFICIAL REPORTS:

Winslow, John A., Captain, U.S. Navy, Commanding Officer, USS *Kearsarge*; *USS Kearsarge's Engagement with CSS Alabama*; Official Union Reports; U.S. Government Printing Office; Official Records of the Union and Confederate Navies in the War of the Rebellion, Series 1, Vol. 3, pp. 59–82; Washington, D.C., 1896. Note: This official report also includes the signed reports and correspondence from the following:

Gideon Welles, Secretary of the Navy

John M. Browne, Surgeon, U.S. Navy

James S. Thornton, LCDR, U.S. Navy, Executive Officer

William H. Cushman, Chief Engineer, U.S. Navy

J. C. Walton, Boatswain, U.S. Navy

Franklin A. Graham, Gunner, U.S. Navy

James R. Wheeler, Acting Master, U.S. Navy

E. M. Stoddard, Acting Master, U.S. Navy

D. H. Sumner, Acting Master, U.S. Navy

Edward E. Preble, Midshipman and Acting Master, U.S. Navy

Hon. Charles Francis Adams, Envoy Extraordinary and Minister Plenipotentiary, U.S. State Dept.

INTERNET RESOURCES:

"CSS *Alabama* Wreck Site (1864)," Naval History and Heritage Command, https://www.history.navy.mil/research/underwater-archaeology/sites-and-projects/ship-wrecksites/css-alabama.html.

Holloway, Don. "High-Seas Duel." *Civil War Quarterly*, 2014, http://donhollway.com/alabama-kearsarge.

Reidy, Joseph P. "Black Men in Navy Blue During the Civil War," https://www.archives.gov/publications/prologue/2001/fall/black-sailors-1.html.

Stevens, Danny, and Jennie Ashton. "The Search for Seaman Joaquin Pease," Naval History and Heritage Command, Feb. 2020, https://usn

history.navylive.dodlive.mil/2020/02/18/the-search-for-seaman-joachim-pease.

Veit, Chuck. "How the U.S. Navy Won the American Civil War," http://navyandmarine.org/historicalref/HowNavyWonWar.htm.

INDEX

Stewart, Charles, 73
Strahan, Robert H., 273
Stribling, John, 50
Sumner, David, 236
CSS *Sumter*
    achievements of, 60, 66, 111,
        117
    construction of, 48–49
    in Gibraltar, 59–60, 60n27,
        68, 173
    limitations of, 42–43, 52
    prize crews from, 54–56
    raids conducted by, 54–59
    recruitment of crew for, 49–51
    Semmes as captain of, 48–52,
        54–60, 117
Symonds, T. E., 179

T
CSS *Tallahassee,* 179–181
Taylor, John M., 21, 36, 150, 204,
    266
Taylor, Zachary, 31, 98, 180
Teach, Edward (Blackbeard), 82
Tebbutt, John, 53
Thornton, James Shepard
    on Bickford's spy mission, 140
    in Cherbourg battle, 229, 233–
        234, 245–246, 250, 281
    death of, 281
    on *Deerhound* escape, 259
    education at Naval Academy,
        136
    family background, 135–136
    hunt for Confederate cruisers,
        174
    injuries sustained by, 281
    in Mississippi River campaigns,
        137, 193
    preparations for battle, 225–227

    promotion to commander, 265,
        271, 281
    Queenstown Incident and, 171,
        172
    supervision of crewmen by, 167,
        170, 261
Thornton, Matthew, 135
Tonawanda (cargo ship), 151–152
Tremlett, Francis, 267, 268
Tremlett, Louisa, 267–268
Trent affair (1861), 118, 118n51
CSS *Tuscaloosa,* 145, 184, 200,
    200n76
USS *Tuscarora,* 59, 75, 151
290. See CSS *Alabama*
Tyler, John, 27n9, 93, 94

U
Union. *See also* Civil War; Union
    Navy; *specific battles*
    manufacturing abilities of, 46,
        111, 116–117, 164
    merchant ships of, 45, 47–48,
        54–55, 116–117, 146–149
    Mississippi River campaigns
        of, 122–130, 137, 164, 193
Union Navy. *See also specific ships*
    Black crewmen in, 140–142
    blockades by, 46–48, 47n18,
        51, 64, 113–116, 164
    Mohican class warships of,
        75–79
    size and strength of, 37–38, 74,
        116
U.S. Naval Academy, 22n5, 23,
    27n9, 29n10, 136
U.S. Navy. *See also specific ships,
    squadrons, and naval yards*
    autocratic nature of, 33
    Black crewmen in, 140–142